For too long, U.S. higher education has viewed ESL students as a homogeneous (and needy) population. This volume explicitly challenges such views and encourages us to see the successes of ESL students as integral to the wider success of the institution. Going further, it provides accessible resources for collective thinking on how to promote such success.

Dudley W. Reynolds, *Carnegie Mellon University Qatar*

This important and timely volume combines literacy skills (reading and writing), which are often separated in books on second language learners. It will be useful for TESL programs as well as a reference for other higher ed administrators looking to support second language students at their institutions.

Sarah Rilling, *Kent State University, USA*

D1131883

ESL READERS AND WRITERS IN HIGHER EDUCATION

ESL Readers and Writers in Higher Education describes the challenges ESL students in U.S. postsecondary institutions face when studying in a second language, and offers suggestions for how teachers, advisors, tutors, and institutions might provide support that meets the reading and writing needs of this very important student population.

Because the ESL profession as a whole, including what professionals are doing in the classroom, sits under the umbrella of an institutional response to a language-related challenge, some solutions aimed at helping students achieve optimal proficiency lie outside of the classroom. As such, this book is based on the assertion that language development support is not the sole responsibility of language teachers. Everyone on campuses that host ESL students bears some responsibility for these students' language development. Chapters are therefore intentionally adapted to appeal to a wide variety of readers from classroom teachers, and teachers in training, to admissions officers, academic advisors, and international student advisors.

Norman W. Evans is Associate Professor, Department of Linguistics and English Language, and Coordinator, English Language Center, Brigham Young University, USA.

Neil J Anderson is Professor, Department of English Language Teaching and Learning, Brigham Young University–Hawaii, USA.

William G. Eggington is Ludwig-Weber-Siebach Humanities Professor, Department of Linguistics and English Language, Brigham Young University, USA, and Visiting Professor, Kyung Hee University, Global Campus, South Korea.

ESL & Applied Linguistics Professional Series
Eli Hinkel, Series Editor

Evans/Anderson/Eggington, Eds. • *ESL Readers and Writers in Higher Education: Understanding Challenges, Providing Support*

Hinkel • *Effective Curriculum for Teaching L2 Writing: Principles and Techniques*

Farrell • *Promoting Teacher Reflection in Second-Language Education: A Framework for TESOL Professionals*

Nunan/Richards • *Language Learning Beyond the Classroom*

Christison/Murray • *What English Language Teachers Need to Know Volume III: Designing Curriculum*

Turner • *Using Statistics in Small-scale Language Education Research: Focus on Non-parametric Data*

Hong/Pawan • *The Pedagogy and Practice of Western-trained Chinese English Language Teachers: Foreign Education, Chinese Meanings*

Lantolf/Poehner • *Sociocultural Theory and the Pedagogical Imperative in L2 Education: Vygotskian Praxis and the Research/Practice Divide*

Brown • *Pronunciation and Phonetics: A Practical Guide for English Language Teachers*

Birch • *English Grammar Pedagogy: A Global Perspective*

Liu • *Describing and Explaining Grammar and Vocabulary in ELT: Key Theories and Effective Practices*

deOliviera/Silva, Eds. • *L2 Writing in Secondary Classrooms: Student Experiences, Academic Issues, and Teacher Education*

Andrade/Evans • *Principles and Practices for Response in Second Language Writing: Developing Self-Regulated Learners*

Sayer • *Ambiguities and Tensions in English Language Teaching: Portraits of EFL Teachers as Legitimate Speakers*

Alsagoff/McKay/Hu/Renandya, Eds. *Principles and Practices of Teaching English as an International Language*

Kumaravadivelu • *Language Teacher Education for a Global Society: A Modular Model for Knowing, Analyzing, Recognizing, Doing, and Seeing*

Vandergrift/Goh • *Teaching and Learning Second Language Listening: Metacognition in Action*

LoCastro • *Pragmatics for Language Educators: A Sociolinguistic Perspective*

Nelson • *Intelligibility in World Englishes: Theory and Practice*

Nation/Macalister, Eds. • *Case Studies in Language Curriculum Design: Concepts and Approaches in Action Around the World*

Johnson/Golumbek, Eds. • *Research on Second Language Teacher Education: A Sociocultural Perspective on Professional Development*

Hinkel, Ed. • *Handbook of Research in Second Language Teaching and Learning, Volume II*

Nassaji/Fotos • *Teaching Grammar in Second Language Classrooms: Integrating Form-Focused Instruction in Communicative Context*

Murray/Christison • *What English Language Teachers Need to Know Volume I: Understanding Learning*

Murray/Christison • *What English Language Teachers Need to Know Volume II: Facilitating Learning*

Wong/Waring • *Conversation Analysis and Second Language Pedagogy: A Guide for ESL/EFL Teachers*

Nunan/Choi, Eds. • *Language and Culture: Reflective Narratives and the Emergence of Identity*

Braine • *Nonnative Speaker English Teachers: Research, Pedagogy, and Professional Growth*

Burns • *Doing Action Research in English Language Teaching: A Guide for Practitioners*

Nation/Macalister • *Language Curriculum Design*

Birch • *The English Language Teacher and Global Civil Society*

Johnson • *Second Language Teacher Education: A Sociocultural Perspective*

Nation • *Teaching ESL/EFL Reading and Writing*

Nation/Newton • *Teaching ESL/EFL Listening and Speaking*

Kachru/Smith • *Cultures, Contexts, and World Englishes*

McKay/Bokhosrt-Heng • *International English in its Sociolinguistic Contexts: Towards a Socially Sensitive EIL Pedagogy*

Christison/Murray, Eds. • *Leadership in English Language Education: Theoretical Foundations and Practical Skills for Changing Times*

McCafferty/Stam, Eds. • *Gesture: Second Language Acquisition and Classroom Research*

Liu • *Idioms: Description, Comprehension, Acquisition, and Pedagogy*

Chapelle/Enright/Jamieson, Eds. • *Building a Validity Argument for the Test of English as a Foreign Language*™

Kondo-Brown/Brown, Eds. • *Teaching Chinese, Japanese, and Korean Heritage Language Students Curriculum Needs, Materials, and Assessments*

Youmans • *Chicano-Anglo Conversations: Truth, Honesty, and Politeness*

Birch • *English L2 Reading: Getting to the Bottom, Second Edition*

Luk/Lin • *Classroom Interactions as Cross-cultural Encounters: Native Speakers in EFL Lessons*

Levy/Stockwell • *CALL Dimensions: Issues and Options in Computer Assisted Language Learning*

Nero, Ed. • *Dialects, Englishes, Creoles, and Education*

Basturkmen • *Ideas and Options in English for Specific Purposes*

Kumaravadivelu • *Understanding Language Teaching: From Method to Postmethod*

McKay • *Researching Second Language Classrooms*

Egbert/Petrie, Eds. • *CALL Research Perspectives*

Canagarajah, Ed. • *Reclaiming the Local in Language Policy and Practice*

Adamson • *Language Minority Students in American Schools: An Education in English*

Fotos/Browne, Eds. • *New Perspectives on CALL for Second Language Classrooms*

Hinkel • *Teaching Academic ESL Writing: Practical Techniques in Vocabulary and Grammar*

Hinkel/Fotos, Eds. • *New Perspectives on Grammar Teaching in Second Language Classrooms*

Hinkel • *Second Language Writers' Text: Linguistic and Rhetorical Features*

Visit **www.routledge.com/education** for additional information on titles in the ESL & Applied Linguistics Professional Series

ESL READERS AND WRITERS IN HIGHER EDUCATION

Understanding Challenges, Providing Support

Edited by Norman W. Evans,
Neil J Anderson, and
William G. Eggington

Routledge
Taylor & Francis Group

NEW YORK AND LONDON

First published 2015
by Routledge
711 Third Avenue, New York, NY 10017

and by Routledge
2 Park Square, Milton Park, Abingdon, Oxon OX14 4RN

Routledge is an imprint of the Taylor & Francis Group, an informa business

© 2015 Taylor & Francis

Library of Congress Cataloging-in-Publication Data
ESL readers and writers in higher education : understanding challenges, providing support / edited by Norman W. Evans, Neil J Anderson, & William G. Eggington.
  pages cm
  Includes bibliographical references and index.
  1. English language–Study and teaching (Higher)–Foreign speakers.
  I. Evans, Norman W., editor. II. Anderson, Neil J., editor.
  III. Eggington, William, editor.
  PE1128.A2E7687 2015
  428.0071–dc23   2014049066

ISBN: 978-1-138-79170-1 (hbk)
ISBN: 978-1-138-79171-8 (pbk)
ISBN: 978-1-315-76265-4 (ebk)

Typeset in Bembo
by Wearset Ltd, Boldon, Tyne and Wear

Printed and bound in the United States of America by Publishers Graphics, LLC on sustainably sourced paper.

CONTENTS

Preface   xi
Acknowledgments   xiv

PART I
Understanding Challenges   **1**

1 Understanding Challenges, Providing Support:
   ESL Readers and Writers in Higher Education   3
   Norman W. Evans and Maureen Snow Andrade

2 Perceptions and Realities of ESL Students in Higher
   Education: An Overview of Institutional Practices   18
   Maureen Snow Andrade, Norman W. Evans,
   and K. James Hartshorn

3 Focusing on the Challenges: Institutional Language
   Planning   36
   William G. Eggington

4 Writing Centers: Finding a Center for ESL Writers   49
   Lucie Moussu and Nicholas David

5 Writing Instruction for Matriculated International
   Students: A Lived Case Study   64
   Tony Silva

6 Familiar Strangers: International Students in the U.S.
Composition Course   80
Elena Lawrick and Fatima Esseili

7 Academic Reading Expectations and Challenges   95
Neil J Anderson

PART II
Providing Support   **111**

8 Developing Self-Regulated Learners: Helping Students
Meet Challenges   113
Maureen Snow Andrade and Norman W. Evans

9 The Research–Instruction Cycle in Second Language Reading   130
William Grabe and Xiangying Jiang

10 Supporting Multilingual Writers through the Challenges
of Academic Literacy: Principles of English for Academic
Purposes and Composition Instruction   147
Dana Ferris

11 Assisting ESP Students in Reading and Writing
Disciplinary Genres   164
Fredricka L. Stoller and Marin S. Robinson

12 Corpus-Based Vocabulary Support for University
Reading and Writing   180
Mark Davies and Dee Gardner

13 When Everything's Right, but It's Still Wrong: Cultural
Influences on Written Discourse   198
William G. Eggington

14 Using Technology to Teach ESL Readers and Writers   209
Greg Kessler

15 Integrated Reading and Writing Assessment: History,
Processes, and Challenges   223
Mark Wolfersberger and Christine Coombe

Contributors   236
Index   239

PREFACE

This volume began as a lecture series in the Department of Linguistics and English Language at Brigham Young University. We invited prominent scholars to our campus to share their insights on the challenges second language readers and writers face once they transition into demanding discipline studies in higher education. After only the second lecture, we realized the need to share this scholarship more broadly in order to increase understanding of the linguistic challenges that nonnative English speakers (NNESs) encounter in academic reading and writing contexts, and offer professionally informed suggestions for support. To do this, we have assembled the writing of 20 different authors, all of whom are professionally involved in various aspects of ESL related to reading and writing in higher education.

This book is based on three premises. First, ESL students in higher education, while certainly skillful second language users (the majority have likely "passed" language admission requirements), may not have fully developed the English language skills, especially academic reading and writing, that are necessary to meet the demands that higher education exacts of them. Second, a student's success is directly related to the degree of support that is available for the challenges at hand. In other words, the amount of challenge a person can abide is highly correlated to the available support. Third, both students and institutions share a common goal: student success.

From the outset, we wanted to make this volume accessible to the many in higher education who work with NNESs. It is our assertion that language development support is not the sole responsibility of language teachers. Everyone on campuses that host ESL students bears some responsibility for these students' language development from the time they enter the university until they exit. We have, therefore, intentionally adapted the chapters to appeal to a wide variety of readers from classroom teachers, and teachers in training, to admissions officers, academic advisors, and international student advisors.

The concept of challenge and support is based on the work of Nevitt Sanford (1967), a preeminent scholar on college student development. Sanford maintains that learning occurs best in an environment of optimal dissonance. By this he means that an appropriate balance of challenge and support is needed in an environment for positive development to occur. This is a concept similar to Vygotsky's Zone of Proximal Development. A setting with too much challenge, such as the situations many NNESs face in higher education, can be overwhelming, resulting in limited or no development. With too little challenge, students may feel safe, but their development is restricted as a consequence. As Eggington quotes in Chapter 3, "there is no growth in a comfort zone, and there is no comfort in a growth zone."

Overview

The volume is divided into two parts: Understanding Challenges and Providing Support. This dual focus is used to build a culture of inclusion, so that all involved in NNESs' education, teachers and administrators alike, understand the difficulties these students face and at the same time are informed of helpful pedagogical practices.

Part 1 presents a number of relevant issues primarily from the institutional perspective. In Chapter 1, Evans and Andrade provide an overview and profile of the NNES population and the various challenges these students face, as well as some of the most common misperceptions of these students' linguistic needs and lacks. Andrade, Evans, and Hartshorn (Chapter 2) follow with an overview based on a national survey of what support services are actually being offered in higher education across the country and how much more can and needs to be done. Following on the needs described in Chapter 2, Eggington (Chapter 3) reports on a commitment made by a small U.S. university to help its NNESs by developing and implementing a comprehensive language plan that follows established language planning procedures. And in the spirit of providing meaningful support, Moussu and David (Chapter 4) discuss one of the most common kinds of institutional support, the Writing Center, and how it must be reconceptualized to meet the growing NNES population. In Chapters 5 and 6, Silva and Lawrick and Esseili provide valuable insights from Purdue University, which has one of the largest NNES student populations in the country. In these two chapters we see essential characteristics of Purdue's writing program, such as its history, goals, and its relationship to other units, specifically the graduate programs Introductory Composition Program and the Writing Lab. In Chapter 6, Lawrick and Esseili present findings from data collected from Purdue's students to provide a current profile of second language writers and the skills, abilities, and attitudes they bring to a first-year writing course. Finally, Anderson reports in Chapter 7 on data from a national survey that answers several valuable research questions related to reading challenges: How much and what kinds of reading are expected of students in their first semester in their major, and how might these expectations vary across majors?

Part II considers the issues of challenge and support from a pedagogical perspective. Each of the chapters offers insight on practices that can help NNESs develop their English skills as readers and writers. In Chapter 8, Andrade and Evans introduce self-regulated learning (SRL) to the English language teaching context with the objective of helping learners help themselves. Grabe and Jiang conceptualize in Chapter 9 the second language reading research and instruction relationship as a cyclic process that eventually leads to improved student learning outcomes. Dana Ferris (Chapter 10) then presents valuable principles for teaching composition in an "English for academic purposes" (EAP) context. Professors Stoller and Robinson (Chapter 11) address the challenges NNESs face in the various reading genres they face in higher education. They explore a *read–analyze and write* instructional approach as a viable form of assistance for students making transitions into various disciplines. In Chapter 12, Davies and Gardner provide concrete examples of the ways in which university-level students can use the freely available, 425 million word *Corpus of Contemporary American English* (COCA) for individualized, independent vocabulary learning. The foundational assumption of Eggington's chapter (Chapter 13) is that understandings of what we consider to be universal qualities of clear writing are actually bound to particular cultural values and rhetorical contexts. Eggington takes this foundation, and illustrates how it can help teachers better understand and thus support their students to develop as writers.

No volume such as this would be complete without a discussion of technology and assessment. Kessler (Chapter 14) argues that teaching reading and writing skills requires teachers to develop a critical perspective on the use of digital tools and the skills and practices associated with their use. Finally, Wolfersberger and Coombe review in Chapter 15 current trends in assessing reading and writing for academic purposes, with a particular focus on integrated assessment. Their aim is to provide useful information for EAP teachers and curriculum designers and university personnel who must make competent decisions.

Finally, to make this book more applicable to a classroom context, we have included at the end of each chapter discussion questions that the authors think might be considered to further the readers' understanding of critical, related issues. In addition, the authors have provided suggested chapters, articles, and books for further reading on the subject presented in their chapters.

Reference

Sanford, N. (1967). *Where colleges fail: A study of the student as a person.* San Francisco, CA: Jossey-Bass.

ACKNOWLEDGMENTS

We wish to thank Naomi Silverman and Eli Hinkel from Routledge, Jennifer McDaniel and Mel Thorne from Brigham Young University and their team of editors in the Faculty Editing Service at Brigham Young University, and the Brigham Young University College of Humanities for their input and support. We are also indebted to each of the authors for their contributions to this volume.

PART I
Understanding Challenges

1

UNDERSTANDING CHALLENGES, PROVIDING SUPPORT

ESL Readers and Writers in Higher Education

Norman W. Evans and Maureen Snow Andrade

Vignette

A small but rapidly growing U.S.-based company is expanding into various Asian countries. They are seeking new employees who have three essential qualifications: solid academic training from a reputable business school, native proficiency in an Asian language, and very strong English skills—particularly in speaking and writing. Since "native proficiency" in an Asian language is required, a number of promising applicants are citizens of Asian countries who studied business abroad in the United States. To determine the quality of the applicants' English skills, the committee has face-to-face interviews with applicants and asks them to respond in writing to a memo that outlines a proposed business plan. The search committee soon discovers that these applicants' English skills, especially in writing, are not at all what they expected from people who have spent years in the United States studying at accredited universities. In some cases, the low level of English is disturbing.

Introduction and Overview of the Challenges

Students for whom English is a second language (ESL) not only benefit individually from higher education but contribute globally to the human condition and public good.

> There is a wealth of evidence that increased [educational] attainment improves health, lowers crime rates, and yields citizens who are both globally aware and participate more in civic and democratic processes such as voting and volunteering, all of which have enormous implications for our democracy.
>
> *Lumina Foundation, 2013, p. 3*

Recognizing these benefits, postsecondary institutions around the world are providing access to greater numbers of individuals from diverse backgrounds rather than limiting opportunity to an elite few.

By the year 2020, 65% of all jobs in the United States will require a postsecondary certificate or degree (Lumina Foundation, 2013). Currently, only 38.7% of Americans aged 25 to 64 possess a two- or four-year degree (Lumina Foundation, 2013). In other countries, such as the United Kingdom, governments are widening participation by raising awareness, increasing aspirations, motivating students, and supporting attainment (Grundy, 2007). To prepare individuals for future professions, promote global economic development, and build a worldwide knowledge community, populations previously underrepresented for reasons of race, gender, socioeconomic status, or low levels of academic preparation must be both welcomed and supported.

Increasing access for diverse student populations, and specifically, nonnative English language speakers (NNESs), entails careful consideration of linguistic skills. Institutions may do little to provide, encourage, or require further development of English language skills beyond requiring specific admission scores on standardized proficiency tests. NNESs, consisting of both international students and residents, may receive minimal attention aside from possible ESL courses prior to or immediately after admission (see Chapter 2). These courses predominantly focus on international students rather than residents, though residents may also lack the English language proficiency needed for academic tasks.

Consistent with this book's theme of challenges and support, this chapter first provides information related to challenges with common assumptions about NNESs in higher education. It then explicates issues related to NNESs' linguistic and cultural needs, details current support practices, and discusses related theory. The chapter ends with implications for support.

Common Assumptions

Many institutions operate on faulty assumptions about the language needs and abilities of NNESs. This is true for both international and resident students. These assumptions are based on a lack of understanding of language testing and what standardized test scores represent, and the need for further language development post-admission and how to support this. Following is a discussion of the two most common assumptions.

Assumption 1

The first major assumption that institutions make is that once NNESs meet admission requirements, they have adequate English language skills to succeed in postsecondary-level academic work. In reality, NNESs come from different backgrounds with varying language skill sets; some are international students in the United States on a short-term basis, while others—often referred to as Generation 1.5—are residents who arrived as children (early arrivals) or in their preteen or teenage years (late arrivals) (Ferris, 2009; Kanno & Harklau, 2012). Though international students must generally pass an English proficiency exam to be admitted, they face significant cultural and linguistic challenges for which their developing language skills may be inadequate (Andrade & Evans, 2009; Ferris, 2009). Resident students also enroll with varying levels of English language proficiency, often insufficient for the linguistic rigors of postsecondary education (Ferris, 2009), yet these students are not typically required to establish their level of English language proficiency prior to admission or even declare themselves as NNESs.

The TOEFL and similar exams, required for international NNESs, are designed to be a *minimal* indicator of the linguistic skill necessary for academic success. These "institutional English language entry requirements can assist but do not ensure that students will enter university at a sufficiently high level of proficiency" (Barrett-Lennard, Dunworth, & Harris, 2011, p. 100). Resident NNESs' linguistic skills may be similar to or even weaker than those of international students, yet institutions may not assess these students. In some cases, post-admission basic skills screening occurs. Even then, however, these students may be directed to remedial reading and writing courses that do not address their linguistic needs. Additionally, testing requirements may differ depending on institutional type (e.g., community college or four-year university), although students have similar linguistic needs across institutional type.

This situation is largely due to misunderstanding what second language learners must accomplish in terms of academic language once they have been admitted to college. Both groups of NNESs have significant language development needs. As such, though they meet required admission standards, many of these students are likely to require further language development and instruction, as indicated in the following statement:

> Successful participation in academic and professional discourse communities such as business, science, engineering, and medicine requires a strong foundation of very advanced language and common core academic skills. To participate successfully at the postsecondary level, learners require additional knowledge and expertise in content, specialized vocabulary, grammar, discourse structure, and pragmatics.
>
> *Teaching English to Speakers of Other Languages [TESOL], 2010, p. 1*

Assumption 2

The second major assumption that institutions make is that since second language students are immersed in an English-speaking environment once they enroll, their academic language skills (i.e., reading and writing) will naturally continue to develop as they progress through their studies at the institution; by extension, these students will be proficient English users by the time they graduate. This assumption is not supported by language acquisition theory. The reality is that many students' writing skills plateau once they complete their first-year English courses (Ferris, 2009; Storch, 2009). While some students in majors with extensive writing requirements generally do improve their skills, many others do not. Additionally, writing demands for specific disciplines may differ from what is taught in ESL preparatory programs, or students may fail to apply these strategies effectively and consistently (Anderson, Evans, & Hartshorn, 2014; Counsell, 2011). In other cases, the general academic skills taught in ESL programs may not prepare students adequately for study in their chosen disciplines (Benzie, 2011). Faculty members expect students to be linguistically capable of managing the rigors of coursework; however, they find that NNESs lack the linguistic skills necessary for them to function on par with their native-English-speaking peers. Even so, the faculty do not alter their curriculum to accommodate NNESs' limited linguistic skills and indicate having little, if any, time to help students with their English language needs (Andrade & Evans, 2007).

Compounding this is the fact that "individual learners develop language proficiency at variable rates influenced by factors such as educational background, first language, learning style, cognitive style, motivation, and personality, as well as sociocultural factors" (TESOL, 2010, p. 2). The development of linguistic proficiency is gradual and requires complementary programming and support across the institution (Barrett-Lennard et al., 2011). Indeed, faculty members feel strongly that it is the institution's responsibility to provide support services such as tutors, learning centers, and special English classes for NNESs (Andrade & Evans, 2007).

Linguistic and Cultural Issues

A fairly extensive amount of literature on international students indicates their linguistic, cultural, and social challenges (Andrade, 2006, 2008; Andrade & Evans, 2009; Ritz, 2010; Russell, Rosenthal, & Thomson, 2009; Tochkov, Levine, & Sanaka, 2010). Levels of English language proficiency can compound or alleviate cultural and social transitions (Galloway & Jenkins, 2009; Lee, Park, & Kim, 2009; Sherry, Thomas, & Chui, 2010) as well as affect academic adjustment. The same is true of resident NNESs. In both cases, "incoming students must ... negotiate a new range of sociocultural situations such as faculty office hours, team work, public presentations, and frequently, independent living" (TESOL, 2010, p. 1). Mismatches between teaching and learning styles and related expectations also cause difficulties (Huang, 2009; Xiao, 2006). NNESs may struggle with academic vocabulary, written and oral discourse patterns, expectations for synthesis and critical analysis, classroom interaction patterns, class participation, and the amount and difficulty level of reading materials, among other issues (see Chapter 13).

Recent findings at a community college point to another very real problem: though nearly 86% of immigrants who attended high school in another country needed to attend remedial classes, only 25% actually enrolled in these classes during their first semester. Possibly, this is because they did not want to be considered remedial and believed that "over time the natural acquisition of English language skills might enable them to test out of remedial requirements" (Conway, 2010, p. 229). These findings indicate that students are not taking advantage of the help they need, even when it is available, and supports Assumption 2, mentioned earlier, related to misunderstanding about language acquisition.

Linguistic Theory

As a foundation to understanding these challenges, a brief background in the theory of language acquisition is needed—specifically, what it means *to learn* versus *to acquire* a language and what level of proficiency is required for academic success. An important distinction in language learning is the level of proficiency or functionality students have with the language. Many language teaching methodologies focus on teaching students about a language rather than teaching them how to use it (Celce-Murcia, 2014). As such, the endeavor becomes a study of content like history or biology, rather than a study of managing tasks in a second language. While this can produce learners who know much about a language, it does not result in learners who have acquired a language. When learners acquire language, they have gone beyond simply being able to explain or understand a linguistic feature; they are able to use it automatically. Using a second language in such a spontaneous way requires years of practice and extensive exposure (DeKeser, 2007; Ellis, Sheen, Murakami, & Takashima, 2008).

To address the issue of what level of proficiency a learner needs in order to succeed at a university and how long this takes to achieve, we turn to the work of Cummins (2008). The level of English proficiency needed for daily interpersonal interactions is quite different from the English proficiency needed to study the complex and abstract concepts encountered in university courses. The former is referred to as BICS (basic interpersonal communication skills) and the latter as CALP (cognitive academic language proficiency). NNESs who have attained a high degree of fluency and accuracy in everyday spoken English cannot be assumed to have a comparable level of academic language proficiency. It takes NNESs two to three years to acquire BICS and five to seven years in sum to gain CALP, and possibly longer depending on the age of the learner, with older learners requiring more time (Collier, 1987; Collier & Thomas, 1989).

A similar line of research in determining how long it takes to acquire a language is the distance between the first and second languages (R. Clifford, personal communication, September 2008; Omaggio Hadley, 2000). The greater the distance between the two languages, as measured by such factors as syntactic, morphological, or phonological characteristics, the longer it takes to acquire the second language. This is especially relevant when considering student origins. Given the dramatic differences between Korean and English, for example, Korean speakers will likely have greater challenges attaining academic-level English than Spanish speakers.

Self-Theories

Self-theories, or beliefs about oneself and how these beliefs guide behavior, are also relevant to the success of NNESs. Self-theories affect motivation and account for views about learning, effort, and intelligence. In particular, two views of intelligence—fixed or entity and malleable or incremental—are influenced by educational and cultural background. Learners who hold an entity theory of intelligence believe that they are born with a certain amount of intelligence, which cannot be changed (Dweck, 2000). According to this theory, learners focus on performance goals, or easy, low-effort tasks that make them look smart and win praise from peers, teachers, and parents. They avoid challenging tasks at which they fear they cannot succeed and miss valuable learning opportunities to master new concepts and skills. These learners focus on grades as a sign of intelligence and a source of motivation. In contrast, learners with an incremental theory of intelligence believe intelligence can be enhanced through effort. They are willing to take on challenges to increase their levels of knowledge and skill. They focus on learning and are not concerned with how others may perceive their intelligence. Difficult tasks are viewed as opportunities to learn.

Many educational systems have traditionally focused on rote learning, test scores, and grades. International students or recently arrived immigrants may be accustomed to these systems, as are NNESs coming from U.S. high schools, which also emphasize performance based on grades; such students feel that the surest way to succeed is to not take on anything that is too challenging. Language learning does not lend itself well to a performance orientation, as it involves risk-taking, making mistakes, trial and error, and a willingness to show a lack of knowledge or ability. NNESs in higher education may mask their linguistic incompetence or lack of confidence by not participating, avoiding challenging courses or majors, not asking questions, or not seeking help.

One framework to address the need to change students' views of intelligence is self-regulated learning (SRL), defined as the learner's ability to control the factors and conditions that affect learning (Dembo, Junge, & Lynch, 2006; also see Chapter 8). A practical application of this theory can be accomplished through activities related to the six dimensions of SRL: motive (reasons for learning and goal-setting), methods (learning strategies), time (time management and avoiding procrastination), physical environment (external and internal distracters), social environment (seeking and evaluating help), and performance (monitoring, reflecting, and revising goals). These dimensions have been linked to academic achievement in a variety of contexts (Dembo et al., 2006; Zimmerman 1994; Zimmerman & Risemberg, 1997), including language learning—specifically L2 writing (Andrade & Evans, 2013) and distance English language learning (Andrade & Bunker, 2011).

Support Issues

Institutions cannot serve a population of whom they are unaware (Kanno & Harklau, 2012). Although NNESs constitute a significant portion of higher education enrollments, benchmarks specific to this population are largely unavailable. Approximately 95% of international students come from countries where English is not the predominant language (Institute of International Education, 2011), and 21% of elementary and secondary-level students speak a language other than English at home, with 5% speaking English with difficulty (Aud et al., 2011); however, this information is obscured in higher education data sets. National and institutional tracking of NNESs is based on broad categorizations (e.g., White, Black, Hispanic, Asian; see Table 1.1; Aud et al., 2011) that do not indicate linguistic status. This lack of information regarding the success of NNESs places institutions and students at a distinct disadvantage.

The impact of NNESs on individual institutions varies depending on the percentage of the total enrollment they represent. However, even a small percentage of these students represent hundreds or even thousands of individuals who need linguistic support. The fact that information about the success of NNESs is not readily available, at least according to common benchmarks, points to a general lack of awareness of this population.

Additionally, institutions typically do not identify English language proficiency as an at-risk factor. At-risk factors are defined by poor high school or

TABLE 1.1 Participation and Graduation Rates (%)

	Participation	Graduation (Six-year)
All students	Not applicable	55.4
White	62	58.1
Black	15	38.9
Hispanic	13	45.7
Asian/Pacific Islander	7	63.4
American Indian	1	38
Non-resident alien	2	Not available

transfer grade point averages, first-generation or nontraditional status, low college entrance or placement test scores, and minority/ethnicity categories. Although students from minority or ethnic groups may be NNES, they are not specifically identified as such. In essence, NNESs are invisible at the institutional level in terms of their English language proficiency, and therefore, appropriate programming is typically not designed to address their needs, and these needs are not accounted for as a possible factor impacting poor academic performance or lack of persistence.

Implications and Applications

Due, in large part, to faulty assumptions, institutions frequently lack a campus-wide approach to helping NNESs develop their reading and writing skills after admission, or, if an approach exists, it fails to distinguish among variations in nonnative English-speaking populations and their linguistic and cultural needs (see Chapter 3 in this volume). Research suggests that "only at an institution-wide level is it possible to map language development across the whole university, and to identify broad graduate attributes that incorporate high-level English language proficiency and communicative competence in a disciplinary environment" (Barrett-Lennard et al., 2011, p. 102). Leaving English language support to faculty members and departments may have some efficacy; however, research indicates that the former expect a comprehensive and structured plan to ensure that NNESs receive the appropriate linguistic support (Andrade & Evans, 2007). Without this institution-wide approach, NNESs will not only struggle during their higher education experience but graduate with inadequate professional English language skills.

A first step to supporting NNESs is for institutions to gather and track data that identify NNESs and provide a clear understanding of their needs and levels of success. Without this, substantive and lasting change will not occur, nor will it reflect actual needs (Kanno & Harklau, 2012). This information will inform the development of appropriate programming. Considerable institutional resources are directed at first-year programming and retention on most campuses. These initiatives must consider both individual students and specific populations needing support. They must also differentiate among the needs of various populations, rather than trying to incorporate the same best practices at all institutions. This section delineates examples of support related to the issues raised. These can be a starting point for further discussion, exploration, and development.

One innovative approach to addressing needs specific to Generation 1.5 students is to identify their competencies through appropriate testing and require a combination of course work, including a basic skills course for reading and writing, an ESL course for grammatical accuracy, and supplemental support through tutoring (Miele, 2003). This type of intervention demonstrates institutional flexibility and responsiveness to meeting the linguistic needs of a specific population rather than forcing NNESs into courses that may only partially address what they lack in terms of English proficiency, a challenge discussed earlier.

Other examples of academic support programming include embedded instruction, which involves teaching language and academic skills along with content (Brooman-Jones, Cunningham, Hanna, & Wilson, 2011; Harris & Ashton, 2011), collaborations between professors and learning advisors to help local and international students navigate academic tasks and align assessments with course objectives (Stratilas, 2011), and the use of technology to support literacy development (Yakimchuk, 2010). Additionally, institutions may offer preparatory English courses (Green & Agosti, 2011; Rosenstiel, Taafee, & Thomas, 2009), tutorials, and support groups for thesis writing (Sundstrom, 2009). First-year seminars assist with linguistic and cultural transitions (Andrade, 2006, 2009), and collaborative programming involving both student affairs and academic affairs offers a holistic approach (Andrade & Evans, 2009).

Language learning encompasses more than linguistic features; it requires a comprehensive approach. Entity and SRL theories, discussed earlier, address affective factors and beliefs about learning to help learners use different lenses, adopt new views of themselves and their potential, and make needed changes. Training NNESs in these areas can increase their awareness and understanding of their behaviors and their learning and cultural approaches. This training must involve identifying student beliefs about intelligence, how these beliefs have been informed, and how to help students adopt approaches that enable learning (Dörnyei & Ushioda, 2009). Faculty need to probe student views of learning and help them reflect on and understand the goals of higher education: learning not performance.

A well-known approach—the SIOP Model (Vogt & Echevarria, 2005)—is commonly used to support NNESs in K–12 contexts. This model involves identifying language and content objectives in each lesson and encouraging learning by using strategies such as providing background, simplifying content, focusing on strategy instruction, organizing pair and group work for interaction purposes, and providing opportunities for practice. Unfortunately, no similar teaching and learning models exist to support NNESs in U.S. institutions of higher education, nor are any widespread discussions occurring related to this direction.

Other countries, however, have made some progress on this issue. In Australia, for example, increasing numbers of NNESs entering postsecondary institutions (24% of the total higher education enrollment is international; Choudaha, Chang, & Kono, 2013) has resulted in the development of Good Practice Principles for English Language Proficiency for International Students (Arkoudis, Baik, & Richardson, 2012; Australian Universities Quality Agency, 2009). These principles are being adopted across disciplines, are applied across learner populations, and are resulting in discussions of how to define, measure, and develop English language proficiency in academic and professional contexts (Barrett-Lennard et al., 2011; Harris & Ashton, 2011). Centralized language and skills workshops have not addressed NNESs' needs, thus alternative approaches that define communication practices within a discipline and integrate related language and academic skills in individual courses are becoming increasingly common.

Conclusion

The goal to increase higher education opportunities and successes has resulted in a more diverse population in colleges and universities, and this trend will only continue. The benefits of this diverse population are readily acknowledged; however, despite this, institutions of higher education have not fully recognized that NNESs need post-admission support related to language skills, particularly the development of academic reading and writing competencies.

This inattention may be due, in part, to a misunderstanding of NNESs' linguistic limits. However, as the vignette at the beginning of this chapter points out, until these issues are addressed, NNESs will not graduate with the skills needed to fully benefit from their experience, institutional reputations may be at stake, and society will likely not reap the full rewards of a well-educated citizenry. Hosting institutions bear the responsibility of providing NNESs with the educational resources necessary for academic success (Green & Agosti, 2011, Kennelly, Maldoni, & Davies, 2010). Arguably no other factor is more central to the success of NNESs than their facility with the English language (Andrade & Evans, 2007; Ferris, 2009, Grabe, 2009).

Summary

- Many institutions of higher education assume that if NNESs meet the language proficiency requirement for admissions, they have the language skills necessary to succeed at the university.
- Similarly, many institutions assume that when NNESs are immersed in a higher education English-speaking environment, their English skills will naturally develop along with their academic skills.
- The interaction between linguistic competency and cultural adjustment cannot be ignored when considering NNESs' abilities to adjust and succeed in their academic endeavors. This includes the concept of self-theories, which often develop from students' educational and cultural backgrounds.
- One possible explanation for institutions operating on the fallacious assumptions presented in this chapter is a lack of understanding of how languages are learned and acquired.

- While there are clear indications that appropriate institutional attention to NNESs' language development needs is lacking, there are many possibilities for training and programming. This chapter, as well as this volume, present possible ideas and directions.

Discussion Questions

1. This chapter presents two assumptions. The first states that once NNESs meet admission requirements, they have adequate English language skills to succeed in postsecondary-level academic work. This can have far-reaching consequences for students and institutions alike. What are some consequences NNESs may face? How might an institution be impacted? Can you think of others who might be impacted?
2. The second assumption presented in this chapter states that because second language students are immersed in an English-speaking environment once they enroll, their academic language skills (i.e., reading and writing) will naturally continue to develop as they progress through their studies. Why is this thinking flawed? Can you think of specific examples to illustrate this?
3. A major concern identified in this chapter is that many institutions do not track the progress of NNES students. Discuss this concern in terms of what may be causing this institutional neglect and specifically how it may impact the students.
4. The impact linguistic limitations have on cultural adjustment cannot be overlooked. How might an institution address the issue to ensure students make successful adjustments?
5. Suggestions for helping NNESs often focus on the students. What are some possible ways support might be focused on faculty and administrators to help students achieve academic success?

Further Reading

Andrade, M. S., & Evans, N. W. (Eds.). (2009). *International students: Strengthening a critical resource*. Westport, CT: ACE/Rowman Littlefield.

Andrade, M. S., Evans, N. W., & Hartshorn, K. J. (2014). Linguistic support for nonnative English speakers: Higher education practices in the United States. *Journal of Student Affairs Research and Practice, 51*(2), 207–221.

Arkoudis, S., Baik, C., & Richardson, S. (2012). *English language standards in higher education: From entry to exit*. Camberwell, Australia: Australian Council for Educational Research.

Kanno, Y., & Harklau, L. (2012). *Linguistic minority students go to college: Preparation, access, and persistence*. New York, NY: Routledge.

References

Anderson, N. J., Evans, N. W., & Hartshorn, K. J. (2014, March). *Discipline-specific expectations of faculty for reading and writing*. Paper presented at the American Association for Applied Linguistics (AAAL), Portland, OR.

Andrade, M. S. (2006). International students in English-speaking universities: Adjustment factors. *Journal of Research in International Education, 5*(2), 131–154.

Andrade, M. S. (2008). International graduate students: Adjusting to study in the United States. In K. A. Tokuno (Ed.), *Graduate students in transition: Assisting students through the first year* (pp. 71–88). Columbia, SC: National Resource Center for the First Year Experience & Students in Transition.

Andrade, M. S. (2009). The value of a first-year seminar: International students' insights in retrospect. *Journal of College Student Retention: Research, Theory, & Practice, 10*(4), 483–506.

Andrade, M. S., & Bunker, E. L. (2011). The role of SRL and TELEs in distance education: Narrowing the gap. In G. Dettori & D. Persico (Eds.), *Fostering self-regulated learning through ICTs* (pp. 105–121). Hershey, PA: IGI Global.

Andrade, M., & Evans, N. (2007). University instructors' views of ESL students: Implications for training. In G. Poedjosoedarmo (Ed.), *Teacher education in language teaching, anthology series 48* (pp. 224–249). Singapore: SEAMEO Regional Language Centre.

Andrade, M. S., & Evans, N. W. (Eds.). (2009). *International students: Strengthening a critical resource*. Westport, CT: ACE/Rowman Littlefield.

Andrade, M. S., & Evans, N. W. (Eds.). (2013). *Principles and practices for response in second language writing: Developing self-regulated learners*. New York, NY: Routledge/Taylor & Francis.

Arkoudis, S., Baik, C., & Richardson, S. (2012). *English language standards in higher education: From entry to exit*. Camberwell, Australia: Australian Council for Educational Research.

Aud, S., Hussar, W., Kena, G., Bianco, K., Frohlich, L., Kemp, J., & Tahan, K. (2011). *The condition of education 2011* (NCES 2011-033). U.S. Department of Education, National Center for Education Statistics. Washington, DC: U.S. Government Printing Office. Retrieved February 10, 2015, from http://nces.ed.gov/pubsearch/pubsinfo.asp?pubid=2011033.

Australian Universities Quality Agency (AUQA). (2009). *Good practice principles for English language proficiency for international students in Australian universities*. Report to the Department of Education, Employment and Workplace Relations, Canberra. Retrieved February 10, 2015, from www.auqa.edu.au/files/otherpublications/good%20practice%20principles%20for%20english%20language%20proficiency%20report.pdf.

Barrett-Lennard, S., Dunworth, K., & Harris, A. (2011). The good practice principles: Silver bullet or starter gun? *Journal of Academic Language & Learning, 5*(2), A99–A106.

Benzie, H. (2011). A pathway into degree program: Forging better links. *Journal of Academic Language & Literacy, 5*(2), A107–A117.

Brooman-Jones, S., Cunningham, G., Hanna, L., & Wilson, D. N. (2011). Embedding academic literacy: A case study in business at UTS: Insearch. *Journal of Academic Language & Literacy, 5*(2), A1–A13.

Celce-Murcia, M. (2006). Language teaching approaches: An overview. In M. Celce-Murcia (Ed.), *Teaching English as a second or foreign language* (3rd ed., pp. 3–11). Boston, MA: Heinle & Heinle.

Choudaha, R., Chang, L., & Kono, Y. (2013, March). International student mobility trends 2013: Towards responsive recruitment strategies. *World Education News & Review, 26*(2). Retrieved February 10, 2015, from www.wes.org/ewenr/13mar/feature.htm

Collier, V. P. (1987). Age and rate of acquisition of second language for academic purposes. *TESOL Quarterly, 21,* 617–641.

Collier, V. P., & Thomas, W. P. (1989). How quickly can immigrants become proficient in school English? *Journal of Educational Issues of Language Minority Students, 5,* 26–38

Conway, K. M. (2010). Educational aspirations in urban community college: Differences between immigrant and native student groups. *Community College Review, 37*(3), 209–242.

Counsell, J. (2011). How effectively and consistently do international postgraduate students apply the writing strategies they have been taught in a generic skills-based course to their subsequent discipline-based studies? *Journal of Academic Language & Literacy, 5*(1), A1–A17.

Cummins, J. (2008). BICS and CALP: Empirical and theoretical status of the distinction. In B. Street & N. H. Hornberger (Eds.), *Encyclopedia of Language and Education,* (2nd ed., Vol. 2, pp. 71–83). New York, NY: Springer.

DeKeser, R. M. (2007). *Practice in a second language: Perspectives from applied linguistics and cognitive psychology.* New York: Cambridge University Press.

Dembo, M. H., Junge, L. G., & Lynch, R. (2006). Becoming a self-regulated learner: Implications for web-based education. In H. F. O'Neil & R. S. Perez (Eds.), *Web-based learning: Theory, research, and practice* (pp. 185–202). Mahwah, NJ: Lawrence Erlbaum Associates.

Dörnyei, Z., & Ushioda, E. (2009). *Motivation, language identity and the L2 self.* Bristol: Multilingual Matters.

Dweck, C. S. (2000). *Self-theories: Their role in motivation, personality, and development.* New York, NY: Psychology Press.

Ellis, R., Sheen, Y., Murakami, M., & Takashima, H. (2008). The effects of focused and unfocused corrective feedback in an English as a foreign language context. *System, 36,* 353–371.

Ferris, D. R. (2009). *Teaching college writing to diverse student populations.* Ann Arbor, MI: University of Michigan Press.

Galloway, F. J., & Jenkins, J. R. (2009). The adjustment problems faced by international students in the United States: A comparison of international students and administrative perceptions at two private, religiously affiliated universities. *NASPA Journal, 46*(4), 661–673.

Grabe, W. (2009). Reflections on second language reading: Research and instruction. In Z. H. Han & N. Anderson (Eds.), *Second language reading: Research and instruction* (pp. 192–205). Ann Arbor, MI: University of Michigan Press.

Green, T., & Agosti, C. (2011). Apprenticing students to academic discourse: Using student and teacher feedback to analyse the extent to which a discipline-specific academic literacies program works. *Journal of Academic Language & Learning, 5*(2), A18–A35.

Grundy, S. (2007). *Higher education related learning framework: Toward a universal framework.* London: Specialist Schools and Academies Trust. Retrieved February 10, 2015, from www.docstoc.com/docs/129379399/Higher-Education-Related-Learning.

Harris, A., & Ashton, J. (2011). Embedding and integrating language and academic skills: An innovative approach. *Journal of Academic Language & Learning, 5*(2), A73–A87.

Huang, J. (2009). What happens when two cultures meet in the classroom? *Journal of Instructional Psychology, 36*(4), 335–342.

Institute of International Education. (2011). Top 25 institutions hosting international students, 2010/11. *Open Doors Report on International Educational Exchange*. Retrieved February 10, 2015, from www.iie.org/opendoors.

Kanno, Y., & Harklau, L. (2012). *Linguistic minority students go to college: Preparation, access, and persistence*. New York, NY: Routledge.

Kennelly, R., Maldoni, A., & Davies, D. (2010). A case study: Do discipline-based programmes improve student learning outcomes? *International Journal for Educational Integrity, 6*(1), 61–73.

Lee, S. A., Park, H. S., & Kim, W. (2009). Gender differences in international students' adjustment. *College Student Journal, 43*(4), 1217–1227.

Lumina Foundation. (2013, February). *Strategic plan 2013 to 2016*. Retrieved from www.luminafoundation.org/publications/A_stronger_nation_through_higher_education-2013.pdf.

Miele, C. (2003). Bergen Community College meets Generation 1.5. *Community College Journal of Research and Practice, 27*, 603–612.

Omaggio Hadley, A. (2000). *Teaching language in context* (3rd ed.). Boston, MA: Heinle & Heinle.

Ritz, A. A. (2010). International students and transformative learning in a multicultural formal educational context. *The Educational Forum, 74*, 158–166, doi:10.1060/0013172100360S497.

Rosenstiel, E. D, Taafee, J., & Thomas, L. J. (2009). The graduate preparation program at the Ohio State University. In M. S. Andrade & N. W. Evans (Eds.), *International students: Strengthening a critical resource* (pp. 147–151). Washington, DC: ACE/Rowman Littlefield.

Russell, J., Rosenthal, D., & Thomson, G. (2009). The international student experience. *Higher Education, 60*, 235–249.

Sherry, M., Thomas, P., & Chui, W. H. (2010). International students: A vulnerable student population. *Higher Education, 60*, 33–46. doi:10.1007/s10734-009-9284-z.

Storch, N. (2009). The impact of studying in a second language (L2) medium university on the development of L2 writing. *Journal of Second Language Writing, 18*(2), 103–118.

Stratilas, K. (2011). The evolving nature of support: A new horizon. *Journal of Academic Language & Literacy, 5*(2), A44–A49.

Sundstrom, C. J. (2009). Graduate support program: The least we owe international graduate students. In M. S. Andrade & N. W. Evans (Eds.), *International students: Strengthening a critical resource* (pp. 157–162). Washington, DC: ACE/Rowman Littlefield.

Teaching English to Speakers of Other Languages, Inc. (TESOL) (2010). *Position statement on the acquisition of academic proficiency in English at the postsecondary level*. Washington, DC: Author. Retrieved February 10, 2015, from www.tesol.org/about-tesol/press-room/position-statements/higher-education-position-statements.

Tochkov, K., Levine, L., & Sanaka, A. (2010). Variation in the prediction of cross-cultural adjustment by Asian-Indian students in the United States. *College Student Journal, 44*(3), 677–689.

Vogt, M., & Echevarria, J. (2005). *Teaching ideas for implementing the SIOP model*. Glenville, IL: Lesson Lab/Pearson Education, Inc.

Xiao, L. (2006). Bridging the gap between teaching styles and learning styles: A cross-cultural perspective. *TESL-EJ, 10*(3), 1–15.

Yakimchuk, D. T. (2010). Literacy-based technology support for post-secondary second language learners. *Canadian Journal of Educational Administration and Policy, 112*, 1–21.

Zimmerman, B. J. (1994). Dimensions of academic self-regulation: A conceptual frame-work for education. In D. H. Schunk & B. J. Zimmerman (Eds.), *Self-regulation of learning and performance* (pp. 3–21). Hillsdale, NJ: Lawrence Erlbaum Associates.

Zimmerman, B. J., & Risemberg, R. (1997). Self-regulatory dimensions of academic learning and motivation. In G. D. Phye (Ed.), *Handbook of academic learning: Construction of knowledge* (pp. 105–125). San Diego, CA: Academic Press.

2

PERCEPTIONS AND REALITIES OF ESL STUDENTS IN HIGHER EDUCATION

An Overview of Institutional Practices

Maureen Snow Andrade, Norman W. Evans, and K. James Hartshorn

Vignette

The director of international services at a large university has requested a meeting with the vice president of student life. He is concerned that the university's initiatives to internationalize the campus over the past three years have had consequences that the administration may be unaware of. For instance, the decision to keep the Test of English as a Foreign Language (TOEFL iBT) at 70 allows the university to meet targets for enrollment and tuition revenue, but it also seems to allow students into the university with language skills below what is necessary for them to succeed academically.

The support services and faculty don't know how to help. This is evidenced by the fact that directors of the writing and learning centers have reported that their staffs have no English as a second language (ESL) training. They tell him, "We don't know what to do for the international students who are constantly coming in for help," and they struggle particularly with those whose needs seem to differ from those of the student body who are native speakers. Faculty in the business, engineering, and English departments have frequently communicated similar concerns. "We have many international students that need help with their writing and speaking," they say. The international services director's first question for the vice president is "Beyond enrollment numbers, does the university track these students?" The director is startled by her reply: "Once students have been admitted with the appropriate score, we have found no reason to track this group of students."

Overview of the Challenges

Though the United States ranked first for two- and four-year degree attainment in 1960 (Lumina Foundation for Education, 2010), it now ranks sixth in the world for the percentage of 25- to 64-year-olds with an associate degree or higher (Lee & Rawls, 2010). Despite this, increasing numbers of individuals are pursuing postsecondary education in the United States. From 2000 to 2009, enrollments of undergraduate students rose by 34%—from 13.2 to 17.6 million students (U.S. Department of Education, National Center for Education Statistics, 2011). These numbers will increase even further, as 66% of all jobs in the United States are projected to require some form of postsecondary education by the year 2020 (Carnevale, Smith, & Strohl, 2010).

To support the need for further education, completion goals have been set by federal and state governments as well as nonprofit educational institutions and organizations (e.g., Lumina Foundation for Education; Commission on Access, Admissions and Success in Higher Education; the National Governor's Association). These goals include increasing the percentage of college graduates by anywhere from 55% to 60% within the next several years (Lee & Rawls, 2010; Lumina Foundation for Education, 2010). To achieve these goals, higher education institutions must be prepared to expand access to students from a wide range of backgrounds and to provide related support services to ensure success.

Access and success are familiar concepts on both two- and four-year campuses. Degree completion, in particular, is receiving more attention than ever before in the history of U.S. higher education. The Lumina Foundation for Education (2010) notes that 22% of Americans, more than 37 million people, have enrolled in college without achieving a degree. Lumina's goal, and that of others, is not only to increase the number of college degrees for Americans, but to close the gap in attainment for underrepresented students. The latter includes ethnic minorities, first-generation students, and low-income students.

The current focus on the attainment gap (providing access to those previously marginalized from higher education and recognition of the range of challenges that affect completion) has not yet addressed those who may lack adequate preparation or struggle with educational pursuits due to limited academic English language proficiency. Both national and global discussions on access and success must include those for whom English is not a first language. English language proficiency is not recognized as contributing to a lack of participation or completion, primarily because the ESL population is generally not identified or tracked at institutional or national levels.

The literature reveals fairly extensive information on the experiences of nonnative English speakers (NNES) in higher education (see Chapter 1), particularly international students; however, national data are lacking regarding documenting institutional practices for admitting and testing, supporting, and tracking these students. A recent study reveals common themes among these areas (Andrade, Evans, & Hartshorn, 2014). The remainder of the chapter will summarize these findings to illustrate how some institutional practices may exacerbate the challenges that ESL populations face and will then discuss practices that may help institutions ensure greater success for this population.

Insufficient Admissions and Language Testing

The challenges facing any student entering higher education can be daunting. To counter this, most universities go to great lengths to ensure that admitted students are academically prepared for the rigors of a university, imposing multiple measures of academic readiness such as test scores, class rankings, and grade point averages (GPAs). Multiple measures ensure accuracy in the admission process. Logic suggests that multiple measures of linguistic readiness of NNES would also be a good idea; unfortunately, such is generally not the case. It is not uncommon for NNES to be deemed linguistically ready for university based on a single measure, such as a language test or country of origin.

The potential problems with such a practice are substantial. Andrade et al. (2014), gathered data from 138 U.S. institutions with high enrollments of international students (comprising approximately 33% of the total international student population in the United States). These sources indicate that more than half of the institutions identify prospective students as NNES in the admissions process based on criteria such as the applicant's country of origin or the applicant's claim of English prevalence in the home. More than three-fourths of the institutions excuse students from English language testing during admission screening if English is considered the native language in the potential student's country of origin, and more than two-thirds of these institutions exempt students if they attended an educational institution in which English was the predominant language. Where language testing is required in the admission process, only two-thirds of the institutions require a writing sample and hardly any require a speaking sample.

These practices seem reasonable in contexts of limited resources. However, on closer examination, critical issues emerge. For example, that a student comes from a country where English is predominantly used or obtained some education in an English-medium environment may have little bearing on that individual's English language proficiency. It is not unreasonable, for example, to expect that a student might come from a country where English is predominant but grew up in a rural setting where opportunities for English development were extremely limited. In this case, the student's language skills may be well below the average language proficiency profile of students from that country. Exempting students from needed language support by not properly assessing their abilities may not be in the best interests of the student or the institution.

Deficient Language Support

NNES in higher education need language support, and this is evidenced by the various forms of language support offered by many institutions. Andrade et al. (2014) report that nearly 80% of the institutions they surveyed provide language support of some kind for their undergraduate students, and about half provide services for graduate students. It is encouraging that these needs are recognized at some institutions; however, several facts cannot be ignored. First, institutional support is lacking for 20% of the undergraduate and 50% of graduate NNES. Furthermore, and perhaps more importantly, the support that is offered may not be contributing to the long-term language development needs of NNES.

While some institutions offer language support in the form of skill centers, coursework, tutoring programs, workshops, and modules (Andrade et al., 2014), a close inspection of how institutions offer these services is informative. For example, most language support services are optional. This suggests that, in general, there is no systematic approach to supporting language development for NNES over the course of their study in a university. Support services seem to be tangential to students' course of study. This approach is based in the "deficit model of language learning" (Arkoudis, Baik, & Richardson, 2012, p. 2), which assumes that once students have passed or are exempt from language admission requirements, they have the necessary language skills to cope with the demands of their studies. Such a model ignores two important facts: learning a language is a long-term developmental process and an institution has a basic role to make sure that the students it admits are appropriately supported to achieve success.

Inadequate Tracking

Data gathered by Andrade et al. (2014) from institutions across the United States with high percentages of international students also suggest that tracking the success of NNES is sorely lacking. Andrade et al. inquired to what extent institutions used key indicators such as GPA, retention, or persistence to graduation to determine student success. Some institutions employed various methods of tracking the success of NNES, but 40% of the institutions did not track success in any way. Many of the survey participants perceived this as an institutional weakness. Responses varied in explaining why this population was not tracked. Some reasons were rather pragmatic. For example, one respondent indicated, "We don't have the manpower or resources to track these students," while another declared, "They all tend to do exceptionally well" (Andrade et al., 2014, p. 215).

If we accept the premise that an institution has an ethical obligation to admit only those students who are linguistically prepared or who are adequately supported by the institution, then systems that carefully monitor key indicators of student success ought to be in place. Nationwide data further suggest that the deficit model of language learning is commonly accepted. Comments made by several survey participants illustrate this attitude succinctly: "If they meet our admissions criteria, they have demonstrated adequate English understanding and as such no further monitoring is performed"; "Once students have been admitted with the appropriate score [note the use of the singular form], the

Admissions Office has found no reason to track students" (Andrade et al., 2014, p. 214). Clearly, there is much room for improvement in the tracking procedures on the part of institutions that admit and educate NNES.

A Web of Disconnects

While the factors described are interconnected, they result in an overall disconnect in terms of NNES in higher education. Obviously, if students are not identified as NNES in the admission process, they will not be required to demonstrate their proficiency in English. Consequently, they will not receive needed support. If they are not tracked as a distinct group (or two distinct groups—international and resident), the institution can only assume they are succeeding. Thus, institutions may be completely unaware of the challenges these students face, and the students may be excluded from institutional, national, and global discussions regarding student success.

Even if students are identified as NNES, which generally occurs for international students, lenient criteria often exempt them from pre-admission testing. Frequently, further assessment after admission is not required. However, such testing could be used with standardized proficiency tests to identify potential weaknesses in academic reading and writing skills and types of support needed. These oversights increase the likelihood that these students will face challenges that could have been avoided. Such administrative practices also point to the very real possibility that learners will graduate from the institution with weak English skills, such as has been occurring in Australia, where 21.4% of higher education enrollments consist of international students, most of them NNES (Institute of International Education [IIE], 2012).

Australia represents an interesting case. Australian higher education institutions admit NNES based on a standardized proficiency exam (Birrell, 2006). They also offer residency to international students who graduate from Australian universities in order to address work sector needs. However, these students have had difficulty finding jobs due to their weak English language skills. Therefore, the country instituted an English language proficiency test score requirement that must be met to qualify for permanent residency. Nearly one-third of those applying could not pass the test, even though the same score was required for university admission.

Some of these students may have entered the country for other types of educational programs (e.g., intensive English language study or high school) and then entered universities. As such, they would not have had to submit scores from a standardized English language proficiency test. Additionally, anecdotal evidence suggests that universities may have lowered the English demands in their courses and that students cope by getting help from native English speakers (Birell, 2006). This is because universities do not want to require supplementary English courses due to competition with English-medium universities in other countries to attract students. They believe that remaining competitive would be difficult if they required students to spend additional time and money taking English language courses.

This case powerfully demonstrates the effects of institutional decisions related to admission practices (e.g., a single score from a standardized proficiency test, no identification of resident NNES), assessment of English language proficiency (e.g., no post-admission testing), support (e.g., reluctance to require further English language study), and tracking (e.g., lack of awareness that students' proficiency was too low for employment after graduation and that one-third of students had lower English proficiency scores after graduation than when initially accepted to the institution).

Findings of the national study cited earlier (Andrade et al., 2014) indicate that similar practices are prevalent in the United States. However, this issue remains hidden due to the fact that only 3.7% of the total enrollment in U.S. higher education institutions is international (IIE, 2012), in contrast to the 21.4% in Australia. However, the former figure represents over 700,000 international students. Additionally, the United States is still the premier destination for international students, attracting the largest market share at 19%, well ahead of the United Kingdom at 12%, which is in second place (IIE, 2012). Furthermore, the number of resident students in U.S. higher education institutions who are NNES is unknown, which indicates even further need for improved systems related to ESL populations in higher education, particularly in the context of access and completion initiatives.

This issue is clearly not only a national higher education issue but a global one. As nations compete with each other to attract international students, rigor and standards may be compromised. Figure 2.1 illustrates current practices and summarizes the key issues of challenges identified in the national study. We refer to these challenges as a web of disconnects—a series of poorly informed practices that create a disconnected experience, leading to unknown outcomes for the considerable population of NNES in higher education.

Implications and Applications

Institutions will need to consider context- and mission-appropriate responses to the challenges identified in the previous section. To assist in this process, we introduce an institutional framework for English language development. The framework encourages institutions to establish structures that enable collaboration among stakeholders in order to establish a foundation from which to identify and implement specific English language development strategies.

This section introduces the foundational steps in the framework, followed by an overview of concepts that potentially influence institutional action. It then provides examples of possible implementation strategies that specifically address the challenges identified by the research findings cited earlier. These include

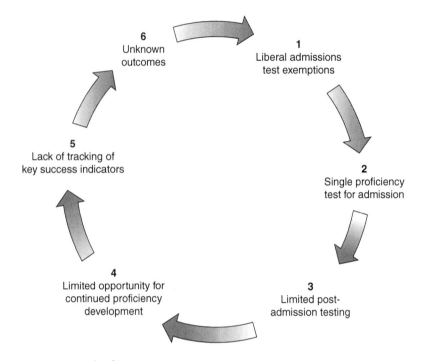

FIGURE 2.1 A Web of Disconnects.

incomplete indications of learners' proficiency levels, lack of success indicators for NNES, non-innovative forms of English language support, and failure to provide ongoing English language development opportunities.

An Institutional Framework for English Language Development

The foundation to the framework consists of a sequence of four steps as follows: examine views and beliefs; establish guiding principles; base policies and practices on principles; and design an assessment plan (see Figure 2.2). These components serve as a point of reference for institutions to consider as they determine how to best demonstrate their commitment to English language development for NNES.

Views and Beliefs

Institutions must examine and address stakeholders' views and beliefs about language learning (e.g., see Andrade & Evans, 2007). Furthermore, they must determine how faculty members see their role in terms of responsibility for helping students further their English language skills. In order for change to be

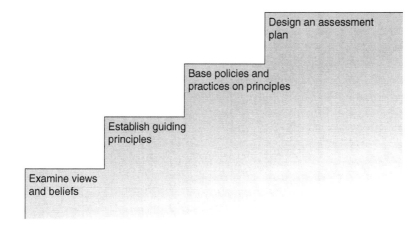

FIGURE 2.2 Foundational Steps to the Framework.

successful, it is critical to recognize the linguistic and transitional issues faced by NNES and to understand the implications for institutional practice. This awareness must be shared by decision makers and by the faculty and staff who develop policies and procedures, provide support, teach, or interact with NNES to any extent.

Guiding Principles

Institutions should identify guiding principles (e.g., see Australian Universities Quality Agency, 2009, in Appendix A) that support a philosophy of success specifically related to English language proficiency development for NNES. These principles must be informed by linguistic theory in terms of language acquisition, general academic and discipline-specific English language proficiency, the length of time required to develop these proficiencies, and expected outcomes. Principles should be aimed at shifting the focus from a philosophy of support to a philosophy of English language development (Arkoudis et al., 2012). This support must extend to all areas of the institution, from the classroom to academic services to social engagement.

Policies and Practices

Institutions need to examine policies and practices for admission, assessment, English language development, and tracking outcomes in terms of the guiding principles to determine where adjustments should and can occur. Furthermore, they should consider how current systems and practices support underrepresented and ethnic minority students and examine their strengths and weaknesses related to developing the English language skills of NNES. Institutions must have an inclusive approach that extends to all of the students they admit and that focuses on specific areas where additional development must occur for students to be academically successful.

Assessment Plan

Institutions must determine and implement a process to measure students' English language skills at entrance, exit, and post-enrollment (see Figure 2.3). They must also determine criteria to determine which students need to be tested on entry and to ensure this information is communicated clearly to students and other stakeholders prior to admission. To avoid the criticism that post-admission assessment is retesting or repeating the testing required for admission purposes, institutions should ensure that the plan has diagnostic characteristics that enable support systems and further opportunities to be activated. They should develop assessment tasks relevant to specific disciplines accompanied by feedback to students and recommendations for directed learning opportunities (Arkoudis & Starfield, 2007; Arkoudis et al., 2012). Finally, institutions should consider how to require or incentivize participation in exit and post-enrollment assessments. (See the Influencing Concepts section in this chapter for an explanation of weak vs. strong in Figure 2.3; see the Strategies section in this chapter for more information on ongoing data collection and analysis.)

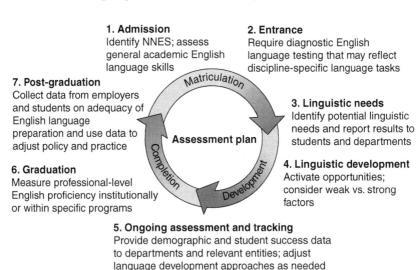

1. Admission
Identify NNES; assess general academic English language skills

2. Entrance
Require diagnostic English language testing that may reflect discipline-specific language tasks

7. Post-graduation
Collect data from employers and students on adequacy of English language preparation and use data to adjust policy and practice

3. Linguistic needs
Identify potential linguistic needs and report results to students and departments

6. Graduation
Measure professional-level English proficiency institutionally or within specific programs

4. Linguistic development
Activate opportunities; consider weak vs. strong factors

5. Ongoing assessment and tracking
Provide demographic and student success data to departments and relevant entities; adjust language development approaches as needed with ongoing measurement and analysis

Matriculation
Assessment plan
Completion
Development

FIGURE 2.3 Assessment Plan.

Influencing Concepts

The next four components of the framework demonstrate concepts that influence action and must be considered once the foundational steps (i.e., examining views and beliefs, establishing guiding principles, basing policies and practices on the principles, and designing an assessment plan) are in place. Figure 2.4 illustrates the relationship among all of the parts of the framework. The influencing concepts are layered over the foundational steps to demonstrate the next level of action required in order to fully implement the framework. The final component of the framework is the specific implementation strategies, examples of which are discussed in the Implementation Strategies section.

Optional vs. Required

Related to support practices, remember the adage "Students don't do optional." Often, the students who need the most help are the least likely to access it. They need all of their available time to focus on passing their courses, and they don't recognize that stronger skills would facilitate their success and decrease the amount of time needed for study. Typically, NNES do not want to spend more time and money on add-on models such as stand-alone credit or noncredit

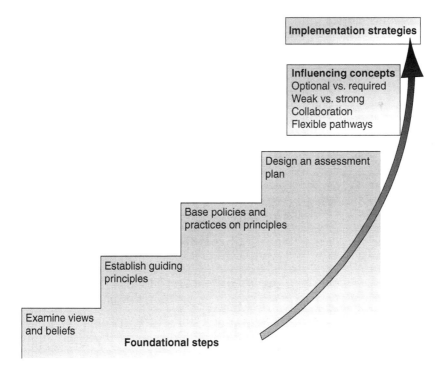

FIGURE 2.4 Institutional Framework for English Language Development.

English language courses. They have an instrumental orientation characterized by doing what is needed to pass their courses, to obtain their qualifications, and to enter the workforce to earn money. As such, institutional expectations must be clear regarding the realities of English language requirements in the discipline and profession. Integrating proficiency development into coursework addresses student resistance and focuses instruction on discipline and professional needs, thus making it more meaningful to students.

Weak vs. Strong

Cost and efficiency factors need consideration (e.g., comparing the cost of providing one-on-one tutoring to large numbers of students as opposed to implementing integrated forms of support embedded within courses). Andrade et al. (2014) found that institutions typically provide what has been called "adjunct weak models of collaboration" (Arkoudis et al., 2012, p. 45; Jones, Bonnano, & Scouller, 2001). These are characterized by approaches (e.g., workshops, credit and noncredit courses, individual tutoring) that are generic in nature rather than discipline-based and that are provided outside students' major courses. General English language skills may not prepare students for the English language needs of specific majors, students may not transfer the skills to new learning tasks or see the relevance of these approaches, and students' skills will likely plateau without further structured opportunities for English language development. In contrast, strong models of development are integrated into coursework and are discipline-specific, since students tend to resist add-on initiatives.

Collaboration

Removing structural and cultural barriers to enable collaboration between Teaching English to Speakers of Other Languages (TESOL) professionals and faculty will help to identify English language challenges represented in the curriculum and options for further development. Examples of collaboration include coteaching, in which a TESOL professional provides discipline-specific workshops or class sessions related to English language development as part of a course in a major; integrated models, in which English language support is built into the curriculum; content-based instruction, such as the adjunct model, in which students are dually enrolled in a discipline course and an ESL course, with the latter providing English language development specific to the content course (Brinton, Snow, & Wesche, 2003); or required stand-alone supplemental support components. Consider that TESOL professionals have traditionally been in the margins of the institution with a lower profile and heavier teaching loads and have been viewed as fulfilling remedial or service needs (Arkoudis et al., 2012). These barriers must be overcome for effective collaboration to occur.

Flexible Pathways

Institutions must determine which students need English language skill development and where and to what extent English language skill development is needed. Then they must provide multiple pathways to related opportunities that are sufficiently flexible to accommodate needs in majors with large numbers of NNES, individual courses with perhaps one or two struggling students, or individuals (faculty and students) independently seeking opportunities and services. These pathways should be part of the institution's overall plan for English language development, should indicate various levels and types of intervention, as well as points of intervention, and should specify how coordination among units will occur (see the Resources section in this chapter). This plan would be the result of a needs analysis based on collected data.

Implementation Strategies

Depending on individual contexts, infrastructures, and resources, the following strategies are possibilities for implementing the guiding framework. As institutions typically have budget constraints, choices for how to best commit to continued English language development must be strategic. Priorities need to be set and approaches evaluated in order to make these decisions. Many of the suggestions that follow could be implemented with faculty reassigned time or considered within the parameters of faculty service. Another option is to redirect how opportunities are provided (e.g., rather than stand-alone general ESL courses, TESOL professionals could develop English language strands within discipline-based curriculum and teach modules in courses in a major program). Other approaches might entail refocusing existing budgets on specific projects related to English language development for NNES (e.g., institutional research, marketing, learning assistance center or faculty center training, or resource development projects).

Entry Testing

Institutions must provide required training for admission staff related to English language proficiency instruments, test scores, score comparisons, score interpretations, processes for setting cut scores, and test limitations. Furthermore, standard measures of error related to proficiency tests must be recognized, along with the extent to which gains on standardized proficiency tests can be expected. Institutions should also create opportunities for TESOL professionals to collaborate in this training and should establish systems that support collaboration between TESOL professionals, admissions officers, and decision makers involved in setting English language entrance and matriculation standards.

Awareness-Raising

Providing regularly scheduled and required training (possibly incentivized) will help staff who interact with NNES (e.g., learning assistance personnel, multicultural and international center staff, faculty, and peer tutors). Training should be tailored to the staff's roles and should be focused on raising their awareness of language acquisition and transition issues. Campus TESOL professionals should also be involved in this training.

Teaching Strategies

Institutions must create a system through which teaching strategies can be accessed and shared. While more intensive and formal professional development initiatives can be provided, for those who may not be able to invest the time, a discussion forum, database, or website with straightforward strategies can be provided. These strategies will likely benefit not only NNES, but all enrolled students and would reflect overall good teaching practice. For example, strategies might include ideas on lecturing, using small groups, encouraging class participation, developing students' critical thinking skills, addressing plagiarism, and planning interaction (Arkoudis et al., 2012). Strategies should demonstrate a range of possibilities from those that require minimal intervention to those that involve a greater level of intervention (Arkoudis et al., 2012). Examples of strategies involving minimal work include simply listing language learning development expectations on a course syllabus (indicating both language and content objectives as part of a class session; Echevarria, Vogt, & Short, 2008) or identifying language proficiency standards on grading rubrics or other assessment measures. A more intensive intervention would be revising the curriculum to include English language support or attending workshops to learn more about how to respond to the needs of NNES.

Resources

Institutions attuned to the needs of NNES should offer resources to faculty and staff that help them create materials and implement services that support development of both general and discipline-specific English language skills. These might include learning assistance resources, websites or databases, e-learning tools or modules (commercial or proprietary), and embedded workshops offered by TESOL professionals or faculty development and innovation center staff. Experts from across campus—TESOL professionals, technology experts, learning assistance and curriculum office specialists—could be called on to develop and provide these resources. Additionally, a centralized office for English language support would coordinate these efforts and serve as a first point of reference for faculty, staff, and students. Many institutions have a student success and retention center of some sort; it is therefore appropriate to have a center focused on English language development or include this as a part of a student success unit.

Ongoing Data Collection and Analysis

Institutions must establish data collection and analysis processes to ensure they can provide relevant data to programs; these data should include major-specific information on NNES, including the number enrolled in a program, GPAs, first-year retention, graduation rates, and job placement. It should also evaluate various English language proficiency development models that may be in place institutionally or within programs. The latter can provide crucial data for making decisions about the viability and efficiency of specific approaches. Institutions should also provide resources to departments, particularly those with substantial percentages of NNES, so they can conduct research on transition and success issues through surveys, student and faculty focus groups, and other means; they should also receive resources to ensure departments can act on their findings and implement appropriate opportunities for English language development. Institutional research could be conducted to determine faculty and student perspectives on the English language skills of NNES and how the latter view their own skills and experiences.

Postgraduation Feedback

When possible, institutions should obtain employer and alumni feedback through surveys or other means to determine the use of and satisfaction with NNES English language skills in their chosen professions. This monitoring will help institutions determine their success in terms of English language development and preparing students with professional skills. Institutions must also determine clear standards for ensuring that students graduate with the English proficiency needed for their future careers by coordinating with employers and examining job placement rates for NNES in English-speaking contexts. These data should then be used to convince students of the importance of attaining strong English language proficiency during their postsecondary education.

Communication

Finally, institutions should work with faculty, staff, and others committed to English language development to promote, market, and disseminate information about the institutional principles of support, the expectations for NNES to develop discipline-specific and professional English language skills, the available resources, and the institutional commitment to English language learning outcomes. Public relations campaigns could include employer and alumni feedback and findings from institutional data. These needs, plans, opportunities, and successes should be clearly communicated across campus.

Conclusion

We began this chapter by describing the all too common situation of universities typically admitting international students on a limited language proficiency profile, usually a single language test, and then assuming that these students have the English language necessary to succeed. This deficit model is flawed in a variety of ways: admission screening for language skills is often insufficient, support for language development is lacking, tracking of this population is frequently nonexistent or limited at best. This model is based on the idea that language deficiencies can be corrected by providing support services that are tangential, not central, to the curricular needs of these students.

While NNES represent only 3.7% of the total enrollment in U.S. higher education, that percentage equates to nearly three-fourths of a million students whose hopes and futures are based on success in the university. As Seidman (2006) has correctly admonished, "do not recruit students to your campus who will not be successful unless you are willing to provide programs and services to help overcome deficiencies. Philosophy does not have to follow finance" (p. 32). The aim of this chapter has been to present a model that will provide programs and services to ensure NNES success by focusing on language development from the time students enter the university until they graduate. This design is based on such foundational steps as identifying beliefs and principles that inform policies and practices that can then be used to create an institutional assessment plan. These foundational steps then allow for influencing concepts such as collaboration and flexible pathways to lead to implementation strategies. Each of these steps are intended to help an institution centralize English language development within the various curricula of the disciplines that NNES study. NNES' academic and linguistic attainment are the objectives of this model.

Summary

- The enrollment of NNES at English-medium institutions of higher learning is on the rise.
- Many institutions of higher learning lack adequate methods to identify NNES, to confirm that they are linguistically prepared for their coursework, and to track their success.
- Students who are NNES and who are not properly identified or tracked are not likely to receive the linguistic support needed to ensure adequate language development and employment following graduation.

- Institutions of higher learning who accept tuition from NNES should re-evaluate their commitment to NNES and should establish principles and strategies that better ensure the language development, academic success, and future employability of this population.
- The initial, foundational steps institutions should take include examining views and beliefs, establishing guiding principles, basing policies and practices on those principles, and designing an assessment plan.
- With the foundational steps in place, institutions need to determine whether resources to facilitate language development will be optional or required, align with weak or strong models of English language development, benefit from effective collaboration, and utilize flexibility in accommodating student needs.
- Institutions will also benefit from various implementation strategies such as entry testing, raising awareness, specific teaching strategies, allocation of resources, ongoing data collection and analysis, post-graduation feedback, and effective communication across the institution.

Discussion Questions

1. What are the key issues identified in this chapter related to admitting, assessing, supporting, and tracking NNES in higher education?
2. How do these issues present challenges for NNES and the institutions that host them?
3. What do you see as the difference between English language support and English language development as explained in this chapter? What implications do these two philosophies have for NNES and higher education institutions?
4. Review Figure 2.4 regarding the institutional framework for English language development. How does the figure address the challenges presented in this chapter? What challenges might arise in implementing this model? What processes and levels of support would need to be in place for successful implication of the framework?
5. Analyze your own institution or one with which you are familiar and identify its processes for admitting, assessing, supporting, and tracking NNES. Gather further information as needed, and then create a plan for implementing the framework. Note the individuals who would need to be involved. Also note potential barriers, but do not let these prevent innovative thinking at this point.

Appendix A: 10 Good Practice Principles

1. Universities are responsible for ensuring that their students are sufficiently competent in the English language to participate effectively in their university studies.
2. Resourcing for English language development is adequate to meet students' needs throughout their studies.
3. Students have responsibilities for further developing their English language proficiency during their study at universities and are advised of these responsibilities prior to enrollment.
4. Universities ensure that the English language entry pathways they approve for the admission of students enable these students to participate effectively in their studies.
5. English language proficiency and communication skills are important graduate attributes for all students.
6. Development of English language proficiency is integrated with curriculum design, assessment practices, and course delivery through a variety of methods.
7. Students' English language development needs are diagnosed early in their studies and addressed, with ongoing opportunities for self-assessment.
8. International students are supported from the outset to adapt to their academic, sociocultural, and linguistic environments.
9. International students are encouraged and supported to enhance their English language development through effective social interaction on and off campus.
10. Universities use evidence from a variety of sources to monitor and improve their English language development activities.

Australian Universities Quality Agency, 2009, p. 3

Further Reading

Andrade, M. S. (2008). International graduate students: Adjusting to study in the United States. In K. A. Tokuno (Ed.), *Graduate students in transition: Assisting students through the first year* (pp. 71–88). Columbia, SC: National Resource Center for the First Year Experience & Students in Transition.
Andrade, M. S., & Evans, N. W. (Eds.). (2009). *International students: Strengthening a critical resource*. Westport, CT: ACE/Rowman Littlefield.
Andrade, M. S., Evans, N. W., & Hartshorn, K. J. (2014). Linguistic support for non-native English speakers: Higher education practices in the United States. *Journal of Student Affairs Research and Practice, 51*(2), 207–221.
Arkoudis, S., Baik, C., & Richardson, S. (2012). *English language standards in higher education: From entry to exit*. Camberwell, Australia: Australian Council for Educational Research.

References

Andrade, M. S., & Evans, N. (2007). University instructors' views of ESL students: Implications for training. In G. Poedjosoedarmo (Ed.), *Teacher education in language teaching, anthology series 48* (pp. 224–249). Singapore: SEAMEO Regional Language Centre.

Andrade, M. S., Evans, N. W., & Hartshorn, K. J. (2014). Linguistic support for non-native English speakers: Higher education practices in the United States. *Journal of Student Affairs Research and Practice, 51*(2), 207–221.

Arkoudis, S., Baik, C., & Richardson, S. (2012). *English language standards in higher education: From entry to exit.* Camberwell, Australia: Australian Council for Educational Research.

Arkoudis, S., & Starfield, S. (2007). *In-course English language development and support.* Canberra, Australia: Australian Education International.

Australian Universities Quality Agency (AUQA). (2009). *Good practice principles for English language proficiency for international students in Australian universities.* Canberra, Australia: Department of Education, Employment and Workplace Relations. Retrieved February 10, 2015, from www.teqsa.gov.au.

Birrell, B. (2006). Implications of low English standards among overseas students at Australian universities. *People and Place, 14*(4), 53–64.

Brinton, D. M., Snow, M. A., & Wesche, M. B. (2003). *Content-based second language instruction.* Ann Arbor, MI: University of Michigan Press.

Carnevale, A. P., Smith, N., & Strohl, J. (2010, June). *Help wanted: Projections of jobs and education requirements through 2018.* Retrieved February 10, 2015, from http://files.eric.ed.gov/fulltext/ED512538.pdf.

Echevarria, J., Vogt, M., & Short, D. (2008). *Making content comprehensible for English learners: The SIOP model.* Boston, MA: Pearson Education, Inc.

Institute of International Education. (2012). *Project atlas.* Retrieved February 10, 2015, from www.iie.org/Research-and-Publications/Project-Atlas.

Jones, J., Bonanno, H., & Scouller, K. (2001). Staff and student roles in central and faculty-based learning-support: Changing partnerships. In B. James, A. Percy, J. Skillen, & N. Trivett (Eds.), *Changing identities: Proceedings of the Australian language and academic skills conference.* Retrieved February 10, 2015, from http://learning.uow.edu.au/LAS2001/selected/jones_1.pdf.

Lee, J. M., & Rawls, A. (2010). *The college completion agenda, 2010 progress report.* Retrieved February 10, 2015, from: http://advocacy.collegeboard.org/sites/default/files/Progress_Report_2010.pdf.

Lumina Foundation for Education. (2010, September). *A stronger nation through higher education.* Retrieved February 10, 2015, from https://cew.georgetown.edu/wp-content/uploads/2014/12/fullreport.pdf .

Seidman, A. (2006). A retention formula for student success. Retrieved April 15, 2015, http://r.search.yahoo.com/_ylt=A86.J7_36S9VvB0AVSsnnIlQ;_ylu=X3oDMTByNzhwY2hkBHNlYwNzcgRwb3MDMgRjb2xvA2dxMQR2dGlkAw--/RV=2/RE=1429232248/RO=10/RU=http%3a%2f%2fwww.cscsr.org%2fdocs%2fRetentionFormulaUpdateForWeb2006.pdf/RK=0/RS=.B0Ug8JGPrW2XFtbeDQoSXc8h2E-

U.S. Department of Education, National Center for Education Statistics. (2011). *The condition of education 2011* (NCES 2011-033). Washington, DC: Government Printing Office. Retrieved February 10, 2015, from http://nces.ed.gov/pubsearch/pubsinfo.asp?pubid=2011033.

3

FOCUSING ON THE CHALLENGES

Institutional Language Planning

William G. Eggington

Vignette

Joung Won is returning to South Korea after completing a four-year undergraduate degree at an American university. Despite typical student struggles, she has enjoyed the experience. However, a growing wave of apprehension has begun to sweep over her. She knows that her next challenge will be to find quality employment in a weakened South Korean economy, the type of employment that would justify the significant financial sacrifices her family has made to support her during her U.S. education. But of more concern is the worry that she will fail her family's expectations in her primary rationale for coming to the U.S., namely the acquisition of high-proficiency English to a level that will open significant career-path doors in Korea. In her own slightly edited words, she tells of:

> *[her] grandfather who told me a true story before he died about the necessity of language. In the Korean colonial period when the Japanese ruled [1910–1945], my grandfather lived in a small village. There was one bridge that connected to the place where people could earn money. But several Japanese police officers always stood there and let Koreans pass by the bridge only when they could speak Japanese. My grandfather, who has seven children, learned Japanese so he could earn enough money and have a high status. He later became the principal of the major high school in the city. There was a language battlefield which required the survival of the fittest. These days in Korea, English is my grandfather's Japanese, although not as intense. There is an English bridge in Korea, and to pass over it, we need good English.*

It was her grandfather's post-colonial, English-as-success orientation, an orientation shared by most Koreans (see Dudden, 2005; Lee, Min & McKerrow, 2010), that led her family to decide to send Joung to the U.S. even though she could have studied at many top-tier Korean universities. In the beginning of her U.S. experience, Joung applied herself to English acquisition as well as to the content of her major. But she became consumed by struggles to understand her textbooks, the lectures, and the study necessary to pass examinations, most of which came in multiple-choice format with very little demand to write extended English prose. Corrective feedback on writing assignments that she did submit was minimal.

By the time she reached upper-level classes, Joung's days were devoted to attending lectures and then sitting with fellow Korean classmates in study sessions struggling to understand the lectures and textbooks. These sessions were all conducted in Korean. Sometimes she studied with other non-Korean English language learners functioning in a non-standard English as Lingua Franca mode. Extended interaction with native English speakers was rare. Professors in some classes tried to involve her in class discussions, but she knew if she sat toward the rear corner of the class farthest from the professor's podium, and behind some taller students, and showed a "please don't ask me" expression, she would seldom be called upon. Her professors needed to keep the class going and so they sub-consciously preferred to interact with native English speakers. Socially, it was easier to room with fellow Koreans. In fact, it was easier to spend all of her time outside of her studies functioning in Korean rather than in English. In many ways, the metaphorical language acquisition device in her brain was residing in Korea, but with occasional forays into an English-speaking world. With the impending return to her homeland, an uncomfortable realization was settling into her psyche involving notions of opportunities lost, forthcoming shame, and disappointment.

Introduction

Joung's apprehension concerning her English language proficiency even after extensive study in a supposed immersion context is not rare. A variation in Australia, for instance, involves ESL university students who, instead of returning home after completing their studies, apply for and receive immigrant status so they can work in their chosen career in Australia. This scenario led to a recent interesting discovery by Dr. Bob Birrell of Monash University's Centre for Population and Urban Research based in Melbourne, Australia (Birrell, 2006).

Prior to 2005, students who had completed a degree at an Australian university could apply for immigrant status to work in their disciplinary field without having to take the International English Language Testing System examination (IELTS), an examination required of immigrants applying from overseas. For example, potential nonnative English-speaking immigrants with university degrees applying from overseas, under the same immigrant status pathway had to sit for the IELTS and receive a minimum of a Band 6 rating. The testing waiver for in-country ESL university graduates was based upon the premise that ESL students who had completed their studies at an Australian university would have, of necessity, sufficient English proficiency to function in an employment context within their discipline (approximately IELTS Band 7).

However, in 2005 the Australian government changed the language testing regulations, requiring an IELTS score even for in-country ESL graduates. This policy change allowed Dr. Birrell to investigate the English language proficiency of ESL graduates from Australian universities who had applied for immigrant status. To the discomfort of many, he found that approximately one-third of these ESL graduates from Australian universities could not achieve a Band 6 rating—a rating below the minimum required for entry into most Australian or U.S. universities, and yet all these students had graduated from an Australian university.

Upon publication of these findings, there was the predictable public angst directed at universities, teachers, and students followed by predictable responses that focused on the validity and reliability of the testing instrument, as well as researcher and general public anti-immigrant bias. Underlying the turmoil, however, are the uncomfortable professional realizations that perhaps many ESL students in Anglo-American university contexts are not developing sufficient English language proficiency to function in their fields even after receiving a four-year degree; that perhaps, Joung Won's experience mentioned above is more typical than we would wish; and that perhaps ESL specialists such as teachers, administrators and researchers may be failing our ESL students in their students' ultimate goals of achieving a level of English fluency sufficient for them to function within their disciplines. But how are we failing? We are second language teaching professionals. We are highly trained, well-experienced artisans, thoroughly supported by a wealth of quality research that informs us of the best pedagogical practices, the most current second language acquisition theories, and the most salient knowledge about the English language.

The underlying argument and related possible provocative challenge of this chapter is that, regardless of these outstanding professional foundations, we are failing in the ultimate objective, at least as defined by many of our students; that is, we are not helping our students achieve a level of English fluency sufficient for them to function within their disciplines. I suggest below that part of this failure is caused by the limits we have placed upon our professional selves. Within this limited concept of our defined selves, a more apt label for our profession should be "*classroom* teachers of English to speakers of other languages" with an emphasis on "classroom." I make this claim because, in spite of a wealth of second language acquisition research that tells us that so much acquisition happens outside of the classroom (O'Malley & Chamot, 1990), we have chosen to limit the scope of our responsibility and expertise to the classroom.

Being an elitist, ivory-tower armchair critic of our profession, as some may claim I am, is hollow unless one is prepared to offer an alternative pathway that, if followed, could expand our professional influence and ultimately assist students in achieving their proficiency objectives. This is my goal for the remainder of this chapter. I will begin by providing a theoretical overview of language planning and policy development that, if applied to our shared contexts, may offer some guidance. I will then briefly describe how a language planning approach was implemented in a U.S.-based university. The chapter will conclude with suggestions for implementing such an approach in other settings. Not surprisingly, many of the chapters in this book are examples of teachers and professionals inserting their professional orientation and expertise into their learners' world beyond the ESL classroom, a much larger and complex world than that contained within the four walls of the typical ESL classroom.

Language Planning and its Relationship to ESL Teaching

Language Planning is an applied linguistics field devoted to developing planned approaches to language-related challenges and opportunities (see Kaplan & Baldauf, 1997 for a thorough overview of the field). Language planning occurs when a governing agency such as a national, state, or regional government, a corporation, or an educational system detects or forecasts a language-related problem or challenge within a particular speech community. Language planners then develop and implement an informed solution to the language-related problem or challenge facing the speech community. These solutions follow established planning procedures. In the past, language planning challenges, and related research were mostly seen as involving a government-sponsored national or regional scope, a macro-language planning orientation. However, more recent emphasis in the field has focused on micro-language planning or planning that addresses institutional concerns (Baldauf, 2005, 2006; Chua & Baldauf, 2011). Baldauf (2012) outlines a four-part framework for language planning goals. I review three of these goals below and provide some ESL-related examples.

1. Status Planning is concerned with raising the status of a language within society. Many of our students, such as Joung Won, the Korean young lady introduced at the beginning of this chapter, come from nations where national language plans have been implemented designed to raise the status of the English language. In South Korea, Japan and just about every nationality represented by our students, high English proficiency has been promoted as a gateway to national modernization, and to individual success (Lee et al., 2010), often at the expense of first language maintenance. In a very real sense, ESL teachers in these nations and in English-as-first-language nations such as the U.S., Canada, and Australia are front-line deliverers of national status-raising language planning. Usually, it is the status of the English language that is being raised, often at the expense of local, national and regional languages As such, it behooves ESL teachers to know what those plans are, and to be involved in critiquing and developing them—but that is a discussion beyond the scope of this chapter.

2. Corpus Planning is concerned with the development of linguistic elements of a language with respect to language standardization, language orthography, dictionary making, terminological creation, and so on. In this respect, the creation of English for Specific Purposes corpora, and the development of general corpus-based studies (see Stoller and Robinson in this volume; Davies and Gardner in this volume; Biber & Reppen, 2002; Gardner & Davies, 2007) are examples of Corpus Planning in educational language planning contexts.

3. Language-in-Education Planning is concerned with language-related policy development, personnel, curriculum, methods and materials, and evaluation policies, among others. The ESL profession fits directly under this labeled umbrella. Chapters in this volume by Andrade and Evans, Silva, and Andrade, Evans, and Hartshorn are examples of planned responses to educational needs that focus on conditions outside of the ESL classroom. As noted above, we are the implementers of national language policies. In addition, we implement institutional policies involving the treatment of students at particular proficiency levels, the types of materials appropriate for various purposes, and the testing and evaluation of students and programs. As claimed in the introduction to this chapter, I contend that we have taken a limited classroom orientation to our role in implementing the language-in-education policies within our universities. The following discussion will elaborate on this point.

Language-in-Education Planning within Higher Education Contexts

Sociolinguists and language planners have an established interest in linguistic variations that exist in the relationships between language and society, often in terms of who speaks what to whom for what purpose under what conditions (Fishman, 1965). For a long time, sociolinguists have been aware that, in some societies, in some language domains, there is a way of communicating in high-prestige, performance-related, status-conscious registers of language that is very different than "normal" contexts such as the type of colloquial language used between family members and friends (Eggington & Eggington, 2010; Ferguson, 1959). This "diglossic" situation distinguishes between high-code and low-code language use. It can be argued that a diglossic-like, low-code/high-code usage pattern is discernable in the English language (Eggington, 2013).

Take, for example, a simple sentence such as, *I looked at the ball*. This is a message delivered in low-code English suitable for most normal spoken registers. It exhibits simple syntax, with Germanic-origin words. However, as one gains greater educational standing in the English-speaking world, it become more apparent that using such language is inappropriate, especially when one begins to enter specialized "discourse communities" (Swales, 1990) and especially when one moves from spoken registers to academic written registers. Our sample sentence must undergo a series of transformations involving lexical choice (from Germanic to Latinate vocabulary such as *ball* becoming *sphere* then becoming *spherical object*), morphological adjustments (lexical choice and nominalization process that change a verb such as *looked* to *observed* to a noun equivalent such as *observations*), and syntactic transformations (from active to passive voice). These adjustments, among others, move *I looked at the ball* to *Personal observations were conducted* vis-à-vis *a designated spherical object* (see Eggington, 2013, Eggington & Eggington, 2010).

Of course, this is an exaggerated example, but in many ways it represents the language of the academic high code in the English language. For native English-speaking students, this code is acquired through a mostly informal language-in-education planning process that commences in secondary schooling and continues throughout the undergraduate and graduate college experience. Required university-level composition courses, writing across the curriculum programs, reading and writing centers, class term papers, senior papers required for graduation, master's theses, and PhD dissertations are all necessary tasks within a gradated language acquisition process that ultimately lead to students and eventually "scholars" gaining some level of proficiency, depending upon how far individuals choose to proceed within their formal education objectives.

The acquisition of such a code is not easy even for native English speakers. Generally, however, native English-speaking college students have sufficient meta-linguistic awareness to successfully take advantage of the informal language-in-education opportunities noted above. However, it is my contention that, for many ESL college students, the informal, almost laissez-faire, disconnected and scattered language-in-education planning pathways established for native English-speaking students do not provide sufficient structure for these students to attain a desired English language proficiency, especially in the academic high code. For ESL college students, the informal needs to be formalized through the development of college-level language planning procedures. How can this be done?

A Case Study: Toward the Development of a University Language Plan for ESL Students

Space does not permit an exhaustive examination of the processes involved in developing a language plan. I will, instead, provide the most salient, rudimentary principles relevant to the task at hand by reporting on a language-in-education planning process I was involved with at a small U.S.-based university that had a relatively large ESL student population mostly from Asia and the South Pacific. For convenience sake, and to maintain institutional privacy, I will henceforth refer to this case study university as XYZ University or XYZU.

Administrators at XYZU were aware that many of their ESL students were graduating without sufficient English to be employable upon return to their home country. This perceived failure was affecting the reputation of the university throughout its targeted future student base. Upon realizing that their informal language-in-education plans for their ESL student population were failing, XYZU administrators placed initial blame upon the university's ESL program, its administrators and teachers. Such a response is common. As noted above, ESL teachers are the front-line implementers of a language plan. Consequently, if that plan is unsuccessful, ESL teachers, administrators and their students are on the receiving end of a range of misinformed finger pointing. Fortunately, upon investigation, enlightened administrators at XYZU realized that the ESL sector was doing all it could do within a reasonable time frame and within acceptable resource allocations. Perhaps more could be done at the institutional level to enhance ESL acquisition. This understanding led to me being asked to spend a semester at the university as a visiting professor in order to help the university develop a more formal response to the challenges faced by the university and its ESL students. I advocated that the university create a language-in-education plan, and received permission to do so.

At approximately the same time, the university was preparing its "self-study" for accreditation purposes. One self-study requirement was to identify institutional themes that the university would be assessed on. University administrators decided to include an institutional theme labeled "Effective communication in English for second language students." This theme was described as follows:

> In order to create an environment more conducive to English language learning at XYZU, we are proposing two distinct action steps: extensive data collection, and the development of a campus-wide language plan. The first step will be used to inform the second step: our language planning process will be grounded in data that describe English use and competence across campus. We will make use of three types of data to direct language planning.
>
> 1. Archival search and presentation of current levels of student proficiency and usage.
> 2. Post-[Intensive English Program] English development.
> 3. Qualitative data.
>
> These data will then lead to the development of a university language plan that:
>
> • provides students with maximum second language learning opportunities and at the same time respects the rich diversity of their first languages;

- informs and is informed by all corners of the campus—from employment to curriculum, from Housing to Admissions, and from [service] responsibilities to Student Life;
- systematically collects data on students' language development at all stages of their university career;
- is managed by a standing L2 committee that broadly represents campus life—a committee that has already been constituted and will manage our investigation of English language acquisition on the XYZU campus;
- is built on a model that allows for constant assessment, evaluation, and modifications.

My initial involvement was to assist in data collection with respect to laying the foundation for a viable language plan. Through hard experience, language planners have determined that the ultimate success of any language plan depends upon a sense of involved ownership of that plan by all who are affected by that plan. In the university context, this inclusive orientation would involve not only ESL students, but also native English-speaking students, faculty, administrators, and support personnel. To this end, the development of a language plan must first consider the language behavior (language proficiency, language use, and language acquisition processes), as well as behavior toward language (motivations, attitudes) of the relevant speech communities. Kaplan and Baldauf (1997) suggest that the creation and administration of a sociolinguistic survey lies at the heart of any language planning enterprise. Consequently, with the help of concerned faculty within the ESL sector of the university, one of my first tasks was to create a series of sociolinguistic surveys to be administered to the university community. One goal was to develop a language-use profile of the university community and sub-communities. In other words, we wanted to know who was speaking, reading, writing, listening what, to whom, in what language, in what context, for what purposes, at what proficiency.

Separate written surveys were targeted to native English-speaking students, ESL students, faculty, and administrators. We received funding to reward respondents with free ice-cream at a university store upon completion of an acceptable survey. At the same time, I taught a class in sociolinguistics consisting of 30 mostly senior students. As part of the class, I instructed them on how to conduct oral focus group surveys and individual interviews revolving around issues touched on in the written surveys. One class assignment required students to conduct a number of interviews and focus groups, collect and analyze the data and write reports. Their work proved invaluable.

Written survey participation was reasonably high across campus, with approximately 450 ESL students and 360 native-English speakers responding. Results indicated that many ESL students were frustrated with their inability to acquire English. In addition, cross-tabulation with country of origin produced two distinctive ESL groups in terms of language behavior and behavior toward language. Group 1 consisted of students from South Korea, Japan, Hong Kong, Taiwan, and the People's Republic of China. Group 2 consisted of students from Southeast Asia, the Pacific Islands, and an "other country" category.

In almost every survey topic, Group 1 students reported on behaviors or attitudes that contributed to a greater sense of frustration and disappointment with their English language acquisition experience. Group 1 students had significantly fewer interactions with native English speakers, far less time functioning in English, and far more friends from their home countries. They were far more likely to live, eat, work, relax and study with students from their own language backgrounds.

Responses from native English-speaking students indicated that they were generally sympathetic toward the challenges faced by their ESL peers. Some expressed frustration when trying to develop close friendships with them. Each survey contained a final open-ended request for input on how to improve the English proficiency of ESL students. The following response from a native English speaker was particularly telling (quoted verbatim except where indicated):

> The problem with the international students is that they come here to learn English, yet they only hang out with people from their country, and speak their native language. It alienates them even more – it's like they have their own mini-country here. [XYZU] needs to make moves to break up those cliques. Don't let them house together in the dorms – put English speakers with each non. Give them jobs where they have to work with English speaking students, and class assignments with [native English speakers] too. It's good for both sides. They're way cliquey in the cafeteria too, but I'm not sure what you could do about that. Maybe just put up some funny signs telling everyone to "have a cultural dining experience – stop sitting with the same people!!"

As noted, a survey was also developed for university faculty. Among other findings, faculty responses were cross-tabulated with the presence or absence of "some ESL training." Faculty with some ESL training were less likely "to grade native English speakers and L2 speakers by the same standard." On the other hand, these faculty were more likely "to alter my method of delivery to accommodate my ESL students," and "to adjust the depth and difficulty of content covered in my class to accommodate my ESL students." Furthermore, faculty with some ESL training were less likely to agree with the proposition that "the University should be satisfied with the current level of English proficiency of ESL students," and that "the University should implement an English-only policy." They were also more likely to agree with the notion that, "the university should focus on motivating ESL students to improve their language skills rather than establish an English-only policy." These findings suggest that general content faculty training in basic ESL teaching, and even sheltered instruction models such as the Sheltered Instruction Observation Protocol (SIOP) (Eggington & Eggington, 2010) would significantly assist ESL students.

The data from these surveys were compiled into a report. Subsequently, a faculty Second Language Committee was established with the following mission statement:

> The mission of the Second Language (L2) Committee is to ensure that the entire campus works together to make XYZU a place where non-native speakers of English develop clear competence in the English language. We will accomplish this goal by developing and implementing a comprehensive language plan which:
>
> • Demonstrates an understanding of English language behavior, (including language use, language proficiency, and language acquisition), and attitudes towards the English language as based on data collected from stakeholders.
> • Establishes an ongoing system for collecting and analyzing data related to English language behavior and attitudes towards the English language.
> • Endorses the highest standards of learning and teaching the English language on campus.
> • Promotes extensive English language development opportunities in all areas of student life including academic, residential, employment, social, and [service], yet respects the rich diversity of the students' first languages.
> • Is subject to continuing evaluation and refinement.

My direct involvement with XYZU ended at this point. I was confident that the recently established Second Language Committee would build upon survey results and implement many of the suggestions received from students and faculty. Hopes were high and some initial innovations were introduced. Unfortunately, after a number of years, changes in university upper administration and the departure of key ESL program faculty resulted in a slow dilution of the whole language planning concept. I recently returned to the campus for a two-day visit. Basically, other than a few innovations, the language planning initiative was a fading memory. Promises were made to revive it. Perhaps that will be the case.

I have thought much about how such a positive series of developments could have dissolved. A subjective evaluation suggests that the goals of the language plan were asking students and faculty to reach beyond a long-established series of comfort zones. Perhaps students, faculty and administrators share a silent social contract; namely, "I won't demand too much from you, if you don't demand too much from me." Semi-retired friends recently returned from a three-year, very demanding, overseas religious "mission" where they were challenged to function far beyond their capabilities. In her homecoming speech, Candilyn shared with us a most profound insight: "There is no growth in a comfort zone, and there is no comfort in a growth zone." Even the process of developing an institutional language plan can move all involved out of conscious and subconscious comfort zones. Thus, one lesson learned is that any language planning enterprise within an educational setting requires a long-term institutional commitment independent of personnel.

Implications and Applications

As one of the editors of this volume, my chapter contributions are most vulnerable to total-volume maximum word-count requirements. Thus severe space restrictions demand that I be brief in drawing implications and suggesting applications regarding the foregoing overview of institutional language planning and a related case study. By way of a summary, I have attempted to show that we should see our professional commitments as stretching beyond our immediate classrooms and intensive English programs. Language planning processes provide an established mechanism for such enterprises. If, for example, after the administration of various sociolinguistic surveys we were to find that matriculated ESL students at our universities were eager to acquire English, but frustrated in that desire; that native English-speaking students were willing to reach out to their ESL peers, but didn't know how; and that faculty and administrators with some ESL training and experience were far more capable in helping their ESL students, a series of innovations could be enacted. These might include:

- an ESL study/writing buddy program;
- the establishment of writing and reading centers dedicated to serving ESL students;
- the very successful "foreign language residential house" model extended to the establishment of English-only residential housing where volunteer native English-speaking students room with volunteer ESL students within an English-only environment;
- the implementation of a specialized ESL Teaching Assistant program where native English-speaking students are assigned to specific classes to mentor ESL students;
- incentivizing continued English development among ESL students by providing a minor in English language;
- the creation of ESL testing protocols that track the language development of ESL students across their four-year journey toward graduation;

- the provision of "Certificates in English Language Proficiency" given immediately before graduation that would enable students to better market their English competency upon return to their homeland;
- the training of general content-area faculty in basic sheltered instruction models.

This list is provided to show what can be "planned" within an institutional language planning framework. Each institute would develop its own approaches based upon the data derived from their sociolinguistic surveys. Regardless of the details, such an institutional language planning approach will result in our ESL students such as Joung Won returning to their home countries with a greater sense of success, and a more positive view of their U.S.-based academic institutions, and of the ESL profession, a profession that sees its professional scope as encompassing not just the classroom, but the institution as well.

Discussion Questions

1. How might an institutional language plan be developed at your institution?
2. Some may say that an institutional language plan is a form of unwanted social engineering. In what ways is it? In what ways is it not?
3. The case study provided in this chapter ended in a less-than-successful outcome. How could an institutional language plan be developed that would ensure sustained success independent of administrative and personnel changes?

Further Reading

Baldauf, R. (2012). Language planning: Where have we been? Where might we be going? *Revista Brasileira de Linguistica Aplicada, 12*(2), 233–248.
Baldauf, R. (2005). Micro language planning. In P. Bruthiaux, D. Atkinson, W. G. Eggington, W. Grabe, & V. Ramanathan (Eds.), *Perspectives on applied linguistics: Essays in honor of Robert. B. Kaplan* (pp. 227–239). Clevedon: Multilingual Matters.
Chua, S., & Baldauf, R. (2011). Micro language planning. In E. Hinckel (Ed.), *Handbook of research in second language teaching and learning* (Vol. 2, pp. 936–951). New York, NY: Routledge.
Kaplan, R. B., & Baldauf, Jr., R. (1997). *Language planning: From theory to practice.* Clevedon: Multilingual Matters.
Swales, J. (1990). *Genre analysis.* New York, NY: Cambridge University Press.

References

Baldauf, R. (2005). Micro language planning. In P. Bruthiaux, D. Atkinson, W. G. Eggington, W. Grabe, & V. Ramanathan (Eds.), *Perspectives on applied linguistics: Essays in honor of Robert. B. Kaplan* (pp. 237–239). Clevedon: Multilingual Matters.
Baldauf, R. (2006). Rearticulating the case for micro language planning in a language ecology context. *Current Issues in Language Planning, 7*(2&3), 147–170.

Baldauf, R. (2012). Language planning: Where have we been? Where might we be going? *Revista Brasileira de Linguistica Aplicada, 12*(2), 233–248.

Biber, D. and R. Reppen (2002). What does frequency have to do with grammar teaching. *Studies in Second Language Acquisition, 24*(2), 199–208.

Birrell, R. J. (2006). Implications of low English standards among overseas students at Australian universities. *People and Place, 14* (4), 53–64.

Chua, S., & Baldauf, R. (2011). Micro language planning. In E. Hinckel (Ed.), *Handbook of research in second language teaching and learning* (Vol. 2, pp. 936–951). New York, NY: Routledge.

Dudden, A. (2005). *Japan's colonization of Korea: Discourse and power.* Honolulu: University of Hawaii Press.

Eggington, W. (2013). Using English corpora to Teach and learn high-code/low code register variation. In *Proceedings of the 2013 Korea Multi-media Assisted Language Learning (KAMALL) International Conference,* Seoul, South Korea. October 2013.

Eggington, K., & Eggington, W. (2010). Teacher research used to evaluate sheltered instruction in a science classroom setting. *Electronic Journal of Literacy Through Science, 9,* 1–24.

Ferguson, Charles A. (1959). Diglossia. *Word, 15,* 325–340.

Fishman, J. (1965). Who speaks what language to whom and when? *La Linguistique, 1*(2), 67–88.

Gardner, D., & Davies, M. (2007). Pointing out frequent phrasal verbs: a corpus-based analysis. *TESOL Quarterly 41* (2), 339–359.

Kaplan, R. B., & Baldauf, Jr., R. (1997). *Language planning: From theory to practice.* Clevedon: Multilingual Matters.

Lee, J., Min, W., & McKerrow, R. (2010). English or perish: How contemporary South Korea received, accommodated, and internalized English and American modernity. *Language and Intercultural Communication, 10*(4), 337–357.

O'Malley, J., & Chamot, A. (1990). *Learning strategies in second language acquisition.* New York, NY: Cambridge University Press.

Swales, J. (1990). *Genre analysis.* New York, NY: Cambridge University Press.

4

WRITING CENTERS

Finding a Center for ESL Writers

Lucie Moussu and Nicholas David

Vignette

It is a scene played out at many college campuses. An international student receives feedback from the teacher concerning grammar errors and the general need for revision. This ESL student goes to the college Writing Center for assistance, hoping that the tutor can help fix these grammar errors. However, the student quickly finds that the Writing Center's policy is to work not on grammar but on higher-order or "global" concerns like organization and content. If the student insists on working on grammar, the tutor helps the student using an indirect, Socratic questioning method. Unfortunately for the ESL student, this style of feedback is unclear and ineffective. Other times the tutor might address the errors more directly, but in doing so, the tutor feels guilty for not following the policy of the Writing Center. What is lost in either case is a common meeting place, a center where both grammar and content concerns are effectively addressed by Writing Center tutors.

Background

As the number of ESL students registering at U.S. and Canadian postsecondary institutions increases (Institute of International Education, 2014), so does the supplementary role of support systems put in place for them at these institutions. For example, more and more faculty members send undergraduate and graduate ESL students to their institution's Writing Centers (WCs) for help with grammar.

Indeed, faculty and ESL students alike often believe that learning English involves mastering the language's grammar; accordingly, they prioritize feedback on grammatical issues (Leki, 1991). Their belief in the effectiveness of this type of corrective feedback (Diab, 2005) often leads ESL students to view WCs as "grammatical repair shops." However, most WC tutors are instructed to look at texts globally and to verify that students understand the broader components of their assignments (e.g., organization) before helping with grammar (North, 1984). This philosophical approach of placing organization and content before grammar ends up causing conflicts with ESL students who are specifically looking for the type of assistance that the WC may be unwilling to provide.

Introduction and Overview of the Challenges

Certainly, assisting ESL writers at the postsecondary level is a complex task. ESL writers often struggle with the linguistic demands of writing in a second language as well as with the cultural and rhetorical norms expected in academic discourse (see CCCC Statement on Second Language Writers and Writing, 2001; Silva, 1993). Often, ESL students know grammatical rules but lack the linguistic proficiency as well as the rhetorical and cultural knowledge needed to effectively revise and self-edit their papers (e.g., Hyland, 2003; Matsuda, 1999).

Across the United States and Canada, WCs are feeling the impact of increasing ESL student enrollment. This impact can be measured by the amount of literature on ESL writers in the WC. Before 1990, fewer than five articles existed in the literature, whereas now over 100 published works concerning the topic span eight journals and multiple books, theses, and dissertations. The growing body of ESL-WC research attests to the increasing ESL student population in WCs and the interest in meeting this population's unique needs (see Blau & Hall, 2002; Harris, 1997; Powers, 1993).

Despite ESL students' increased use of WCs, WC pedagogy can conflict with effective ESL tutorial practices. North's (1984) seminal article, "The Idea of a Writing Center," emphasizes that WCs are not editing services and encourages WCs to focus primarily on higher-order concerns (e.g., organization). This pedagogical concept, focusing on process and not product, was crystallized in North's call for "better writers, not better writing" (p. 438). Additionally, current WC pedagogy stresses that tutors be non-directive, non-editing, and collaborative in their approach. When researchers realized that these general WC practices did not work for ESL students, they began studying ESL students in WCs (see Harris & Silva, 1993; Powers, 1993; Thonus, 1993). This research found that non-directive tutoring is ineffective with ESL students because it presupposes knowledge of conventions and rhetorical norms of writing that ESL students simply do not have (Blau & Hall, 2002; Harris & Silva, 1993; Moussu, 2013), and that some directiveness concerning grammar and other areas is warranted (Taylor, 2007).

While much of this research can be found in WC-focused publications, the taboo of working on grammar still remains in many WCs, and as a result, many ESL students are still seeking a "center" to call their own. To better understand and approach ESL tutorials in WCs, and to "find a center" for ESL writers, we investigate four questions in this chapter: first, what the backgrounds of the ESL students using the WC are; second, what tutors do differently in tutorials with ESL students and tutorials with native speakers of English (NS); third, what ESL students do during their tutorials; and fourth, how ESL issues are addressed by different WCs on their websites. The discussions in these different areas will provide an overview of the challenges that postsecondary ESL students face in U.S. and Canadian WCs and set the stage to discuss the implications and suggestions of support that are offered in the final section of this chapter and the second part of this book.

ESL Students' Backgrounds

Despite university and college entrance requirements (e.g., TOEFL, IELTS) intended to ensure some homogeneity in English language skills, ESL students in U.S. and Canadian institutions often have dissimilar language skills (Gradman & Hanania, 1991; Harris & Silva, 1993). For example, ESL students are dissimilar in the amount of time they have lived in an English-speaking country, the amount of contact they have had with the English language, and their level of experience with their first language (L1). Some students are highly literate in their L1, while others may be illiterate in their L1 or have not done any work in academic writing. Some students have learned English extensively in their home countries, some students have attended U.S. or Canadian high schools, and others still come to the United States or Canada with limited English skills and may choose to first attend ESL intensive courses. Above all, most ESL students are unaware of or unfamiliar with the writing requirements, stylistic conventions, and specific genres used in their academic discipline (Angelova & Riazantseva, 1999), and their attitudes toward writing in L2 might need to be challenged or constructed (Ismail, Elias, Safinas, Perumal, & Muthusamy, 2010; Petric, 2002; see also Chapter 6). Also, factors such as affective variables (e.g., self-confidence, motivation), first language, age, language practice, educational levels, reasons for being abroad, learning styles, and sociocultural variables also influence students' language skills and their familiarity with and attitudes toward writing (Angelova & Riazantseva, 1999; Ellis, 1994; Gradman & Hanania, 1991; Qian & Krugly-Smolska, 2008; Reid, 1987).

Whatever their backgrounds, the majority of ESL students entering U.S. and Canadian colleges and universities today have learned English in skill-based courses by means of rote memorization, drills, and practice in the use of grammatical rules, multiple-choice exams, and a strong focus on language accuracy (Cheng, Chang, Chen, & Liao, 2010). As Qian and Krugly-Smolska (2008) say about their study's participants:

> The formation of [the belief that the ability to produce grammatically correct sentences is an important indicator of good writing skills] can be

traced back to their experiences of learning English as a foreign language in China. Grammar-focused teaching and learning activities can lead students to pay particular attention to specific details at the sentence level.

p. 77

These students also lack academic writing strategies and resources, do not understand how to learn the language in a more communicatively effective manner, are often unfamiliar with their teachers' (and by extension, WC tutors') expectations (Chang & Swales, 1999), and see their writing difficulties as problems with form rather than with content (Bitchener & Basturkmen, 2006).

As a result, ESL students coming into WCs often ask for help on "lower order" concerns (grammar, spelling, etc.) while neglecting "higher order" issues of rhetoric, organization, and genre (Taylor, 2007); in fact, the students' expectations are so high for feedback related to grammatical correctness that WC tutors can lose credibility in students' eyes if they don't offer it (Bitchener & Ferris, 2011; Diab, 2005; Ferris, 1995; Lee, 2005). These expectations, of course, go against the tutoring philosophy that requires tutors to work on higher-order concerns first, to favor the development of ideas above grammatical accuracy, and to encourage all students to take ownership of their writing (Gillespie & Lerner, 2000).

Keeping students' backgrounds in mind, the following section seeks to address the other side of the tutorial experience, namely, tutors' perceptions of tutorial sessions with ESL students, and how tutors perceive time is spent in both native speaker and ESL tutorials. By better understanding how WC tutors respond to ESL students in the WC, we gain a clearer sense of what is needed to find a center for ESL students.

Tutor Perceptions of Their Tutoring Sessions

To clarify how ESL students' background expectations might affect WC tutorials, this section summarizes what occurs during tutorials with NSs and ESL students. It also examines how those tutorials differ, if at all.

To determine how tutors perceive their tutoring sessions with NSs and ESL students, an online survey was distributed to community college WC tutors in the United States. Community colleges were selected based on their underrepresented status in much of the ESL literature and because they offered a cross-section of not only international ESL students but also domestic ESL students, or Generation 1.5 students.

This survey sought to determine tutors' perception of how time is broken down in tutorials, or the amount of time tutors spend on organization, content, and correctness for NSs and ESL students. Eighty-five tutors responded to the survey. Additionally, interviews were conducted with six WC tutors from three community colleges to determine more holistically how tutors view ESL tutorials and what differences may exist between ESL and NS tutorials.

The first question asked was *"What percentage of your tutorials is with ESL students?"* As shown in Table 4.1, almost two-thirds of the tutors surveyed reported that they worked with ESL students at least 20% of the time. These numbers corresponded with Powers and Nelson's (1995) initial survey of U.S. postsecondary institutions concerning the prevalence of ESL tutorials. Similar numbers may be expected for universities as well (Williams, 2002).

In a subsequent question, tutors were asked to indicate how much of their tutorial time with NSs was spent on the areas of content, organization, and grammatical correctness.

As shown in Figure 4.1, tutors in NS tutorials reported spending substantial time in all three areas measured. However, the data also suggest that in NS tutorials, tutors tended to work on the area of content slightly more than on organization, and on organization more than on correctness.

TABLE 4.1 Percentage of ESL Tutorials

Percentage of Tutorials with ESL Students	No.	%
0	2	3
1–10	14	19
11–20	11	15
21–40	18	24
41–60	13	17
61–80	11	15
More than 81	6	8
Total	75	100

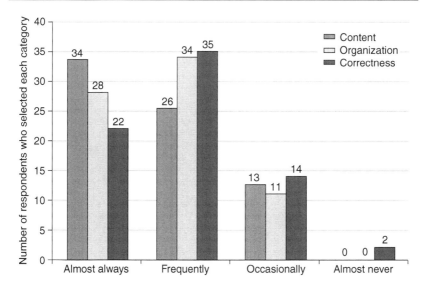

FIGURE 4.1 Tutorial Division of Labor in NS Tutorials.

In contrast, tutors' perceptions of ESL tutorials differed in substantial ways (see Figure 4.2). The most salient difference was in the amount of time spent on correctness. Whereas only 22 respondents stated that they "almost always" worked on correctness with NSs, 50 respondents stated they "almost always" worked on correctness with ESL students.

In order to determine whether there were any statistically significant differences among the areas measured (i.e., content, organization, and correctness with NSs and ESL students), a unilateral ANOVA statistic was used. These results can be found in Table 4.2. It should be noted that the researcher entered the values into the online survey such that 4 = *almost always*, whereas 1 = *almost never*, so the higher the number, the more frequently tutors spent time in this category.

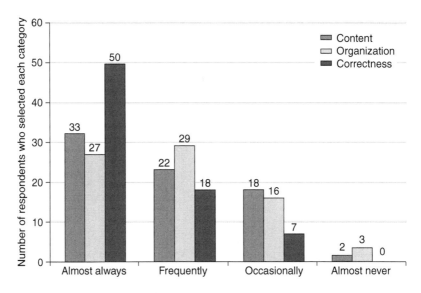

FIGURE 4.2 Tutorial Divison of Labor in ESL Tutorials.

TABLE 4.2 Descriptive Statistics for Tutor Survey Tutorial Division of Labor

Group	Mean	Std. Dev.	N
NS content	3.29	.754	73
NS organization	3.23	.698	73
NS correctness	3.08	.780	73
ESL content	3.15	.877	73
ESL organization	3.07	.864	73
ESL correctness	3.57	.665	73
Total	3.23	.793	438

As indicated in Table 4.2, the categories with the lowest means were time spent with NSs on correctness and time spent with ESL students on organization. The category with the highest amount of time spent was with ESL students on correctness.

An ANOVA statistic also found statistically significant differences among the six groups measured. The level of significance was set at $p < .05$, and the results indicate a p value of $p < .0001$, a statistically significant difference with a high confidence interval. Subsequently, a post hoc Tukey's Test was run to determine where these statistically significant differences occurred. One statistically significant difference was in the area of ESL correctness versus NS correctness. Additional areas of statistical significance were found in the areas of ESL content versus ESL correctness, and ESL organization versus ESL correctness. In both cases, tutors worked significantly more on correctness in ESL tutorials than on either content or organization. There was no statistical difference, though, between tutor work on ESL content and ESL organization or between ESL and NS tutorials in the areas of content and organization.

Thus, to review, the areas of statistical significance are listed as follows. First, tutors reported working significantly more on correctness with ESL students than on correctness with NSs. Second, tutors reported working significantly more on correctness with ESL students than on organization with ESL students. Finally, tutors reported working significantly more on correctness with ESL students than on content with ESL students.

According to the interviewed tutors, some possible reasons as to why they worked with ESL students on the areas of content and organization less frequently than on correctness may be that tutors could only work on so many issues during one tutorial, and ESL errors seem to monopolize time. Additionally, while perception may not precisely reflect how much time was actually spent in tutorials, the significance and high confidence interval of tutors' perceptions indicated that a correlation is very likely. Further research is recommended to determine whether these perceptions match reality.

In the interviews, tutors reported being more directive in their tutorials with ESL students than they would be in NS tutorials. Additionally, many tutors expressed that they preferred working with ESL students because those students were more willing to learn, more engaged in the tutorial process, and more likely to collaborate with individual tutors over time than NSs are. As a result of this collaboration, tutors felt that they were better able to help these students progress.

In summary, the community college tutors in this study worked often with ESL students, and they perceived that they usually work with ESL students in a more directive manner and more frequently with grammar. Furthermore, they reported that work with ESL students tended to include repeat tutorial appointments and sustained one-on-one work. Such perceptions and practices represent positive examples of centers for ESL students.

Student Perceptions of WC Tutoring

To understand the other side of the WC tutorial interaction, it is vital to also investigate ESL students' expectations of, needs for, and reactions to WC support. To accomplish this, researchers conducted a study of 178 students at seven U.S. and Canadian universities. Table 4.3 describes the participants in more detail.

Regarding the students' first language, 52% of the participants answered that they were native speakers of English. Of the ESL speakers, 44.6% responded that their first language was Chinese, Mandarin, or Cantonese; 10.6% spoke Korean; and the remainder of the ESL students spoke other languages, including German, Japanese, French, Spanish, Hindi, and Arabic.

The instrument used for this study consisted of one short questionnaire (see Appendix A). Completion of this questionnaire took five minutes and responses were completely anonymous. Following a series of demographic questions, the questionnaire presented 19 Likert scale statements (ranging from 1 = *strongly disagree*, to 5 = *strongly agree*) based on literature on ESL writers and WC research (e.g., Bell & Elledge, 2008; Taylor, 2007). Questions addressed tutoring expectations, the learning that took place (or did not take place) during the sessions, the roles of tutors, and the role of WCs. Participants were then asked two open-ended questions about additional suggestions and comments they might have.

Descriptive and inferential statistics were calculated for each group of participants. However, because of the differing numbers of participants from every institution, no analysis was performed to compare responses among individual universities. An ANOVA was used to determine if variations within the means could be attributed to students being NSs or ESL students.

In general, the means calculated for every question are very similar between groups. However, the means for NSs tend to be slightly higher than those for ESL students, meaning that NSs generally agreed a little more strongly with most of the statements than ESL students did. One notable exception is Q11 (*A good tutor should fix mistakes and edit your paper*), for which the ESL mean is 4.54 and that of NSs is 4.00, significantly lower ($p < .0001$). The ESL student mean (4.37) is also slightly higher than the NS mean (4.21) for Q15 (*A good tutor should focus on grammar*), showing again that ESL students agree more strongly with the statement. ESL students also agreed significantly more with Q12 (*A good tutor should fix mistakes and edit your paper*), Q13 (*You felt comfortable asking your tutor questions*), and Q17 (*You trusted your tutor's knowledge and expertise*) than

TABLE 4.3 Classification of Participants

	NSs	ESL	Undergrads	Grads	All participants
Total	94	84	169	9	178

the NSs did. These statistically significant differences point to an important trend in how ESL students differ from NSs in their expectations of tutors.

At the end of the questionnaire, an open-ended question asked *How can this WC help you better?* NSs said that they needed more help in the following areas: editing, organization of their ideas, and reading (i.e., texts and assignments). NSs also said that they wanted longer appointments, more tutors, tutors that specialized in the students' specific fields of study, and tutors that expressed their opinions more assertively regarding the quality of students' papers. The majority of NSs were very grateful for the services offered by their WC.

More often than NSs did, ESL students noted that they wanted more help with the organization and structure of their papers, as well as help understanding cultural expectations regarding format (e.g., thesis statements, introductions and conclusions, APA, and MLA) and the writing process in general. ESL students also stated more often than NSs that they needed longer tutoring appointments and more frequent availability for tutoring (even during weekends). A third area of concern for many ESL students was grammar, punctuation, and help with editing their papers. Like NSs, ESL students needed their tutors to express more clearly and strongly what they thought regarding the positive and negative aspects of the students' papers. These findings are echoed in the study reported in Chapter 6. While several ESL students acknowledged that the WC tutoring philosophy was helpful, they also often requested tutors that were more knowledgeable about their field of study. In their final comments about the WC, ESL students thanked their tutors profusely; they often noted that their tutors were friendly and that the students felt comfortable working with them. All students seemed grateful for the help they received and for the very existence of a WC at their institution.

While these results are not surprising, they do confirm that ESL students are more likely than NSs to expect and appreciate receiving extra help with their papers, including grammar-related help, and that, according to the participants, a directive approach works better than a minimalist approach. Effective centers for ESL students would include these elements.

WC Websites and ESL Writers

A final area of interest for both authors of this chapter was the mention of ESL students made (or not made) on the websites of postsecondary WCs in the United States and Canada. We were specifically interested to see how many WC websites mentioned ESL students as a demographic that they served, and whether the WC websites included any additional online resources for ESL students. This overview provided a snapshot of ESL students' use of WCs, and conversely, how committed WCs are toward serving ESL populations. It also determined whether WCs with strong commitment to ESL writers could be found and what resources these centers provide online.

To answer this question, 10 states in the United States and three Canadian provinces were selected randomly, and within each state or province, two universities and two community colleges were chosen at random. The U.S. states chosen were Montana, Indiana, Ohio, Wisconsin, Massachusetts, Oregon, Connecticut, Florida, Virginia, and North Carolina. The Canadian provinces were New Brunswick, Alberta, and Nova Scotia.

This browsing of WC websites focused on three areas: (1) did the institution provide a WC or a place to tutor writing; (2) was there any mention of ESL on the website; and (3) if ESL writers were mentioned, what online resources (if any) were available to these students. The results for each area can be found in Table 4.4.

Of the 52 institutions selected, 88.5% offered writing tutoring to students in at least some capacity (volunteer tutoring, skills centers, etc.). This high percentage marks how widespread the resource of tutoring is at the postsecondary level. However, only 40.4% of the tutoring took place at an actual WC or writing lab. So although tutoring for writing is widespread, the existence of WCs or labs is not. One reason for this is that writing tutorials are often combined with reading or general learning in a tutorial setting.

Next, about 30% of all 52 institutions mentioned ESL students on their websites, with about 25% providing some online resources for ESL students. Of those WCs that provided online resources, all but one posted links to ESL websites, one provided a video about ESL tutoring and resources available to them, and five had in-house materials.

This section indicates that the growing ESL presence in higher education strongly influences postsecondary WCs, both in their approaches and the resources they provide. However, the fact that only a quarter of the tutoring centers we studied included links and resources for ESL students seems to indicate that WCs can do more for these ESL students. The goal of consistently finding a center for ESL students in colleges and universities is one that is yet to be met.

TABLE 4.4 ESL Support Information on WC Websites

Category	Number	Percent
Colleges/universities providing some sort of tutoring help	46/52	88.5
Colleges/universities with an actual WC/lab	21/52	40.4
Mention of ESL students on WC website	16/52	30.8
ESL support materials provided on WC website	13/52	25.0

Implications and Applications

As ESL student populations in the United States and Canada increase, WCs could be poised to serve an ever-expanding role in instructing these students. However, in order for this to take place, we must change the attitude that WC pedagogy is analogous for both ESL and NS tutorials. Understanding ESL students' backgrounds, tutors' perceptions of ESL tutorials, and ESL students' expectations is key for these tutorials to be effective. The results of the studies reported in this chapter underline the importance of grammar correction and feedback in ESL tutorials. This theme can be seen in terms of students' backgrounds, the amount of time tutors report working on grammar correction and feedback, and on ESL students' expectations during tutorials. Nevertheless, tutors should recognize such issues within the broader backdrop of global concerns of organization and content and should prioritize such feedback accordingly. By doing both, tutors need not chose only "better writers, not better writing" (North, 1984, p. 184), but can assist writers in becoming "better writers through better writing." Thus, ESL writers can find a center that effectively addresses and meets their needs.

Summary

- A review of the literature describes the roles of WCs in the United States and Canada and their basic philosophy and practices. The increasing number of ESL students in postsecondary institutions forces WCs to re-evaluate their practices and the pedagogical theories that have guided tutor training and responses to student needs in the last decades.
- The next section provides information about ESL students' backgrounds. It describes how difficult it is to categorize students into groups of similar language skills and cultural knowledge of academic writing. Numerous variables strongly influence students' needs and the type of help they require in WCs.
- The results of the first study are discussed. WC tutors in U.S. colleges were asked to report the frequency of ESL tutorials as well as differences in how time is divided in NS and ESL tutorials. Results indicate that tutors perceive that they spend more time on correctness in ESL tutorials than they do in NS tutorials.
- Results of the second study are also discussed. The study asked NSs and ESL students for their opinions regarding the help they received in seven postsecondary WCs. Results show that ESL students indeed expect more help with grammar-related issues than NSs do.
- Finally, the authors share the results of their own search through a number of WCs' websites in U.S. and Canadian postsecondary institutions. They looked for specific mentions of ESL students as well as any available online resources that are specifically designed for them.

Discussion Questions

1. What kinds of preconceived ideas do people in general have about ESL writers?
2. What are some differences that WC tutors might encounter in working with ESL students versus NSs? How might this affect tutor strategies and assumptions?
3. How might the question of whether to be direct while correcting errors tie into broader concerns about plagiarism and ownership of the text? What steps might WC tutors take to avoid overcorrecting papers and making them inauthentic representations of student proficiency?
4. What steps may WC directors need to take as ESL student populations rise? What kinds of support systems can be created?
5. How might "better writers, not better writing" be best achieved with ESL student writing? Is the "writers versus writing" dichotomy effective for ESL students?

Appendix A: C4W Questionnaire

Please answer the following questions:

1. Are you: (a) an undergraduate student? (b) a graduate student?

2. What languages do you speak? _____

3. Do you consider yourself a: (a) native speaker of English? (b) non-native speaker of English?

4. Is this your first visit to the Writing Center (a) Yes (b) No

   Please circle the numbers below according to your experience at the Writing Center and your opinion regarding our services, using the following scale:

Strongly Disagree	Disagree	Not Sure	Agree	Strongly Agree
1	*2*	*3*	*4*	*5*

	SD	D	NS	A	SA
5. Your most recent session at the Writing Center met your expectations.	1	2	3	4	5
6. You learned a lot from your most recent session at the Writing Center.	1	2	3	4	5
7. A good tutor should know what is most important for you to work on in the session.	1	2	3	4	5
8. You would recommend the Writing Center to a friend.	1	2	3	4	5
9. A good tutor should focus on the organization of ideas in your paper.	1	2	3	4	5
10. You felt motivated by your tutor.	1	2	3	4	5
11. A good tutor should fix mistakes and edit your paper.	1	2	3	4	5
12. You felt comfortable asking your tutor questions.	1	2	3	4	5
13. A good tutor should help you develop all your skills as a writer.	1	2	3	4	5
14. You would definitely come back for more sessions at the Writing Center.	1	2	3	4	5
15. A good tutor should focus on grammar.	1	2	3	4	5
16. You trusted your tutor's knowledge and expertise.	1	2	3	4	5
17. The Writing Center is a good resource for all students.	1	2	3	4	5
18. You collaborated well with your tutor in the session.	1	2	3	4	5

19. How can the Writing Center help YOU (specifically) better?

20. Please include any comments you may have about the Writing Center.

Further Reading

Barnett, R., & Blumner, J. (2008). *The Longman guide to writing center theory and practice.* Toronto: Longman.

Bitchener, J., & Ferris, D. R. (2012). *Written corrective feedback in second language acquisition and writing.* New York, NY: Routledge.

Boquet, E., & Lerner, N. (2008). Reconsideration: After "The idea of a writing center." *College English, 71*(2), 170–189.

Murphy, C., & Sherwood, S. (2003). *The St. Martin's sourcebook for writing tutors.* Boston, MA: Bedford/St. Martin's.

Williams, J., & Severino, C. (2004). Writing centers [special issue]. *The Journal of Second Language Writing, 13*(3).

References

Angelova, M., & Riazantseva, A. (1999). "If you don't tell me, how can I know?" *Written Communication, 16*(4), 491–525.

Bell, D., & Elledge, S. (2008). Dominance and peer tutoring sessions with English language learners. *Learning Assistance Review, 13*(1), 17–30.

Bitchener, J., & Basturkmen, H. (2006). Perceptions of the difficulties of postgraduate L2 thesis students writing the discussion section. *Journal of English for Academic Purposes, 5*(1), 4–18.

Bitchener, J., & Ferris, D. R. (2011). *Written corrective feedback in second language acquisition and writing.* New York, NY: Routledge.

Blau, S., & Hall, J. (2002). Guilt-free tutoring: Rethinking how we tutor non-native-English-speaking students. *The Writing Center Journal, 23*(1), 23–44.

Chang, Y., & Swales, J. M. (1999). Informal elements in English academic writing: Threats or opportunities for advanced non-native speakers? In C. N. Candlin & K. Hyland (Eds.), *Writing: Texts, processes, and practices* (pp. 145–167). London: Longman.

Cheng, M. C., Chang, J., Chen, Y., & Liao, Y. (2010). "Do they want the same thing?" Learner perspectives on two content-based course designs in the context of English as a foreign language. *Asian EFL Journal, 12*(4), 67–84.

Conference on College Composition and Communication (CCCC). (2009). Statement on second language writing and writers. Retrieved February 10. 2015, from www.ncte.org/cccc/resources/positions/secondlangwriting.

Diab, R. L. (2005). Teachers' and students' beliefs about responding to ESL writing: A case study. *TESL Canada Journal, 23*(1), 28–43.

Ellis, R. (1994). *The study of second language acquisition.* Oxford: Oxford University Press.

Ferris, D. R. (1995). Student reactions to teacher response in multiple-draft composition classrooms. *TESOL Quarterly, 29*(1), 33–51.

Gillespie, P., & Lerner, N. (2000). *The Allyn and Bacon guide to peer tutoring.* Boston, MA: Allyn & Bacon.

Gradman, H. L., & Hanania, E. (1991). Language learning background factors and ESL proficiency. *The Modern Language Journal, 75*(1), 39–51.

Harris, M. (1997). Cultural conflicts in the WCs: Expectations and assumptions of ESL students. In C. Severino, J. C. Guerra, & J. E. Butler (Eds.), *Writing in multicultural settings* (pp. 220–233). New York: Modern Language Association of America.

Harris, M., & Silva, T. (1993). Tutoring ESL students: Issues and options. *College Composition and Communication, 44*(4), 525–537.

Hyland, K. (2003). *Second language writing.* New York, NY: Cambridge University Press.

Institute of International Education (2014). *Open doors: Report on international education exchange.* Retrieved August 13, 2014, from www.iie.org/research-and-publications/open-doors/data

Ismail, N., Elias, S., Safinas, M. A. A., Perumal, D., & Muthusamy, I. (2010). Exploring ESL students' apprehension level and attitude towards academic writing. *The International Journal of Learning, 17*(6), 475–483.

Lee, I. (2005). Error correction in the L2 writing classroom: What do students think? *TESL Canada Journal, 22*(2), 1–16.

Leki, I. (1991). The preferences of ESL students for error-correction in college-level writing classes. *Foreign Language Annals, 24*(3), 203–208.

Matsuda, P. K. (1999). Composition studies and ESL writing: A disciplinary division of labor. *College Composition and Communication, 50*(4), 699–721.

Moussu, L. (2013). Let's talk! ESL students' needs and writing centre philosophy. *TESL Canada Journal, 30*(2), 55–68.

North, S. (1984). The idea of a writing center. *College English, 46*(5), 433–446.

Petric, B. (2002). Students' attitudes towards writing and the development of academic writing skills. The *Writing Center Journal, 22*(2), 9–27.

Powers, J. (1993). Rethinking writing center conferencing strategies for the ESL writer. *The Writing Center Journal, 13*(2), 39–47.

Powers, J. K., & Nelson, J. (1995). Second language writers and the writing center: A national survey of writing center conferencing at graduate institutions. *Journal of Second Language Writing, 4*(2), 113–138.

Qian, J., & Krugly-Smolska, E. (2008). Chinese graduate students' experiences with writing a literature review. *TESL Canada Journal, 26*(1), 68–86.

Reid, J. M. (1987). The learning style preferences of ESL students. *TESOL Quarterly, 21*(1), 87–111.

Silva, T. (1993). Toward an understanding of the distinct nature of L2 writing: The ESL research and its implications. *TESOL Quarterly, 27*(4), 657–677.

Taylor, V. (2007). The balance of rhetoric and linguistics: A study of second language writing center tutorials. (Unpublished doctoral dissertation). Purdue University, West Lafayette, IN.

Thonus, T. (1993). Tutors as teachers: Assisting ESL/EFL students in the writing center. *The Writing Center Journal, 13(2),* 13–26.

Williams, J. (2002). Undergraduate second language writers in the writing center. *Journal of Basic Writing, 21*(2), 73–91.

5

WRITING INSTRUCTION FOR MATRICULATED INTERNATIONAL STUDENTS

A Lived Case Study

Tony Silva

Vignette

The number of international students enrolled at institutions of higher learning in the United States has been steadily increasing for more than 65 years (Institute of International Education, 2013b) and so has concern about providing the English language support necessary for these students to succeed in their academic and professional endeavors. Has the offering of language support courses provided for these students by colleges and universities kept up with the growth of the international student population? My professional experience and my inquiry into the situation suggest that the answer to this question varies greatly from institution to institution and that this variation can be described in terms of recognition of need or level of support. As a metric, I offer this five-point scale: 1 (abject denial), 2 (grudging recognition), 3 (token effort), 4 (minimal measures), and 5 (adequate support). I would like to believe that most institutions score at the high end of this scale, but I do not think that this belief is justified at the current time. I offer the story of one particular university's record with regard to its instructional support in a particular area—writing. I leave it to the reader to decide where this university's efforts fall on the scale.

Introduction

What follows is an account of the ESL Writing Program at Purdue University and my role in it. I hope it will be interesting, informative, and helpful for those who are or will find themselves in a similar situation. I have tried to be accurate and fair, but I have no illusions about this being an objective account because, having directed and taught in this program for more than 20 years, I am both the author of and a central character in this story, and because my account relies as much on my perceptions and recollections as on existing documentation.

Purdue University, founded as a land-grant university in 1869, is today a large, full-service, public research university, with nearly 39,000 students at its main campus located in Lafayette/West Lafayette, Indiana (home to roughly 100,000 inhabitants). It is a member of the Big Ten conference and is best known for its programs in engineering, science, and technology. Perhaps most germane here, Purdue has the second-largest international student population— more than 8,700 students—of all public universities in the United States (Institute of International Education, 2013c). Roughly 17% of Purdue's undergraduate and 40% of its graduate students are international students (Purdue University Office of International Students & Scholars, 2013). English language support, in the form of writing instruction, for these students is provided primarily by the Department of English.

In this chapter I will look at the history of the ESL Writing Program during the time I have been involved with it; describe the current state of the program in terms of its administration, instructors, students, and courses; offer an assessment of the program's performance; and consider the challenges it faces at this time and in years to come.

History

I came to Purdue University as a faculty spouse/English department doctoral student in rhetoric and composition and linguistics in 1986. What I brought with me was a BA in Spanish, an MA in teaching English as a second language (from the University of Illinois at Urbana-Champaign), seven years of experience teaching ESL (listening, grammar, and writing) and composition (basic writing), and four years of supervisory experience (overseeing grammar and writing courses at an intensive English institute).

In my first year at Purdue, I taught mainstream first-year composition. Thereafter, I began teaching in and informally coordinating Purdue's ESL writing support courses. I took on this role because no other faculty or staff member had the necessary background (or desire) to do so and because the director of the ESL program requested my help. The ESL courses that were on the books at this time included ENGL 002, an ESL writing class for international graduate students; ENGL 100i, a basic/developmental writing course for undergraduate international students; and ENGL 101i and ENGL 102i, a two-course, first-year composition sequence also for undergraduate international students.

At this time, all graduate students (international and domestic) had to satisfy a writing requirement administered by the Office of Writing Review, which was a small unit in the Department of English. International students who were nonnative speakers of English could satisfy this requirement by achieving a certain score on the TOEFL. If students scored too low, they were given three hours to write a 600-word essay. If the resulting essay was deemed unsatisfactory, they then had to write a series of three 400-word essays, each in the same amount of time, typically working with someone in the Writing Lab as they progressed. Soon, enrolling in and passing ENGL 002 would replace this earlier process for meeting the writing requirement.

ENGL 100i was a noncredit course meant for international undergraduates who, based on their English proficiency and writing abilities, were seen as unready for ENGL 101i. Due to low enrollments, this course was discontinued in 1989, and thus will receive no further treatment in this chapter. ENGL 101i and 102i were part of Purdue's undergraduate Composition program, administered by the English department. They were parallel to ENGL 101 and 102, which were introductory writing courses required for all undergraduate students.

In 1990 I finished my PhD program and went on the job market. I got a position as an assistant professor at Auburn University in Alabama, where I was to develop an ESL support program and teach graduate ESL courses—to be their ESL person. I spent an interesting and enjoyable year (especially the winter) at Auburn. In the meantime, a tenure-track line opened up at Purdue for a specialist in second language writing. I applied, was hired, and headed back to West Lafayette in the fall of 1991.

At Purdue, I would be teaching graduate courses in ESL within the Program in English Linguistics and directing the incipient ESL Writing Program—rethinking and reworking the course offerings, developing curricula, mentoring and supervising teaching assistants, liaising with the Composition Program, the Graduate Program in Rhetoric and Composition, the Writing Lab, the Office of Writing Review, and seemingly, anybody else on campus who had some interest in or questions about ESL writing.

During my first year, I made some changes. I suspected that ENGL 002 would not survive long in its current form—each section required a half-time teaching assistantship and student enrollments were very low. So I made a deal with the head of the English department to make it a three-hour-a-week writing course. This made the course more focused and less expensive for the department. I also bargained to offer, in perpetuity, at least three sections per semester and to cap enrollment at 10 students per section. Also around this time, at the suggestion of one of the ENGL 002 instructors, I created an alternative tutorial form of ENGL 002. The rationale was that it might be better in some cases for students to meet with their teacher/tutor once per week to work on writing they were doing in their other classes—rather than working on writing assignments created for the ENGL 002 (sounds good in theory, no?). Thus ENGL 002T was born. Unfortunately, this new course was short-lived. It turned out (in retrospect, not surprisingly) that many students who enrolled in ENGL 002T were not asked to write much, if at all, in their other classes. ENGL 002T expired in 1993.

Also in 1993, an alternative version of ENGL 101i, the first course in the two-course, first-year writing sequence, was offered for students in the School of Management, which admirably wanted to give their students an international experience. This alternative, ENGL 101m, would be composed of roughly equal numbers of international and domestic undergraduates, and its curriculum would focus on cross-cultural issues (see Reichelt & Silva, 1995/1996; Matsuda & Silva, 1999 for details). Things went well with ENGL 101m, but after several years interest in the course waned. I gave some thought to opening up this option to students campus-wide, but the logistics of getting equal numbers of international and domestic students enrolled in the class proved to be too much for the university to handle at that point in time. ENGL 101m faded away.

The 1990s were to see yet another major change, one that involved the Office of Writing Review (OWR), which, you will remember, tracked international students into ENGL 002. The OWR was itself reviewed. And the reviews were not good. Students were typically not enamored of it—seeing it as yet another hoop of dubious value to jump through. Many students' home departments or schools argued that it wasted their students' time and impeded progress toward their degrees. The Graduate School saw the OWR as an outdated unit, and the English department did not see it as the best use of its limited resources. It was one of those rare occasions in academia where all parties agreed. The OWR was closed in 1997 (with its small budget going into the ESL program and the Writing Lab), but ENGL 002 continued—now as an optional course for interested international graduate students.

The ESL Writing Program (consisting then of ENGL 101i, ENGL 102i, and ENGL 002) moved forward. Curricula were reviewed and revised, a pool of teachers (primarily English department graduate students) was cultivated, and an enrollment cap of 20 was put in place for ENGL 101i and 102i (mainstream composition courses were capped at 27 at the time). As the numbers of international students enrolled at Purdue increased, so did the numbers of sections of ENGL 101i and ENGL 102i; however, ENGL 002 stayed put at three sections per semester with 10 students per section.

In 2003, a major development in the English Composition program caused some significant changes in the undergraduate ESL writing courses. The program moved from the required two-course sequence (ENGL 101 and ENGL 102) to a single required composition course: ENGL 106, a five-day-per-week class. As you might expect, ENGL 101i and ENGL 102i followed suit, morphing into ENGL 106i. The course was also reconceived. In addition to classroom instruction, students would receive instruction in digital technology used for writing and would have regular teacher–student conferences.

This seemed to mean that students would have to do a lot of running around—to a classroom, to a computer lab, and to a conferencing center—each week. Fortunately, it just so happened that, around this time, there was a campus initiative to get computers into all classrooms, and one option was using laptops that would be kept in a secure cart in a single dedicated classroom. The English department offered me this option for ENGL 106i, and I immediately accepted. This meant that sections of ENGL 106i could use the same room every day—for classroom instruction, technology use, and conferencing—and that my teachers and their students would have a much less mobile and confusing experience. Also at this time, based on recommendations from a 2001 Conference on College Composition and Communication position paper on ESL writers and writing (updated in 2009), my department head, a former director of composition, allowed ENGL 106i to cap enrollment at 15 students per section.

In 2006, we conducted another curricular experiment for the ESL Writing program. The chair of a particular department contacted me about providing some writing support for their increasing numbers of international graduate students. I agreed, and I and one of my senior graduate students went to interview the chair and some of the faculty in this department to learn more about these students and to get an idea of their writing needs. This done, we worked up a syllabus for the course (a modified section of ENGL 002) and worked out the logistics with our department's scheduling deputy. Things were set to go for the next semester, and the students signed up. Unfortunately, during the first week of class, seven of the 10 enrolled students from this department dropped the course. I contacted the chair of the department, filled her in on what had happened, and asked her to get the students back in. She refused, saying that staying in or dropping out of the class was up to the students. This left us with an under-enrolled section of ENGL 002—the kind of thing that administrative bean counters see as an opportunity to eliminate courses—and left me with much less enthusiasm about participating in this type of outreach.

The most recent changes in the program came in 2009, when ENGL 002 had a number change to indicate that it was a bona fide graduate course and not a "remedial" offering (it became ENGL 621), and in 2011, when one or two sections of ENGL 106i were included in learning community contexts (situations in which a small cohort of first-semester students with similar academic interests takes a number of courses—including ENGL 106i—together) and when the program hired three continuing lecturers to help staff the growing number of ENGL 106i sections.

The Current State of the ESL Writing Program

Administration

Currently, directing the ESL Writing Program involves the oversight of ENGL 106i and ENGL 621. The director's responsibilities include the ongoing development and modification of the courses and their instructional materials, the hiring of instructors, the mentoring and evaluation of new instructors (which involves a weekly meeting, two class observations of each new instructor, two post-observation conferences, and a review of instructor evaluations), and staff supervision and development.

Instructors

The ESL Writing Program's instructors are almost always students in the PhD program in Second Language Studies/ESL (a relatively new program that grew out of the Graduate Program in English Language and Linguistics). During their first year, these graduate students each teach one section of mainstream composition per semester and receive a lot of support, which includes a week of intensive orientation before they begin their first semester and two semesters of mentoring. The mentoring comprises a three-hour-per-week course, ENGL 505: Teaching First-Year Composition, in each of their first two semesters. ENGL 505 is a practicum in the teaching of writing that involves reading professional literature on the teaching of writing, the study of methodologies, assessment issues, and the relationship between theory and pedagogy. Mentor groups (usually with 8–10 students) are typically led by a faculty member or an advanced graduate student from the Graduate Program in Rhetoric and Composition.

The Second Language Studies/ESL Program typically requires its students to teach and get mentored in mainstream composition (ENGL 106) during their first year so that they can interact with students from the other graduate programs in the English department and to help prepare them to teach a writing course—most of our students come in with quite a bit of ESL teaching experience, but have sometimes not taught writing per se. After students have taught mainstream composition for a year, if they want to teach ESL writing, they must sign up for mentoring (ENGL 502: Practicum in Teaching Written ESL) with the ESL Writing Program director. However, this mentoring is much less extensive. After a two-hour orientation meeting, the group meets for an hour once per week, basically to talk about what has been going on in their ENGL 106i classes in the previous week, to share and discuss student papers (in the manner of a reading group), to address problems that come up, and to preview the week to come. At present, the majority of the ENGL 106i teaching assistants are international students themselves. This includes instructors from Afghanistan, Algeria, China, Colombia, India, Iran, Japan, Korea, Libya, Poland, Russia, Saudi Arabia, Taiwan, Thailand, Turkey, and Ukraine, as well as instructors from the United States. Until very recently, ENGL 106i instructors have been almost exclusively teaching assistants.

Students

Our undergraduate (ENGL 106i) students these days come, for the most part, from East Asia, specifically China and Korea, with small groups of students from a variety of other countries (e.g., Colombia, Ecuador, Egypt, France, India, Indonesia, Japan, Jordan, Kazakhstan, Kuwait, Lebanon, Malaysia, Mexico, Nigeria, Pakistan, Saudi Arabia, Serbia, Singapore, Spain, Sri Lanka, Taiwan,

Thailand, and the United Arab Emirates). They are typically first-year students with a mean age of about 19; on average, they have studied English for more than eight years; they are more often men (58%) than women (42%); and most of them are majoring in science, engineering, or business. These students are the best and brightest from their countries. They are typically well educated, affluent, cosmopolitan, and technologically savvy. Their English proficiency is typically high-intermediate to advanced. However, as most are in an English-dominant country for the first time, it takes a while for their latent English ability to manifest itself.

Our graduate (ENGL 621) students are, for the most part, similar to the undergraduates, except that they are, of course, older, more highly educated and skilled, and they have been working in their disciplines for a substantial amount of time—they are, in short, accomplished professionals. However, their English proficiency is markedly lower than that of the undergraduates, and this often impedes their progress, not only in ENGL 621, but also in the courses they take in their area of expertise.

Courses

ENGL 621

ENGL 621 is a three-credit, three-hour-per-week academic writing course designed especially for international graduate students at Purdue. As mentioned earlier, it has an enrollment limit of 10 students per section; students are graded on a pass/fail basis; and credit for ENGL 621 does not typically count toward students' degree requirements. In general terms, ENGL 621 aims to help international graduate students become more comfortable with and proficient in writing in English and to prepare them for the writing they may need to do in graduate school and in the workplace. The course is open to all matriculated Purdue international graduate students—MA and PhD—from any school, college, department, or program. ENGL 621 is not obligatory; enrolling in it is a choice made by the students in consultation with their advisors.

Instruction focuses on composing processes (strategic options for writing) and written texts (in terms of their generic, rhetorical, and linguistic features). Students work on assigned writing projects and engage in discussions of academic and disciplinary issues and concerns. Course meetings are roughly evenly split between classroom activities and individual conferences with their instructors. Individual conferences are used to respond to the drafts of the students' major assignments. The course requires the completion of eight short activity reports and four major writing projects. The short activity reports require students to address professional development issues in their fields. These reports include descriptions of the students' field, employment opportunities, promotion and tenure opportunities, professional organizations and conferences, research tools, scholarly journals, documentation practices, and research funding sources. The major projects typically include an academic biography, a CV and cover letter, an analysis of a research report, and a proposal for a conference paper or a research proposal. Students typically write three drafts for each major project. The first draft is looked at in terms of content and organization; the second, in terms of language issues; and the third receives a grade with specific comments on strengths and weaknesses, guided by a modified form of an analytic scoring rubric, the English Composition Profile (Jacobs, Zinkgraf, Wormuth, Hartfiel, & Hughey, 1981).

ENGL 621 is taught by instructors—typically advanced PhD students—with experience and expertise in teaching both English as a second language and composition, with international experience, and with an understanding of what it is like to write in a second language. There are typically no required textbooks for ENGL 621; the program director provides basic material for the course to the instructors to use with their students.

ENGL 106i

ENGL 106i is a writing course for nonnative English-speaking undergraduate students who feel they might be at a disadvantage in ENGL 106, the mainstream writing course, due to such factors as level of English proficiency, experience in writing in English, or familiarity with American cultural or educational practices. ENGL 106i is not obligatory for undergraduate international students; enrolling in it is a choice made by the students in consultation with their advisors.

While students are not tracked into ENGL 106i, they are given guidelines for directed self-placement in first-year composition. It is suggested that they should consider enrolling in 106i if their TOEFL total score is below 100 on the internet-based test, if their TOEFL writing subscore is below 26, if English has not been the medium of instruction for most of their education, if their speaking and listening skills in English are not as strong as their writing and reading skills, or if they feel that they are likely to have difficulty with a heavy reading load.

ENGL 106i and ENGL 106 meet the same composition requirement; bear the same amount of credit; require the same amount of writing; share a focus on strategic, rhetorical, and linguistic issues; and integrate classroom instruction, individual or small-group conferencing, and the use of technology. Additionally, ENGL 106i appears as ENGL 106 on students' transcripts so that there will be no stigma attached to taking it. ENGL 106i is designed especially for undergraduate international students, allowing for more focus on language and cross-cultural issues. As with ENGL 621, it is typically taught by instructors with experience and expertise in teaching both ESL and composition, with international experience, and with an understanding of what it is like to write in a second language. In addition, these instructors are mentored and supervised by an ESL writing specialist.

ENGL 106i sections, with an enrollment cap of 15 students, are smaller than sections of ENGL 106, allowing for more teacher–student interaction. All ENGL 106i sections meet in a room set up as a wireless computer lab or in a regular computer lab, giving students and teachers constant and easy access to that technology. ENGL 106i classes meet in the same room at the same time five days per week, permitting greater flexibility in integrating traditional classroom activities, conferencing, and the use of technology. Finally, ENGL 106i students often comment on how comfortable they feel in ENGL 106i because its relatively small size allows them to get to know their classmates better and because of the sense of camaraderie they feel with their international student peers. The primary goal of the course is to help students become more comfortable with and proficient in writing in English.

There is no required textbook, though instructors can use textbooks if they so desire. The program director provides instructors with materials to give to their students—a policy handout, a syllabus, assignment sheets, sample papers for analysis, and a grading rubric similar to the one used in ENGL 621.

ENGL 106i requires the completion of five major writing projects. Students write multiple drafts for each assignment and receive feedback from both the instructors and their peers. As with ENGL 621, course meetings are roughly evenly split between classroom activities and individual conferences with instructors, and individual conferences are used to respond to drafts of students' major assignments, focusing on content and organization in the first draft and on language issues in the second. The third draft receives a grade guided by a modified version of the Jacobs et al. (1981) analytic scoring rubric.

The major assignments begin with a writer's autobiography and then move to a set of sequenced assignments based on work by Ilona Leki in her 1991/1992 article in *TESOL Journal* and in her 1998 textbook, *Academic Writing: Exploring Processes and Strategies*, from which much of our materials and procedures have been adapted. The sequenced writing format requires that students write a total of four papers on the same subject over the course of the semester. The idea of a series of assignments forming a sequenced writing project grows from the belief that students develop their writing skills best when each assignment they do builds quite directly on the experience and knowledge gained from completing the previous assignments.

In the sequenced writing project, students may write on any topic they wish, with the approval of their teacher. However, they must select a topic that meets three requirements: (1) they must be very interested in the topic and want to learn more about it; (2) they must already have had some personal experience with and an investment in the topic; and (3) the topic must be one that will allow them to do all four papers involved. Teachers meet one-on-one with students to negotiate their sequenced writing project topic. The projects include a personal narrative, a literature review, an interview report, and culminate in an argumentative essay.

Program Assessment

Does the ESL writing program work? It seems to. Teachers enjoy working in the program and students give the classes and their teachers good evaluations. I get very few complaints. So, if it works, why does it work? I believe there are a number of reasons. First, we draw support from the Composition Program, the Writing Lab, the Graduate Programs in Second Language Studies/ESL and Rhetoric and Composition, the English Department, and the College of Liberal Arts.

I would like to give a shout out to Purdue's Writing Lab, which is both actual and virtual. Its physical existence began in 1976 and its virtual life in 1994, in the form of the Online Writing Lab or OWL, which annually logs more than 250 million page views from more than 200 countries. The Lab has been a great resource for the ESL Writing Program, offering our students drop-in consultations, weekly appointments, and vast online resources. The Lab helps students with all aspects of writing, and its staff typically includes tutors who specialize in working with second language writers.

We also have outstanding instructors—dedicated, engaged, knowledgeable, experienced, and humane—I am especially pleased to have instructors who are multilingual and have international experience; it is clear that students appreciate being taught by someone who has been in their situation. Finally, we have world-class students—smart, knowledgeable, hardworking, and highly motivated.

Challenges

The program faces three major challenges—now and in the years to come. The first is accommodating the sharply increasing undergraduate international student population (see Table 5.1).

TABLE 5.1 Purdue University International Undergraduate Enrollment: 2008–2013

Academic Year	Undergraduates	Change from Previous Year	% Change
2008–2009	2,360	+318	+15.6
2009–2010	2,818	+458	+19.4
2010–2011	3,420	+602	+21.4
2011–2012	4,544	+1,124	+32.9
2012–2013	4,974	+430	+9.5

Source: Purdue Office of Student Analytical Research, 2014.

Over the past five academic years (2008–2009 through 2012–2013), the total number of undergraduate international students has gone from 2,360 to 4,974—an increase of 2,614 students or 111%. As shown in Table 5.1, the magnitude of this increase, whether in terms of real numbers or percentages, has grown greater year by year. During this period, the growth of the international undergraduate student population has averaged about 586 students or 20% per year. This has, of course, required an increase in the number of sections of ENGL 106i offered. In 2007–2008 and 2008–2009, 20 sections per year were offered; in 2009–2010, 25; in 2010–2011, 30; in 2011–2012, 43; and in 2012–2013, 50.

This rapid growth has put a serious strain on the ESL Writing Program. The program lacks adequate administrative and secretarial support, is having difficulty finding enough classroom space, and is struggling to get enough teachers to cover the added sections of ENGL 106i (even though the university recently provided funding for three continuing lecturers dedicated to ENGL 106i).

The situation has also affected the First-Year Composition Program as a whole. For a long time (at least since I started in 1991), what has been labeled as a "containment model" by Matsuda (2006) has been in effect; that is, for the most part, all of the undergraduate international students who chose to enroll in ENGL 106i (or ENGL 101i and ENGL 102i before 2002) were able to do so. However, due to the increases described above, this is no longer the case. As a result, ENGL 106 teachers, who may have had one or two international students per class, may now have five or more in each of the sections they teach. There is, in essence, a new status quo—all first-year composition teachers have to be, to some extent, second language writing teachers. And this is a tall order.

The second major challenge has to do with providing writing instruction for international graduate students. The situation here is quite different. The population of international graduate students has also been growing, but not by nearly as much or by as many as the international undergraduate population (see Table 5.2).

Over the past five academic years (2008–2009 through 2012–2013), the total number of international graduate students has gone from 3,091 to 3,556—an increase of 465 students or 15%. During this period, the growth of the

TABLE 5.2 Purdue University International Graduate Student Enrollment: 2008–2013

Academic Year	Graduates	Change from Previous Year	% Change
2008–2009	3,091	+169	+5.8
2009–2010	3,144	+53	+1.7
2010–2011	3,315	+171	+5.4
2011–2012	3,359	+44	+1.3
2012–2013	3,556	+197	+5.9

Source: Purdue Office of Student Analytical Research, 2014.

international graduate student population has averaged about 126 students or 4% per year. This relatively small increase has not resulted in more sections of ENGL 621. In fact, due to small advance enrollments and the need for teachers to staff ENGL 106i, no sections of ENGL 621 were offered from fall 2012 through fall 2013. I expected some complaints, but I did not hear any.

It is important to note that, per semester, this course was typically serving only 30 of the more than 3,000 international graduate students enrolled at Purdue. This was and is a very interesting and frustrating situation—especially since Purdue's international graduate students tend to have lower English proficiency and writing ability levels than do its international undergraduates. There is certainly need here. The stumbling blocks seem to be time, money, and turf. First, time; that is, international graduate students, with their challenging class, lab, and research or teaching obligations, tend to have very tight and somewhat unpredictable schedules. This makes it difficult for those who enroll to attend regularly and makes it impossible for others to enroll at all. Also, unlike first-year writing for undergraduates, ENGL 621 is not an obligatory, credit-bearing course that counts on a graduate student's plan of study. Then, there is money. Currently the College of Liberal Arts funds ENGL 621 via the English department, and they are understandably somewhat reluctant to fund graduate classes for students primarily coming from science and engineering departments. And then there is turf—at Purdue, schools, colleges, and departments are very autonomous—their motto could be "Stay out of my business, and I'll stay out of yours." So there is not a lot of coordination or cooperation across units. Alleviating this situation will require a change of the academic culture of graduate programs at Purdue; specifically, these programs will need to acknowledge their students' needs with regard to writing in English; build flexibility into their students' class, teaching, and lab schedules so that students can take advantage of the writing support courses provided; and communicate to their students the value of attending these courses.

The third major challenge is providing adequate language support (in this case, writing instruction) for international students. The rapid increase in the international student population at Purdue is not an accident. While Purdue certainly enjoys a good reputation worldwide, the increases are a result of a concerted effort to bring in more (full-tuition-and-fee paying) international undergraduate students and graduate students (i.e., an inexpensive, yet highly skilled labor force to deploy in Purdue's classrooms and laboratories). Administrators will highlight the fact that increasing numbers of international students results in more diversity and new perspectives and helps make the university a truly global and world-class institution. I believe this, and I strongly support this policy, but it would be foolish to believe that the need to develop new "revenue streams" (at a time when state support is dwindling) has nothing to do with it. My concern is whether international students are getting as much as they give. That is, has the increase in numbers of international students been accompanied by a corresponding level of growth in language support? My conclusion is that it has not—at least not yet.

However, I do not mean to suggest that Purdue is an isolated case. Indeed, numbers of international students at institutions large and small across the United States continue to rise steadily—since 2008, undergraduates at an average of 19,327 students or 7.0% per year; graduates at an average of 7,072 or 2.4% per year (see Tables 5.3 and 5.4; Institute of International Education, 2013a).

Many, if not most, colleges and universities across the United States today are looking to increase their international student populations, and the support (in writing or other areas) they provide for these students varies widely in amount and quality. It is hoped (but not altogether expected) that these institutions will not see international students primarily as cash cows, but rather as the intellectual and cultural assets they are and treat them accordingly.

Epilogue

During the 2013–2014 academic year, numerous units and individuals with a stake in the success of undergraduate international students met to try to develop a plan to better address these students' language needs. It was widely felt that the status quo—a variety of programs working in relative isolation—was counterproductive and untenable. We stakeholders attended a "summit meeting," by

TABLE 5.3 International Undergraduate Student Enrollment: 2008–2013

Academic Year	Undergraduates	Change from Previous Year	% Change
2008–2009	269,874	+26,514	+10.9
2009–2010	274,431	+4,557	+1.7
2010–2011	291,439	+17,008	+6.2
2011–2012	309,342	+17,903	+6.1
2012–2013	339,993	+30,651	+9.9

Source: Institute of International Education, 2013a.

TABLE 5.4 International Graduate Student Enrollment: 2008–2013

Academic Year	Graduates	Change from Previous Year	% Change
2008–2009	283,329	+6,487	+2.3
2009–2010	293,855	+11,526	+4.1
2010–2011	296,574	+2,719	+0.9
2011–2012	300,430	+3,856	+1.3
2012–2013	311,204	+10,774	+3.6

Source: Institute of International Education, 2013a.

the Office of the Provost, where all described their current efforts and offered ideas for what might be done to build on these efforts to move toward a viable, coordinated, and comprehensive plan of action. The discussion was productive and resulted in the formation of working groups designed to address what were seen as the major issues. The working groups met and formulated responses to what would become a steering committee, charged with putting together a comprehensive proposal for consideration by the university administration. The steering committee produced and submitted such a proposal.

The proposal (which, in my view, asked for too much too fast) was rejected by the administration and sent back to the committee for revision. The committee developed a more modest proposal, which was approved by the administration. What the committee got was not what it had hoped for, but it was something—and a rather substantial something in terms of dollars. This whole process was very interesting and revealing, at least for me, and worthy of elaboration—but not here.

To bring this story back home, the ESL Writing Program got funding for three additional continuing lecturers and greatly increased secretarial support. The Writing Lab got funding to make its three-quarter time ESL Coordinator full-time and to hire four additional tutors—two graduate and undergraduate tutors. This is not a bad thing. So, all in all, while these results are, in my opinion, not optimal, they will help us better serve our undergraduate international students. *C'est la vie.* Note, however, that all of this addressed only undergraduate international students, so we may have another interesting year trying to increase language support for graduate international students, who arguably are currently less well served and more in need than their undergraduate counterparts.

Summary

- Sharply increasing numbers of international students at institutions of higher education in the United States require (re)consideration of the level of language support (writing support, in this case) provided for these students. This chapter looks at this issue in a particular context—a large public research university with more than 8,700 international students.
- The author provides an insider's look at the history of the development of writing support instruction at this university. He examines not only the university's actions but his own role as well.
- Program changes and innovations (big and small, successes and failures) over 20-plus years are chronicled. The events and situations that gave rise to these developments are also considered.
- The current status of the program in terms of its administration, instructors, students, and courses is described in detail. An assessment of the program's effectiveness and the resources upon which it draws is provided.

- Three major challenges currently facing the program are presented and discussed. It is suggested that these challenges are probably not unique to the university examined in this chapter.

Discussion Questions

1. Do you trust the writer of this chapter to be fair and accurate, given his personal and professional investment in the program he describes?
2. Do you think the changes that took place in the evolution of this program reflect conscious planning and gradual movement toward a desired goal?
3. Do you feel that the instruction now being offered (ENGL 106i and ENGL 621) is appropriate and adequate for this institutional context at the current time?
4. Do you believe that all writing teachers need to be ESL writing teachers?
5. What actions would you propose to meet the challenges specified at the end of the chapter?

Further Reading

Ferris, D. R., & Hedgcock, J. S. (2013). *Teaching ESL composition: Purpose, process, and practice* (3rd ed.). New York, NY: Routledge.

Leki, I. (Ed.). (2001). *Academic writing programs*. Alexandria, VA: TESOL.

Matsuda, P. K., Fruit, M., Lee, T., & Lamm, B. (2006). Second language writers and writing program administrators [special issue]. *Writing Program Administrators, 30*(1–2), 9–130.

Open Doors/Institute for International Education. www.iie.org/en/Research-and-Publications/Open-Doors.

Williams, J. (1995). ESL composition program administration in the United States. *Journal of Second Language Writing, 4*(2), 157–179.

References

Conference on College Composition and Communication. (2001/2009). *CCCC statement on second language writing and writers*. Urbana, IL: National Council of Teachers of English.

Institute of International Education. (2013a). *In Open Doors report on international educational exchange* [Fast Facts Open Doors 2013]. Retrieved May 13, 2014, from www.iie.org/Research-and-Publications/Open-Doors.

Institute of International Education. (2013b). International student enrollment trends, 1948–2013. *Open Doors report on international educational exchange*. Retrieved from www.iie.org/opendoors.

Institute of International Education. (2013c). Top 25 institutions hosting international students, 2012/13. *Open Doors report on international educational exchange*. Retrieved from www.iie.org/opendoors.

Jacobs, H. L., Zinkgraf, S. A., Wormuth, D. R., Hartfiel, V. F., & Hughey, J. B. (1981). *Testing ESL composition: A practical approach*. Rowley, MA: Newbury House.

Leki, I. (1991/1992). Building expertise through sequenced assignments. *TESOL Journal, 1*(2), 19–23.

Leki, I. (1998). *Academic writing: Exploring processes and strategies* (2nd ed.). New York, NY: Cambridge University Press.

Matsuda, P. K. (2006). The myth of linguistic homogeneity in U.S. college composition. *College English, 68*(6), 637–651.

Matsuda, P. K., & Silva, T. (1999). Cross-cultural composition: Mediated integration of US and international students. *Composition Studies, 27*(1), 15–30.

Purdue Office of Student Analytical Research. (2014). *Fall 2013 international student and scholar enrollment and statistical report.* West Lafayette, IN: Purdue University. Retrieved from www.iss.purdue.edu/resources/Docs/Reports/ISS_Statistical ReportFall13.pdf.

Purdue University Office of International Students and Scholars. (2013). *Fall 2013 international student and scholar enrollment and statistical report.* Retrieved from www.iss.purdue.edu/resources/Docs/Reports/ISS_StatisticalReportFall13.pdf.

Reichelt, M., & Silva, T. (1995/1996). Cross-cultural composition. *TESOL Journal, 5*(2), 16–19.

6

FAMILIAR STRANGERS

International Students in the U.S. Composition Course

Elena Lawrick and Fatima Esseili

Vignette

Many will recognize this sketch of new international undergraduates at a U.S. university: Excited. Jet-lagged. Late to class because they got lost on a big campus. Overwhelmed by myriad things to do on the first days of the semester. Confused by the English language that sounds so different. Thrown into a first-year writing course instrumental to their academic success.

Introduction and Overview of the Challenges

As Leki, Cumming, and Silva (2008) observe, undergraduate ESL writers in the U.S. higher-education context have been a focal group for L2 writing researchers (pp. 28–36). In fact, such groups of ESL writers have been researched from several perspectives, including:

- appropriate curricula options (Braine, 1996; Harklau, 1994; Matsuda, 2006; Silva, 1997; Williams, 1996) and pedagogical approaches (Horowitz, 1986; Johns, 1995; Spack, 1988; Zamel, 1982);
- ESL writing needs as perceived in an English department versus other university departments (Janopoulos, 1992; Leki, 1995, 2003, 2007; Leki & Carson, 1994, 1997);
- L2 composing processes, rhetorical strategies, and textual characteristics (Ferris, 1994; Reid, 1993; Silva, 1993);
- ESL error treatment (Ferris, 1999; Truscott, 1999);
- teacher feedback (Ashwell, 2000; Fathman & Whalley, 1990; Ferris, 1995, 1997; Goldstein, 2005; Leki, 1992; Reid, 1994; Severino, 1993; Zamel, 1985);

- ESL student perceptions, experiences, preferences, and identities (Allaei & Connor, 1990; Christianson & Krahnke, 1986; Leki & Carson, 1994; Nelson & Murphy, 1992; Ortmeier-Hooper, 2008; Zamel, 1995; Zhu, 2001); and
- distinctions among traditional ESL writers, Generation 1.5 ESL writers, and basic native English writers (Doolan & Miller, 2011; Harklau, Losey, & Siegal, 1999; Matsuda, Fruit, & Lamm, 2006; Roberge, Siegal, & Harklau, 2008).

Regardless, international ESL undergraduates proliferating at U.S. colleges remain familiar strangers (Milgram, 1974) passing through their respective campuses. Like strangers repeatedly encountered on the commuter rail, they constitute the most recognizable yet least known student population. Consequently, as Leki (2007) argues, international ESL students are often perceived as the "unidimensional and inferior Other" (p. 261). The "Other" tends to be considered as a homogeneous group of "traditional internationals" or intelligent learners of the English language who struggle to adapt linguistically and culturally (Lawrick, 2013, p. 31).

Considering the amount of relevant research, one might wonder what accounts for this insufficient awareness. In L2 writing scholarship, the focus on international students in U.S. first-year composition courses peaked in the 1990s. (Please note the publication dates of most of the aforementioned studies.) Accordingly, the related findings are contextualized in the assumptions that are based on dated sociolinguistic realities of the 1990s. In that period of time, a distinction between native and nonnative English-speaking countries was unambiguous: Students from nonnative English-speaking countries learned English as a foreign language. Nor did they study English composition or routinely write in English in their home countries.

Since the 1990s, however, two influential processes have drastically changed the sociolinguistic and educational landscapes in nonnative English-speaking countries. First, globalization increasingly continues to interconnect nations through the English language, which has spread into virtually every country. Although the global presence of English is uneven, English is used by nonnative speakers for numerous purposes within diverse linguistic realizations that are much different from the Standard American English or British English (Blommaert, 2010; Schneider, 2011). The other catalyst is the internationalization of higher education, which has caused an English composition course to become an omnipresent requirement in worldwide, higher education contexts (Ide, 2010). To increase international mobility of students and faculty, universities across the globe align their curricula, credit allocation systems, and course offerings. This stimulates the introduction of writing-in-English curriculum at early, often elementary, stages of education in nonnative-English-speaking countries. Concurrently, U.S. universities are aggressively exploring new markets to combat their crumbling budgets. Global extensions of U.S. college campuses promote the writing-in-English curriculum molded in the U.S. tradition, which is further augmented by the global dominance of American English in academic collaboration and scholarly publications.

Put another way, teaching composition to international ESL undergraduates at U.S. colleges is based on assumptions that do not take into consideration the exposure to English that students experience in their home countries. Specifically, it is commonly assumed that international students are English-language learners who had limited experiences in the authentic use of English, who had "little opportunity to write extended texts in English" (Ferris, 2009, p. 89) before taking their U.S. first-year composition course, and, therefore, who had acquired none-to-little knowledge of English composition and rhetoric. This leads to others' perceptions of the ESL student as a *tabula rasa*, thus supporting the premise that "proper" teaching of English writing begins in a U.S. college composition class. Yet it is hardly debatable that writing pedagogy should be founded on up-to-date and empirically supported insights into ESL students' previous experiences with both using and writing English.

This chapter presents selected findings from our study of a well-established ESL writing program at a U.S. university with a large population of international undergraduate students. The study was conducted in all 13 writing sections. The instruments included demographic data from university registrars; one instructor survey, administered at the end of the semester; and two student surveys, one administered at the beginning of the semester and one at the end. The instructor survey response rate was 100% (13 teachers); the student survey response rates were 82.5% (161 students) and 88% (171 students), respectively.[1] The reported findings inform five areas: an ESL course in the university's writing program, placement and student motivation, course structure and practices, instructor feedback, and writing lab (WL). A tripartite discussion of each area includes the observed processes, related findings, and potential implications.

Challenges, Implications, and Applications

ESL Writing Course

Observed Practices

ENGL 106i is a first-year writing course for nonnative English-speaking undergraduate students at Purdue University. The course shares goals and learning outcomes with the non-ESL first-year writing course, fulfills the same requirement, and bears the same amount of credit, while providing additional support for ESL writers (Blackmon, Haynes, & Pinkert, 2012, pp. 9–12). ESL sections are capped at 15 students, scheduled for five times per week in a computer lab setting, and taught by teachers trained in L2 writing. This allows more frequent teacher–student conferencing, more available access to technology, and more prompt responses to student needs as they emerge in the course (see Silva in Chapter 5). This course setting, unfortunately, is barely representative of first-year writing programs at U.S. colleges. Rather, sections with 20 or more students meeting in a regular classroom and being taught by teachers lacking ESL training are more commonplace. Student learning in such an environment is further affected by the little knowledge that such teachers have about the English writing experiences that ESL students had accrued prior to their first-year writing course at a U.S. college. Our study provides germane insight.

Findings from Student Surveys

At the time of this study, 13 ESL writing sections were composed of 195 students who came from 14 countries and spoke 18 native languages along with several additional, nonnative languages. The majority of the students came from Southeast Asia, with the majority of their countries of origin being China (46%), Malaysia (14%), India (12%), and South Korea (11%). Ninety-one percent of the students were international, and 9% were U.S. residents (a detailed student profile is available in Lawrick, 2013, pp. 36–38).

Prior to their U.S. writing course, 81% of students had studied English composition in their home countries. In fact, the majority of students in every national group had previously studied English writing (see Table 6.1).

The following non-U.S. educational settings in which the students studied writing in English were reported:

- a writing course in school combined with a program preparing students for college admission examinations (54% of students);
- a writing course in school (19%);

TABLE 6.1 Students Who Studied English Composition in Their Home Countries by Nationality Groups

Nationality Group	% (n) of Students in the Nationality Group
Malay	100 (23)
Indonesian	100 (8)
Indian	90 (15)
Chinese	88 (143)
Arabic	86 (6)
Korean	71 (12)
Miscellaneous	82 (12)

Note
The miscellaneous group is composed of 1–2 students of six nationalities: Thai, Spanish, Russian, Kazakh, Turkish, and Croatian.

- a program preparing students for college admission examinations (12%);
- a writing course in school combined with a program preparing students for college admission examinations and individual tutoring (11%); and
- tutoring (4%).

In sum, 84% of the students studied English composition in non-U.S. secondary education settings, in which these writing courses lasted from one to 28 semesters (4, 8, and 12 semesters were indicated most frequently). In addition, 77% studied writing for standardized college admission tests, including TOEFL, SAT, ACT, TOEIC, GRE, IELTS, FCE, CAE, and TEPS.[2]

Implications

Our study provides evidence that international ESL undergraduates learn to compose in English in their home countries. Rather than being discarded, their previous backgrounds need to be studied and built upon. It is imperative that U.S.-based writing programs attune to worldwide realities by adjusting their writing pedagogies founded on insights from empirical studies. Although this is challenging due to the diversity of students' backgrounds, much-needed research pertains to (1) English writing curricula in national contexts that supply the largest groups of undergraduates, and (2) international undergraduates in U.S. writing programs that are systematically conducted across U.S. institutions of higher learning and are similar to our study and the research by Andrade, Evans, and Hartshorne in this volume (see Chapters 1, 2, and 8).

ESL Placement

Observed Processes

At Purdue University, matriculated international undergraduates enroll in courses through a guided self-registration system. That is, after meeting with an academic advisor, a student registers for courses through an online system. In this placement process, the decision regarding which writing course (ESL or non-ESL) to pursue is made by the student. Arguably, several factors may affect a student's choice, including the recommendation of an academic advisor, other international students, and the availability of ESL sections. While offering certain advantages, this ambiguous placement process opens several routes to misplacement. Based on anecdotal evidence, academic advisors tend to place international students in non-ESL sections when ESL sections are full, although the course could be postponed until the following semester. Also, a placement based on the advice of other ESL students can hardly be accurate. Finally, the sheer pressure of making an important decision is overwhelming for international undergraduates who are just beginning to figure out a U.S. college life.

Findings from Student Surveys

Our study investigated students' motivations to register for an ESL writing course regardless of the recommendations of their academic advisors. Forty-eight percent of students indicated that they would choose an ESL course over a non-ESL course, 31% would register for a non-ESL course, and 21% were not sure which track they would prefer.

To get deeper insight for this study, the students who indicated their preference for an ESL course were asked to briefly explain their reasons. The explanations were grouped in the four categories presented below. The parentheses show the percentage of students who displayed each respective motivation type; each category is illustrated by student comments.

1. Intention to improve English writing skills (54%): "I want to improve my writing skills as much as possible." "It is a great class in effectively improve English writing." "I love to deal with my papers and essays. It is fun and I learn a lot from it."
2. Awareness of the pragmatic value of writing proficiency in English for academic and professional success (34%): "It's useful for future classes/research papers." "Because English is a tool that I'll be using for the rest of my college career." "I will need to write in other courses. Useful in any job area."
3. Perception of an ESL writing course as a fair learning environment as compared to that of a non-ESL course (9%): "Because I think it is fair to let all International Students take the same level of English. But if I take normal English course [sic] then [sic] I have to work harder since I will be competing [with students] whose native language is English."
4. Other (3%): no comments provided.

One unsettling finding, though, is that some students were motivated by their perception of an ESL course as "easy credits," which reminds us of how delicate the balance between support and challenge can be.

Additional insight comes from two sets of thought-provoking comments volunteered by students who indicated a lack of motivation to take an ESL writing course. First, transfer students from Malaysia and China had taken an English college writing course before: "I took a similar course in a home country university." Second, several students felt overwhelmed and struggled with their course load: "This semester my schedule is too challenging."

Implications

Our study suggests that international ESL students tend to perceive an ESL writing course positively for its practical benefits. This may not be typical of

U.S.-resident ESL students, who may carry over the stigma associated with K–12 ESL. Regardless of their perceptions, ESL students should learn academic writing in the course that addresses their specific needs and provides adequate support so that they will succeed rather than set themselves up to fail in their college studies. Therefore, the development of accurate and fair placement processes is one of the most pressing issues that needs to be addressed.

ESL Course Structure and Practices

Observed Processes

The Sequenced Writing Project (Leki, 1991) provides the framework for the four essays required in this course. The overarching goal is to introduce the foundations of research conduct and academic writing in a continuous, hands-on learning environment. At the beginning of the semester, students choose a topic to examine in a series of four sequenced essays: a personal narrative that addresses the chosen research topic, a literature review that provides practice in secondary research, an interview report that introduces students to original research, and an argumentative essay that builds on the three previous essays. The assumption is that target skills and competencies will be reinforced at each essay phase, building up into the set of competencies that is expected of a college writer.

Instruction includes traditional face-to-face learning (e.g., mini-lectures, discussions and activities in class, small-group, and individual work formats), peer review sessions, suggested sessions with WL tutors, and one-on-one student–teacher conferences. Additionally, as our study found, five out of the 13 instructors occasionally had group sessions, teaching half or one-third of the class at a time. To create a student-centered learning environment, face-to-face teaching is supplemented by e-instruction. At the time of our study, all teachers maintained either a course website or a course e-mail list to share handouts, lecture notes, assignment instructions, and other course materials.

The process of teaching essay writing is grounded in the assumption that academic writing proficiency develops best in the environment that engages a variety of instructional means and emphasizes collaboration between novice and experienced writers. To implement this assumption, the work on each essay begins with an introduction to the genre and guided essay planning in the setting of mini-lectures and classroom activities. After writing Draft 1, students meet with the instructor individually to discuss it, focusing on content, organization, and idea development. After that, the class meets for peer review and, if necessary, for a follow-up session to address any emerged concerns. Then students write Draft 2 and attend the second one-on-one conferences with the instructor to discuss Draft 2, this time shifting to concerns related to language usage, grammar, and mechanics. In both cases, the instructor provides oral feedback during the conference *and* written feedback either before or after the conference. As found from the instructor survey, 11 instructors used the Microsoft Word Commenting feature and two made handwritten notes for written feedback. In addition, all instructors encouraged students to work with a WL tutor. Finally, Draft 3 is submitted for grading, as a digital copy for 10 instructors, both digital and print copies for two instructors, and a print copy for one instructor.

With some alterations, this organization of essay writing is typical of a U.S. college first-year writing course. However, it has yet to be empirically shown whether this course organization aids or hinders the academic success of international ESL freshmen who are unaccustomed to the U.S. traditions of teaching composition.

Findings from Student Surveys

In our study, ESL students were asked to evaluate the educational practices that they experienced in the course as the least, somewhat, or most helpful in their learning to write for academic purposes. Table 6.2 displays the results.

As shown, all students considered a one-on-one conference with the instructor as beneficial, with 90% of students perceiving it as their most beneficial learning experience. Another notable finding is that learning from other ESL students (group work and peer review) had a high perceived value, almost equal to the perceived value of WL tutoring. Overall, the majority of students appreciated the combination of all educational practices experienced in the course.

Furthermore, the study investigated how the students felt about writing an essay in three drafts, a commonplace process in U.S. writing courses. Our finding indicates the preference for multiple drafts. In fact, only 8% (14) of the students would prefer writing just one draft as compared to 92% (157) who would prefer writing numerous drafts.

TABLE 6.2 Students' Perceptions Regarding the Effect of Educational Practices Experienced in the ESL Course on Their Writing Proficiency

Practice	% (n) Least Helpful	% (n) Somewhat Helpful	% (n) Most Helpful
One-on-one conference with instructor	–	10 (17)	90 (154)
Combination of all instructional types	2 (3)	55 (94)	43 (74)
Classroom learning (incl. mini-lectures, class activities, and handouts)	9 (15)	56 (96)	35 (60)
Session with a writing lab tutor	13 (22)	51 (87)	36 (62)
Group work	31 (53)	62 (106)	7 (12)
Peer review	34 (58)	51 (87)	15 (26)

Note
Totals (N = 171). Percentages are rounded.

Implications

Our study suggests that, to be effective, an ESL writing course should provide numerous opportunities for active, hands-on learning. It should balance teacher instruction, peer-to-peer learning, and WL tutoring. It should also blend face-to-face teaching and e-learning, utilizing technology to create supportive learning environments. Importantly, the instructional design of the course should provide adequate time for one-on-one student–teacher interaction.

ESL Instructor Feedback

Observed Processes

In the course, students receive both oral and written feedback from teachers on each of the two ungraded drafts. Oral feedback is provided during two one-on-one conferences and is combined with the instructor's written comments on each draft. In our study, written comments were provided in the following forms:

- corrections on the draft or highlighted erroneous words/phrases with marginal explanatory comments (10 instructors);
- highlighted erroneous words/phrases with identification of an error type (9);
- highlighted erroneous words/phrases (5);
- a combination of marginal comments and end comments (2); and
- end comments (2).

Notably, 12 instructors shared the assumption that the form of written comments should vary depending on the draft and the student's progress, whereas one instructor believed that the same form should be used consistently throughout the course.

Findings from Student Surveys

As discussed in the previous section, the students perceived the oral feedback that they received during one-on-one conferences as the most helpful type of assistance in their essay-crafting process. Similarly, 13 instructors unanimously considered the conference as the most effective type of teaching. Because oral feedback is provided in combination with written comments, our study investigated which form of the written comments listed above the students considered as the most helpful for revising drafts. To accommodate those who would object to written comments, an "Other" comment box was included for an open-ended answer. Table 6.3 illustrates the students' perceptions.

TABLE 6.3 Students' Perceptions Regarding the Form of Written Instructor Comments Most Helpful for Draft Revision

Form	% (n) of Students
Corrections on the draft provided with explanatory marginal comments	65 (111)
Combination of marginal and end comments	62 (106)
Highlighted erroneous words or phrases	58 (99)
Highlighted erroneous words/phrases with identification of error type	49 (84)
End comments	38 (65)
Other: oral feedback	2 (34)

Note
Totals (N = 171). This survey item is a multiple-choice question.

These results clearly suggest the students' preference for written comments. Most notably, the students perceived detailed feedback, as opposed to a paragraph summarizing errors and suggesting revisions, to be more instrumental in their learning to write a college essay. Notice that many students indicated almost equal preference for four different forms of written comments, which is in line with the instructors' shared belief that the form of comments should vary to adjust for emerging skills in revising and editing.

Implications

Our findings clearly suggest that the learning benefits of combining oral feedback with written comments are significant. To implement this effectively, three issues need to be addressed, however. First, it is instrumental to ensure sufficient time for systematic oral feedback, scheduling student–teacher conferences during regular class time rather than office hours. Second, students need to become active collaborators in the essay-crafting process as opposed to playing the regrettably typical role of passive receivers of teachers' comments. Third, this process should connect all involved parties: the student, the teacher, and the WL tutor. One effective sequence may be as follows: A student receives written comments before the conference, processes them, and makes some revisions. At the conference, this student asks questions and the instructor teaches mini-lessons targeting prime concerns or emerged error patterns. The student works on these concerns with the WL tutor.

Writing Lab

Observed Processes

It is not unusual among writing teachers to consider the WL as the key resource for ESL writers. In the examined ESL Writing Program, all instructors encouraged students to utilize this institutional support resource, but only four indicated that their students *regularly* visited the WL throughout the semester. At the university, the WL serves both non-ESL and ESL students. At the time of our study, the ESL angle was at the onset of development. Along with professional staff, the lab is staffed with graduate and (some) undergraduate tutors. Students can have a 30-minute-long session once per week. At the end of a session, the tutor asks whether the student would like the instructor to receive a brief note about the session. If the student agrees, a note is put in the instructor's mailbox. As argued by David and Moussu in Chapter 4 of this volume, it is imperative for writing programs to figure out how to assist ESL writers effectively. Our findings provide relevant insight.

Findings from Student Surveys

To address the concern that an accurate answer may be difficult to obtain, our survey did not inquire whether students visited the WL. Instead, we examined the students' perceptions regarding their experiences in the WL.

Sixty-nine percent (118) of students felt that WL tutoring was beneficial compared to 31% (53) who did not feel this way. The students mentioned mostly working on grammar, spelling, sentence structure, mechanics, and language usage, but several students also mentioned brainstorming, planning, and essay organization.

When asked what kind of help they would like to receive in the WL, the students named both higher-order concerns (HOCs), such as brainstorming, planning, and organization, and lower-order concerns (LOCs), such as transitions, grammar, punctuation, and other aspects of English language usage. Some student comments are as follows:

- HOCs-related comments: "Inspiration (help me figure out) or the main point for the essay"; "the way to write interesting introduction and how to well organize the essay"; "idea problems"; "paper structure"; "suggestion[s] about organization and structure"; "help in building up strong support."
- LOCs-related comments: "grammar and more on sentence structure (with explanation which they usually can't provide)"; "i want my essay more clear"; "the way of editing in American writing style"; "grammar error, word choice, [sentence] structure"; "more native way to write sentences"; "grammar, transitions between paragraph and check errors."

In addition, three requests emerged. The first was to extend the session time or to allow several sessions per week: "More time. I think 30 mins for each time is fine. But, I had hard time because of the limitation of weekly uses. Once a week was uncomfortable [insufficient] for me." The second request voiced students' discontent with the "non-interference" philosophy of Writing Centers that disapproves of error correction and explicit suggestions. In fact, several students expressed the need for more direct guidance:

- "I hope that the tutors *would not be afraid of giving more suggestions* in improving our essays. As personally I can see, some tutors do not dare to point out the whole picture to a student when it comes to improving the student's writing skills. It might be that the tutor does not want to make the student feel offended" (emphasis added).
- "I would like them to *direct me in the way I want to write my essay*. They should also provide their own ideas regarding how to write the essay" (emphasis added).
- "More time and more detailed correction check."

Finally, students asked for a tighter collaboration between instructors and WL tutors: "I'd like the writing lab tutor to emulate the help provided by my instructor. Well to be more specific to emulate the format my instructor helps me in."

Implications

Our findings suggest that ESL students are underserved in Writing Centers, which tend to prioritize errors related to LOCs. Put another way, WLs provide an emergency response to ESL writers in an inadequate time frame. To assist ESL writers more effectively, the pedagogy and practices of WLs need to change, as discussed in detail by David and Moussu in Chapter 4 of this volume. WLs need to become the place where ESL writers *systematically* work on *all* aspects of essay crafting, learning to write through collaboration with writing professionals. Such learning partnerships would help students assume the ownership of essay planning and the revision process, thus molding them into skilled academic writers.

Summary

- Most students studied English composition in pre-higher education settings in their home countries. Most frequently, non-U.S.-based English composition was taught at school and in a program to prepare students for college admission examinations.
- Half of the students opted for an ESL writing course. Most were motivated by practical benefits of English writing proficiency for college studies and professional careers. Others thought that an ESL course levels the playing field with native English speakers.
- A one-on-one student–teacher conference was perceived as the most helpful learning experience.

- A guided essay revision process, combining oral feedback and detailed written comments, was preferred.
- Students indicated that WL tutoring should be more extended, more explicit, and better aligned with the ESL writing course.

Discussion Questions

1. Based on your experience, which instructional practices (traditional face-to-face teaching, one-on-one teacher–student conferences, group work, peer reviews, or WL tutoring) are most effective for L2 writers?
2. In this study the students perceived a one-on-one conference as vital for effectively learning to write in academic English. Can you think of other reasons why students might prefer a one-on-one conference to other instructional practices?
3. Should student self-assessment of learning outcomes inform curriculum decisions in an ESL writing program? If so, to what extent?

Notes

1. In this chapter, the quoted text is presented exactly as written by the students.
2. The reported standardized examinations are as follows: the tests of the U.S. Educational Testing Services including Test of English as a Foreign Language (TOEFL), the Scholastic Aptitude Test (SAT), American College Testing (ACT), Test of English for International Communication (TOEIC), Graduate Record Examinations (GRE); the International English Language Testing System (IELTS); the tests of the U.K. Cambridge English Language Assessment including First Certificate in English (FCE), Certificate in Advanced English (CAE); the South Korean Test of English Proficiency (TEPS).

Further Reading

Cimasko, T., & Reichelt, M. (Eds.). (2011). *Foreign language writing instruction: Principles and practices.* West Lafayette, IN: Parlor Press.
Horner, B., Min-Zhan, L., & Matsuda, P. K. (2010). *Cross-language relations in composition: Understanding the multilingual nature of composition courses.* Carbondale, IL: Southern Illinois University Press.
You, X. (2006). Globalization and the politics of teaching EFL writing. In P. K. Matsuda, C. Ortmeier-Hooper, & X. You (Eds.), *The politics of second language writing: In search of the promised land* (pp. 188–202). West Lafayette, IN: Parlor Press.

References

Allaei, S., & Connor, U. (1990). Exploring the dynamics of cross-cultural collaboration in writing classrooms. *Writing Instructor, 10*(1), 19–28.
Ashwell, T. (2000). Patterns of teacher response to student writing in a multi-draft composition classroom: Is content feedback followed by form feedback the best method? *Journal of Second Language Writing, 9*(3), 227–257.

Blackmon, S., Haynes, L, & Pinkert, L. A. (2012). *Composing yourself: A student guide to introductory composition at Purdue 2012–2013*. Southlake, TX: Fountainhead Press.

Blommaert, J. (2010). *The sociolinguistics of globalization*. Cambridge: Cambridge University Press.

Braine, G. (1996). ESL students in first-year writing courses: ESL versus mainstream classes. *Journal of Second Language Writing, 5*(2), 91–107.

Christianson, K., & Krahnke, K. (1986). Student perceptions of academic language study. *TESOL Quarterly, 33*, 759–763.

Doolan, S. M., & Miller, D. (2011). Generation 1.5 written error patterns: A comparative study. *Journal of Second Language Writing 21*(1), 1–22. doi:10.1016/j.jslw.2011.09.001.

Fathman, A., & Whalley, E. (1990). Teacher response to student writing: Focus on form versus content. In B. Kroll (Ed.), *Second language writing: Research insights into the classroom* (pp. 178–190). New York, NY: Cambridge University Press.

Ferris, D. (1994). Rhetorical strategies in student persuasive writing: Differences between native and non-native English speakers. *Research in the Teaching of English, 28*(1), 45–65.

Ferris, D. (1995). Student reactions to teacher response in multiple-draft composition classrooms. *TESOL Quarterly, 29*(1), 33–53.

Ferris, D. (1997). The influence of teacher commentary on student revision. *TESOL Quarterly, 31*(2), 315–339.

Ferris, D. (1999). The case for grammar correction in L2 writing classes: A response to Truscott (1996). *Journal of Second Language Writing, 8*(1), 1–11.

Ferris, D. (2009). *Teaching college writing to diverse student populations*. Ann Arbor, MI: University of Michigan Press.

Goldstein, L. M. (2005). *Teacher written commentary in second language writing classrooms*. Ann Arbor, MI: University of Michigan Press.

Harklau, L. (1994). ESL versus mainstream classes: Constructing L2 learning environments. *TESOL Quarterly, 28*, 241–272.

Harklau, L., Losey, K. M., & Siegal, M. (1999). *Generation 1.5 meets college composition: Issues in the teaching of writing to U.S.-educated learners of ESL*. Mahwah, NJ: Lawrence Erlbaum Associates.

Horowitz, D. (1986). What professors actually require: Academic tasks for the ESL classroom. *TESOL Quarterly, 20*, 445–462.

Ide, W. (2010, November 14). China passes India as biggest source of foreign students in US. *Voice of America*. Retrieved October 4, 2012, from www.voanews.com/content/china-passes-india-as-biggest-source-of-foreign-students-in-us-108230084/168501.html.

Janopoulos, M. (1992). University faculty tolerance of NS and NNS writing errors: A comparison. *Journal of Second Language Writing, 1*(2), 109–121.

Johns, A. (1995). Faculty assessment of ESL student literacy skills: Implications for writing assessment. In L. Hamp-Lyons (Ed.), *Assessing second language writing in academic contexts* (pp. 167–179). Norwood, NJ: Ablex.

Lawrick, E. (2013). Students in the first-year ESL writing program: Revisiting the notion of "traditional" ESL. *Journal of the Council of Writing Program Administrators 36*(2), 27–58.

Leki, I. (1991). Building expertise through sequenced writing assignments. *TESOL Journal, 1*(2), 19–23.

Leki, I. (1992). *Understanding ESL writers*. Portsmouth, NH: Boynton/Cook.

Leki, I. (1995). Good writing: I know it when I see it. In D. Belcher & G. Braine (Eds.), *Academic writing in a second language* (pp. 23–46). Norwood, NJ: Ablex.

Leki, I. (2003). A challenge to L2 writing professionals: Is writing overrated? In B. Kroll (Ed.), *Exploring dynamics of L2 writing* (pp. 315–331). New York, NY: Cambridge University Press.

Leki, I. (2007). *Undergraduates in a second language: Challenges and complexities of academic literacy development.* Mahwah, NJ: Erlbaum.

Leki, I., & Carson, J. (1994). Students' perceptions of EAP writing instruction and writing needs across the disciplines. *TESOL Quarterly, 28*, 81–101.

Leki, I., & Carson, J. (1997). "Completely different worlds": EAP and the writing experiences of ESL students in university courses. *TESOL Quarterly, 31*, 39–69.

Leki, I., Cumming, A., & Silva, T. (2008). *A synthesis of research on second language writing in English.* New York, NY: Routledge.

Matsuda, P. (2006). The myth of linguistic homogeneity in U.S. college composition. *College English, 68*(6), 637–651.

Matsuda, P., Fruit, M., & Lamm, T. L. B. (Eds.). (2006). Bridging the disciplinary divide: Integrating a second-language perspective into writing programs. [Special issue]. *Writing Program Administration, 30*(1/2).

Milgram, S. (1974). Frozen world of the familiar stranger. *Psychology Today, 8*, 70–73.

Nelson, G., & Murphy, J. (1992). An L2 writing group: Task and social dimensions. *Journal of Second Language Writing, 1*(3), 171–193.

Ortmeier-Hooper, C. (2008). English may be my second language, but I'm not "ESL." *College Composition and Communication, 59*(3), 389–419.

Reid, J. M. (1993). *Teaching ESL writing.* Englewood Cliffs, NJ: Prentice-Hall.

Reid, J. M. (1994). Responding to ESL students' texts: The myths of appropriation. *TESOL Quarterly, 28*(2), 273–292.

Roberge, M., Siegal, M., & Harklau, L. (Eds.) (2008). *Generation 1.5 in college composition: Teaching academic writing to U.S.-educated learners of ESL.* New York, NY: Routledge.

Schneider, E. W. (2011). *English around the world: An introduction.* New York, NY: Cambridge University Press.

Severino, C. (1993). The sociopolitical implications of response to second language and second language dialect writing. *Journal of Second Language Writing, 2*(3), 181–201.

Silva, T. (1993). The distinct nature of second language writing: The ESL research and its implication. *TESOL Quarterly, 27*(4), 657–677.

Silva, T. (1997). On the ethical treatment of ESL writers. *TESOL Quarterly, 31*(2), 359–363.

Spack, R. (1988). Initiating ESL students into the academic discourse community: How far should we go? *TESOL Quarterly, 22*(1), 29–51.

Truscott, J. (1999). The case against grammar correction in L2 writing classes. *Journal of Second Language Writing, 8*(2), 111–122.

Williams, J. (1996). ESL composition program administration in the United States. *Journal of Second Language Writing, 4*(2), 157–179.

Zamel, V. (1982). Writing: The process of discovering meaning. *TESOL Quarterly, 16*(2), 195–209.

Zamel, V. (1985). Responding to student writing. *TESOL Quarterly, 19*(1), 79–101.

Zamel, V. (1995). Strangers in academia: The experiences of faculty and ESL students across the curriculum. *College Composition and Communication, 46*(4), 506–521.

Zhu, W. (2001). Interaction and feedback in mixed peer response groups. *Journal of Second Language Writing, 10*(4), 251–276.

7

ACADEMIC READING EXPECTATIONS AND CHALLENGES

Neil J Anderson

Vignette

Young Mi has declared Biology as her major at a university in the United States and is excited to begin her studies. The first semester of coursework consists of 12 credit hours with the following classes: Writing 150, American History 101, Biology 100, and Math 110. Young Mi purchases all of the books and packets of material for each of the four courses and attends the first week of classes. For homework tonight she has 14 pages to read from a chapter in her Biology book, entitled Campbell Essential Biology *(Simon, Dickey, & Reece, 2013).*

Young Mi reads the introductory information in the chapter with the heading of "Biology and Society: Water as the Chemical of Life," and she encounters 11 new vocabulary words that cause her to pause and look up the words in the dictionary. She keeps reading, using her dictionary every paragraph to look up new words, as she works her way through sections entitled "Some Basic Chemistry," "Water and Life, Can Exercise Boost Your Brain Power?," "The Search for Extraterrestrial Life," and "Chapter Review." There are several figures and tables in the chapter that provide what should be helpful information, including an abbreviated periodic table of the elements.

She responds to the Self Quiz at the end of the chapter, checks her responses in the Appendix, and realizes she has not responded correctly to the majority of the questions. She feels overwhelmed and discouraged by the amount of reading that she has to complete, with how specific the vocabulary is for Biology, and with the recognition that she does not understand what she has just spent three hours reading. How is she going to thrive in her chosen field of study?

Introduction and Overview of the Challenges

English is the academic language of higher education (Arkoudis, Baik, & Richardson, 2012; Coleman, 2006; Phillipson, 2006; Tsui, 2008). Reading is central to academic success, especially for second language (L2) learners (Anderson, 2014; Grabe 2009). Arkoudis et al. (2012) emphasize that "supporting students' learning and growth is one of the fundamental roles of higher education institutions" (p. 17). University faculty, staff, and administrators all play a role in ensuring success of students, especially those who speak other first languages.

International student enrollments on campuses in the United States typify what is happening in other nations throughout the world. The Organisation for Economic Co-operation and Development (OECD) (2013) reports that close to 4.3 million international students were enrolled in 2011 in tertiary institutions worldwide. "Australia, the United Kingdom, Switzerland, New Zealand, and Austria have, in descending order, the highest percentages of international students among their tertiary enrolments" (OECD, 2013, p. 304). In the United States there has been a steady growth for the past seven years (Farrugia & Bhandari, 2013). During the 2012–2013 academic year, enrollments of international students in the United States reached a record high of 819,644 students (Farrugia & Bhandari, 2013). International students who entered the United States for the first time increased by almost 10%. Also during the 2012–2013 academic year, the number of international undergraduate students exceeded the international graduate student enrollments for the second year in a row. International undergraduate student enrollments accounted for 41.5% of the international students in the United States (Farrugia & Bhandari, 2013). During the 2012 calendar year there were 110,870 international students studying in Intensive English Programs (IEPs), which accounts for 13.5% of the total number of international students studying in the United States (Farrugia & Bhandari, 2013).

These statistics illustrate the continued growth experienced in international student enrollments, particularly in the United States. With these increased enrollments come the challenges of ensuring that students are supported in their academic studies and have successful experiences in the university environment so that they can return to their home countries with a degree and the knowledge to contribute in meaningful ways to the world economy (Arkoudis et al., 2012; Graddol, 2006; EducationDynamics, n.d.).

Significant research has been reported over the past several years on English language teaching and learning, but the research participants in the majority of these studies come primarily from IEPs (Anderson, 1991; Carrell, 1984, 1985, 1991; Carrell & Carson, 1997; Carrell, Pharis, & Liberto, 1989; Clarke, 1980; Eskey, 1988). Very little data are available on the actual challenges that international students face in the early courses of a chosen major (Carson, 2001; Horowitz, 1986; Phakiti & Li, 2011). We do not know what the expectations are of university faculty in terms of reading assignments, how much reading is expected in early courses of a major, and what challenges faculty perceive students face as they approach their reading assignments.

Arum and Roksa (2011) point out that faculty have a key role in outlining the course assignments to engage students. They emphasize that faculty have "a professional responsibility to define [course assignments] adequately" (p. 70). They asked students specifically to report "how many times they took a class where they 'read more than 40 pages per week'" (pp. 70–71). One-third of the 2,322 sophomore-year students who participated in their research reported that they had not taken a course the previous semester that required them to read over 40 pages. Their results indicate that when faculty require more than 40 pages of reading per week (along with writing at least 20 pages over the course of a semester) that students' critical thinking, complex reasoning, and writing skills improve (p. 93). Arum and Roksa also point out that "faculty members who have high expectations also tend to have high standards and are approachable" (p. 93).

This chapter is based on a larger project, conducted in collaboration with colleagues at a private university, which focused on the academic reading and writing expectations and challenges identified by university faculty in the first semester of study in five key majors. This chapter will only report the reading expectations and challenges from the larger project. The following three research questions direct the focus of this chapter:

1. How much reading is expected of students in the first course in their selected major?
2. What expectations do faculty have for student reading in the first course in their selected major?
3. What are the faculty perceptions of the greatest reading challenges students experience in the first course in their selected major?

Method

Using *Open Doors* (Chow & Bhandari, 2011), 30 institutions that enroll the largest numbers of international students were selected for the study through a stratified selection process (10 doctorate-granting institutions, 10 master's degree-granting institutions, and 10 bachelor's degree-granting institutions). Five majors that were popular among international students and that were distinct from each other were also identified (Biology, Business, Computer Science, Engineering, and Psychology).

For each major at each institution, one required class was chosen that represented the most essential beginning course for that major. We excluded one-credit survey courses and prerequisites. Course types varied across institutions. For example, the class chosen for the business major included courses in business management, economics, or accounting, depending on the institution.

To facilitate participation, prospective faculty respondents were identified at each institution because of the specific course they taught. They were contacted by telephone and invited to participate. Those who agreed were then sent the survey via an e-mail link. In our telephone contact with the potential respondents, as well as in the survey, we did not specify that we were interested in the reading expectations and challenges of international students. All questions were directed toward the expectations that faculty have for their introductory course in the major and the challenges that they believe their students face in terms of the reading requirements.

Participants

This study reports data from 157 individuals, representing 114 university departments across the five majors. Where multiple individuals from a single institution provided quantitative data, responses were averaged. This created intradepartmental overlaps of varying sizes for each major. Our goal was to obtain data from 20–25 institutions per major. Our original list of 30 institutions was expanded in order to reach this goal. We received institutional responses from the following numbers of programs by major: Biology, 24; Business, 24; Computer Science, 21; Engineering, 24; and Psychology, 21. Table 7.1 provides an overview of the respondents by major.

Results

Amount of Reading

In response to the first research question, the amount of reading expected of students in the first course of their selected major, we learned that there are statistically significant differences across majors in terms of the total number of pages per week that faculty expect students to read. An ANOVA was calculated, $F(4,79) = 4.87$, $p = .001$. A post hoc comparison using the Tukey HSD test was also calculated in order to determine where the differences occurred

TABLE 7.1 Respondents by Major

Major	Individuals	Institutions
Biology	37	24
Business	35	24
Computer Science	23	21
Engineering	34	24
Psychology	28	21
Totals	157	114

across the five majors. The results are reported in Figure 7.1, which includes means (*M*), standard deviations (*SD*), *p*-values, and effect sizes measured in Cohen's *d*.

While, on average, there was no significant difference in the number of pages read weekly by Business majors (*M*=84.74) compared to Psychology majors (*M*=61.21), statistically significant differences were observed when comparing Business with Biology (*M*=44.52), Engineering (*M*=41.68), and Computer Science (*M*=37.5), each of which produced a large effect size.

Another important point to note from Figure 7.1 is the wide deviation across each of the five majors. Based on the data collected from 24 institutions, Business majors read an average of 84.74 pages per week with a standard deviation (SD) of 60.57. This means that in introductory business classes that were 1 SD below the mean they read about 24 pages, while courses 1 SD above the mean read about 145 pages per week. The range of pages read by major per week can be compared in Table 7.2.

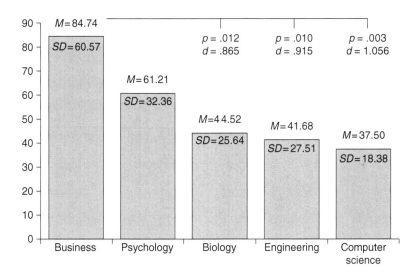

FIGURE 7.1 Total Volume of Reading (Pages per Week).

TABLE 7.2 Range of Pages Read per Week in Each of the Five Majors

Major	Mean	Standard Deviation	1 SD Below	1 SD Above
Biology	44.52	25.64	19 pages	70 pages
Business	84.74	60.57	24 pages	145 pages
Computer Science	37.50	18.38	19 pages	56 pages
Engineering	41.68	27.51	14 pages	69 pages
Psychology	61.21	32.36	29 pages	94 pages

These data suggest that for the programs surveyed in this study, there is great variability within the same major in terms of the reading requirements in introductory courses.

In addition to asking about the total number of pages read per week, we asked about the estimated percentage of digital reading that faculty expect in their introductory courses (see Kessler's discussion in Chapter 12 for more on technology and reading). Because it would be difficult to calculate digital reading in terms of total pages, we asked faculty to estimate the percentage of reading for the semester that is completed digitally. The ANOVA reports that there are statistically significant differences across these five majors in terms of the course percentages of digital reading that is required, $F(4,105) = 10.06$, $p < .001$. Post hoc comparisons using the Tukey HSD test were also run on these data to determine where the differences lie. This information is reported in Figure 7.2, which includes means, standard deviations, p-values, and effect sizes measured in Cohen's d.

The Computer Science majors were expected to read the greatest percentage of their material digitally (an average of 70.76% of the total course reading requirements). The Biology majors read an average of 42.20% of their material digitally, while the Engineering majors read 38.08% of total course material digitally, the Business majors 31.70%, and the Psychology majors 24.11%. It is interesting to note that the majors that required a high volume of hard copy reading have lower percentages of digital reading and the majors that require less reading in terms of hard copy pages tend to report higher percentages of digital reading.

Table 7.3 illustrates the ranges of percentages of material read across the five majors. As with the reading requirements of hard copy materials, there is wide variability within the same major of digitally read materials across institutions.

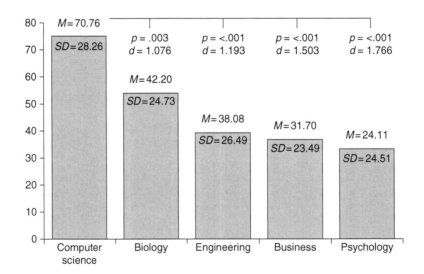

FIGURE 7.2 Volume of Digital Reading (Percent for the Course).

TABLE 7.3 Percentages of Digitally Read Material for the Semester

Major	Percentage of Material Read Digitally	Standard Deviation	1 SD Below	1 SD Above
Biology	42.20	24.73	17.47	66.93
Business	31.70	23.49	8.21	55.19
Computer Science	70.76	28.26	42.50	99.02
Engineering	38.08	26.49	11.59	64.77
Psychology	24.11	24.51	0	48.62

Overall Reading Expectations

One key aspect of this research project was to identify the expectations that faculty have for the reading assignments that they give. One member of the research team carefully reviewed all of the written comments of the faculty (157 faculty members from 114 different institutions) and then synthesized the comments into categories. The categories were then reviewed and consolidated in collaboration with the other two members of the research team to verify that the data fit the themes identified.

Twelve themes emerged from the responses of faculty related to their expectations for reading. Table 7.4 lists the expectations. We highlight here the top three identified expectations. The most frequently expressed expectation of the faculty (57 responses, accounting for 23.08% of all responses) was a desire that students would understand the course content through the reading assignments. The second most frequently expressed expectation was that students would

TABLE 7.4 Overall Reading Expectations

Theme Reference (n = 12)	Percentage of Responses	Number of Faculty Naming the Expectation
Understand course content	23.08	57
Apply new knowledge	21.86	54
Prepare for lectures/labs	16.19	40
Engage in critical thinking	9.72	24
Synthesize information	5.67	14
Understand genre-specific information	5.26	13
Learn/use vocabulary	4.45	11
Demonstrate knowledge through writing	4.05	10
Understand research	3.64	9
Conduct research	2.43	6
Be strategic readers	2.02	5
Use text as a resource	1.62	4
Total	100	247

apply the new knowledge they were gaining from the reading (54 responses, accounting for 21.86% of all responses). Finally, an expectation that the readings would prepare students for the lecture or for lab sessions was identified (40 responses, 16.19% of the total).

It is important to note that there are no statistically significant differences across the five majors for these 12 themes, thus suggesting that they apply equally across the five academic disciplines for the introductory courses.

Using the top three expectations identified by the faculty (understanding course content, applying new knowledge, and preparing for lectures and labs), we can examine some specific comments provided by the faculty to illustrate these expectations. Note that while each of the comments selected will illustrate the focal expectation (highlighted in *italic text*), you will see other expectations included within the comments from the faculty members.

First, in terms of the faculty expectation that students will understand the course content through the reading assignments, Engineering Professor #16 stated:

> "Expect" is too strong a word, as students rarely read what they are assigned anymore. What I "hope" them to gain from the reading is *a familiarity with the concepts of Statics*, which they can in turn use as a springboard for the problem-solving skills that form the foundation of the course. In short, the reading is to inform the acquired skill set.

Next, to illustrate the faculty expectation that students will apply the new knowledge gained from reading (in this specific example, within the context of an exam), Biology Professor #6 indicated the following:

> Students need to read the textbook with ease and apply critical thinking to their problem solving, application questions. For this they must be eloquent in English language and developed readers. If not, they would take too much time to study and probably would *not perform well on the four midterms and the final exam.*

Finally, to show the expectation that students will use the reading assignments to prepare for the lectures and lab sessions, Business Professor #7 stated:

> I expect the students to be able to *read material, attend lectures, integrate the two sources of material,* and *apply them to the assigned work.* I expect them to make small intuitive leaps in recognizing the application of the in class material to choices that they see occurring in their lives.

It is clear from our data that faculty are able to articulate what they expect students to do with the reading material they assign in introductory courses within a major. All L2 speakers of English preparing to enter the university could benefit from being informed of the expectations we have listed here.

Overall Reading Challenges

The final aspect of this research is to highlight the overall reading challenges identified by the 157 faculty members across the 114 institutions for the five academic majors. Table 7.5 lists these overall challenges. We followed the same procedure in identifying the reading challenges as we did for the reading expectations. The written responses of all the faculty who responded to the questionnaire were reviewed carefully by one member of the research team and then reviewed and consolidated in collaboration with the other two members of the team.

Fifteen themes emerged from the data. The top three challenges will be addressed here. First, the students' lack of ability to read the discipline-specific genre was identified by faculty as the top challenge (41 responses, accounting for 20.3% of the total challenges identified by the faculty). Lack of motivation and the inability to be a strategic reader tied for the second and third challenges identified by the faculty (30 responses each, 14.85% of the total comments).

As mentioned above in relation to the reading expectations, there are no statistically significant differences across the five majors for these 15 themes identified as reading challenges by the faculty. All 15 of the themes can be equally important for students in any one of the five majors targeted in this research project.

The top three reading challenges (lack of ability to read discipline-specific genre, lack of motivation, and inability to read strategically) were selected to

TABLE 7.5 Overall Reading Challenges

Theme Reference (n = 15)	Percentage of Responses	Number of Faculty Naming the Challenge
Lack of ability to read discipline-specific genre	20.30	41
Lack of motivation	14.85	30
Inability to read strategically	14.85	30
Taking adequate time to complete the reading	7.92	16
Understanding key vocabulary	7.92	16
Being an ESL student	6.44	13
Lack of academic preparation	4.95	10
Reaching basic comprehension	4.46	9
Reading to learn	3.96	8
Reading graphs	3.47	7
Handling the amount of reading	2.97	6
Lacking critical thinking skills	2.97	6
Relying alone on lectures to get new information	2.48	5
Following directions	1.49	3
Accessing the texts	1.00	2
Total	100	202

provide examples of specific comments from the faculty. Again, the focal challenges will be highlighted in *italic text*. Computer Science Professor #5 provided a comment that illustrates the perceived challenge of reading material within the discipline-specific genre:

> Many appear to be *incapable of reading anything* that isn't on a website, and even then, unwilling to read things unless they take the form of responses to an email or a posting on a blog. And even then, without a video accompanying the email, they seem to be at a loss to comprehend the ideas.

The second most frequently reported challenge identified by the faculty was the students' lack of motivation to engage in reading. A comment from Psychology Professor #11 typifies this challenge:

> Apparently one of the *greatest challenges is sitting down to read the text at all!* I believe many never do this. I think they rely on skimming and memorizing definitions of bolded terms. For students who do make the effort to read the text, I believe there are often problems comprehending vocabulary that one might assume is basic for college students. They also have difficulty extracting key points from the text.

Finally, from the comments of the faculty, the third most frequently identified reading challenge was the students' inability to read strategically. Biology Professor #3 pointed out that

> Students *tend to read texts like a novel and not evaluating their understanding of the information they are exposed to.* We tell them to link everything they read to the learning objectives for that lecture topic, but too many simply refuse to do this.

Faculty are able to identify what they see as the greatest challenges that students face with the reading material required in introductory courses of a major. Faculty preparing L2 speakers of English for entry into full-time university studies should explicitly address these challenges with the students in order to help them be more aware of what faculty see they should do in order to be more successful learners.

Implications and Applications

Given the expectations that faculty have for reading in introductory courses at the university and the challenges that they see their students face, we have identified four major implications from these data. First, there is a need to expose students to greater quantities of expository texts. Next, students need more opportunities to read the discipline-specific genres that they will encounter as matriculated university students. Third, faculty should consider ways to motivate students and, perhaps more importantly, help students take responsibility for their own motivation. Finally, students need to learn to be more strategic readers. We believe that these implications are of particular importance to IEPs that prepare academic readers for success in content-based courses at the university.

First, students need to be prepared to read significant quantities of text in introductory courses within their majors. On average, the data from this research across the five majors shows that faculty expect students to read from 38 to 85 pages per week, supporting the recommendation of Arum and Roksa (2011) that students in university contexts read a minimum of 40 pages per week. We need to inform L2 students enrolled in academic preparation programs of this expectation. Making sure that students have a more realistic idea of the quantity of reading that they will be expected to complete is a first step in helping them prepare for a successful university experience.

This implication could be addressed by developing a stronger extensive reading component in the IEP reading curriculum. Requiring students to read more outside of class is one way to better prepare them for this reality once they transition to university studies.

Next, along with the recommendation of increased quantity of reading, the quality of the reading must also be addressed. The types of academic genres that students will be reading need to be included in reading classes at IEPs. Since students appear to lack abilities in reading discipline-specific genres, academic reading classes within an IEP should provide opportunities to read discipline-specific genres and identify how texts in different academic disciplines differ. By being exposed to texts from biology, business, computer science, engineering, and psychology, students would have a more realistic understanding of how to meaningfully engage in their chosen fields.

Hyland (2000) points out that

> because texts are written to be understood within certain cultural contexts, the analysis of key genres can provide insights into what is implicit in these academic cultures, their routine rhetorical operations revealing individual writer's perceptions of group values and beliefs. Genres are not therefore only text types but imply particular institutional practices of those that produce, distribute and consume them.
>
> *pp. 11–12*

Similarly, Donald (2002) suggests that students need to learn how to think like scholars within specific disciplines. We propose that one of the first steps in learning how to think like a business person, a biologist, a computer scientist, an engineer, or a psychologist is to understand the discipline-specific elements that writers within these disciplines use. Providing L2 readers in an IEP context access to more discipline-specific texts will help better prepare them for academic success at the university. Grabe and Zhang (2013) also emphasize the value of integrating reading and writing for academic preparation. As part of an IEP reading curriculum, there could be more opportunities to combine reading and writing within specific academic genres.

Third, motivation plays a role in any learning context. From our data, faculty identified a lack of motivation as the second most frequently mentioned challenge that readers face in introductory course work. The literature on motivation in second language teaching and learning is clear that teachers play a central role in motivating students in the classroom (Alrabai, 2011; Guilloteaux & Dörnyei, 2008; Thayne, Anderson, Dewey, & Bown, under review). The next step in the research on motivation and language learning is to identify ways to help learners take responsibility for their own motivation. Faculty in IEPs could investigate ways to facilitate the development of learner motivation through a carefully developed curriculum that introduces learners to ways that they can monitor their own motivation. In relationship to this research, much more research is needed within the specific domain of reading and ways that faculty can motivate students in domain-specific reading as well as help students take responsibility for their own motivation to read.

Finally, L2 students need to learn to become more strategic readers. Exposing students to a wide variety of academic reading strategies and, most importantly, providing opportunities for the students to practice using those strategies would better prepare them to successfully meet a reading challenge that they certainly will encounter repeatedly throughout their university experience.

One way to approach the challenge of developing strategic readers is for IEPs to provide more explicit instruction on metacognitive awareness of strategy use (Anderson, 2012). Grabe (2009) outlines eight metacognitive processes for comprehension that can be integrated into a reading curriculum at an IEP. Those eight processes help students:

> (1) set (or reset) reading goals, (2) expect to build a coherent interpretation of a text and establish the main ideas of a text, (3) make inferences as necessary in line with [reading] goals, (4) monitor comprehension to maintain a coherent interpretation and awareness of main ideas, (5) recognize when we are losing coherence of interpretation or the reading output does not match our reader goals, (6) summarize the main ideas of a text, (7) engage various strategies to help repair an incoherent interpretation, and (8) evaluate the reading input in various ways beyond simple understanding.

p. 224

Conclusion

We have conducted this research to address a significant void in academic literature regarding the expectations that faculty have of students in early courses within a university major and to address the lack of information on the challenges that students face in meeting these faculty expectations. IEPs that prepare L2 learners for academic success in a university setting can benefit from these findings by making improvements within the reading curricula for their programs.

Because of the continued growth in international student populations in tertiary contexts around the world, it is incumbent upon faculty to be more aware of the expectations we have of learners in our courses and to provide appropriate support for these learners so that they can complete a degree and be contributing members of the world economy.

Summary

- On average, students are expected to read between 38 and 85 pages per week within the five disciplines addressed in this study.
- Reading requirements vary across majors, with Business majors being required to read significantly more pages per week than students majoring in Biology, Engineering, and Computer Science.
- The three most frequently mentioned expectations that faculty have of students within these five majors in terms of the reading requirements include: (1) understanding the course content; (2) applying the new knowledge gained from reading; and (3) using the reading material to prepare for lectures and lab sessions.
- The top three challenges that faculty perceive that their students face while engaged in the reading include (1) understanding the discipline-specific genres, (2) lacking motivation to engage with the texts, and (3) engaging in strategic reading.

Discussion Questions

1. How could IEPs specifically strengthen the extensive reading component of a curriculum to provide readers with more opportunities to read greater amounts of material?
2. What could IEPs do to provide more opportunities for readers at higher levels of language proficiency to engage in reading discipline-specific genres?
3. What academic reading strategies could be incorporated into a reading curriculum of an IEP to better prepare students to be successful in university reading assignments?

Further Reading

Arum, R., & Roksa, J. (2011). *Academically adrift: Limited learning on college campuses.* Chicago, IL: University of Chicago Press.

Grabe, W. (2009). *Reading in a second language: Moving from theory to practice.* New York, NY: Cambridge University Press.

References

Alrabai, F. A. 2011. Motivational instruction in practice: Do EFL instructors at King Khalid University motivate their students to learn English as a foreign language? *Arab World English Journal, 2,* 257–285. Retrieved February 17, 2015, from http://awej.org/index.php?option=com_content&view=article&id=72:dr-fakieh-abduh-alrabai&catid=19&Itemid=115.

Anderson, N. J. (1991). Individual differences in strategy use in second language reading and testing. *Modern Language Journal, 75,* 460–472.

Anderson, N. J. (2012). Metacognition: Awareness of language learning. In S. Mercer, S. Ryan, & M. Williams (Eds.), *Psychology for language learning: Insights from research, theory and pedagogy* (pp. 169–187). Basingstoke, UK: Palgrave.

Anderson, N. J. (2014). Developing engaged L2 readers. In M. Celce-Murcia, D. M. Brinton, & M. A. Snow (Eds.), *Teaching English as a second or foreign language* (4th ed., pp. 170–188). Boston, MA: National Geographic Learning/Cengage Learning.

Arkoudis, S., Baik, C., & Richardson, S. (2012). *English language standards in higher education.* Victoria, Australia: ACER Press.

Arum, R., & Roksa, J. (2011). *Academically adrift: Limited learning on college campuses.* Chicago, IL: University of Chicago Press.

Carrell, P. L. (1984). The effects of rhetorical organization on ESL readers. *TESOL Quarterly, 18,* 441–469.

Carrell, P. L. (1985). Facilitating ESL reading by teaching text structure. *TESOL Quarterly, 19,* 727–752.

Carrell, P. L. (1991). Second language reading: Reading ability or language proficiency? *Applied Linguistics, 12,* 159–179.

Carrell, P. L., & Carson, J. (1997). Extensive and intensive reading in an EAP setting. *English for Specific Purposes, 16,* 47–60.

Carrell, P. L., Pharis, B., & Liberto, J. (1989). Metacognitive strategy training for ESL reading. *TESOL Quarterly, 23,* 647–678.

Carson, J. G. (2001). A task analysis of reading and writing in academic contexts. In D. Belcher & A. Hirvela (Eds.), *Linking literacies: Perspectives on L2 reading–writing connections.* Ann Arbor, MI: University of Michigan Press.

Chow, P., & Bhandari, R. (2011). *Open doors: Report on international educational exchange.* New York, NY: Institute of International Education.

Clarke, M. (1980). The short circuit hypothesis of ESL reading: Or when language competence interferes with reading performance. *Modern Language Journal, 64,* 203–209.

Coleman, J. A. (2006). English-medium teaching in European higher education. *Language Teaching, 39,* 1–14.

Donald, J. G. (2002). *Learning to think: Disciplinary perspectives.* San Francisco, CA: Jossey-Bass.

EducationDynamics. (n.d.). Full degree programs. Retrieved February 17, 2015, from www.studyabroad.com/programs/full+degree+abroad/default.aspx.

Eskey, D. E. (1988). Holding in the bottom: An interactive approach to the language problems of second language readers. In P. Carrell, J. Devine, & D. E. Eskey (Eds.), *Interactive approaches to second language reading* (pp. 93–100). Cambridge, UK: Cambridge University Press.

Farrugia, C. A., & Bhandari, R. (2013). *Open doors 2013 report on international educational exchange.* New York, NY: Institute of International Education.

Grabe, W. (2009). *Reading in a second language: Moving from theory to practice.* New York, NY: Cambridge University Press.

Grabe, W., & Zhang, C. (2013). Reading and writing together: A critical component of English for academic purposes teaching and learning. *TESOL Journal, 4*(1), 9–24, doi:10.1002/tesj.65.

Graddol, D. (2006). *English next: Why global English may mean the end of "English as a foreign language."* London, UK: British Council.

Guilloteaux, M. J., & Dörnyei, Z. (2008). Motivating language learners: A classroom-oriented investigation of the effects of motivational strategies on student motivation. *TESOL Quarterly, 42*, 55–77.

Horowitz, D. M. (1986). What professors actually require: Academic tasks for the ESL classroom. *TESOL Quarterly, 20*, 445–462.

Hyland, K. (2000). *Disciplinary discourses: Social interactions in academic writing.* Harlow, UK: Pearson.

OECD (2013). *Education at a glance 2013.* Paris: OECD Publishing.

Phakiti, A., & Li, L. (2011). General academic difficulties and reading and writing difficulties among Asian ESL postgraduate students in TESOL at an Australian university. *RELC Journal, 42*, 227–264, doi:10.1177/0033688211421417.

Phillipson, R. (2006). English, a cuckoo in the European higher education nest of languages. *European Journal of English Studies, 10*, 12–32.

Simon, E. J., Dickey, J. L., & Reece, J. B. (2013). *Campbell essential biology* (5th ed.). White Plains, NY: Benjamin Cummings/Pearson.

Thayne, S. W., Anderson, N. J., Dewey, D., & Bown, J. (under review). Facilitating language learner motivation: Teacher motivational practice and teacher motivational training.

Tsui, A. (2008). *Internationalization of higher education and linguistic paradoxes.* Plenary address at the Languages Issues in English-Medium Universities: A Global Concern. The University of Hong Kong, Hong Kong SAR.

PART II
Providing Support

8

DEVELOPING SELF-REGULATED LEARNERS

Helping Students Meet Challenges

Maureen Snow Andrade and Norman W. Evans

Vignette

Erica, from Thailand, enrolls in an online English language course to improve her academic English reading and writing skills. The course not only includes the interaction needed for language development through video postings, group projects, and peer review, but also offers activities that help her take responsibility for learning by setting goals, identifying strengths and weaknesses in English, applying related strategies, and reflecting on performance. As Erica interacts with the materials in the course, she discovers new methods of learning. She states: "My learning improve a lot when I am taking part in this class. I know how to learn and how to use English fluently." Erica's experience overcoming the challenges associated with English-language distance learning entails more than linguistic factors. Taking greater responsibility for learning helps her manage the factors that affect her learning.

Introduction and Overview of the Challenges

Erica's story is not atypical. Institutions must take a holistic approach to ESL student support—English language skills are critical for learners but so are tools with which to manage learning and adjust to academic expectations. Students experience varying degrees of success in higher education depending on their ability to recognize their approaches to learning, identify strengths and weaknesses, set goals, and make needed changes. The possession of the appropriate learning tools will decrease the number of challenges a student will face. Learners who are self-regulated, or have the ability to control the factors and conditions that affect their learning (Dembo, Junge, & Lynch, 2006), have higher levels of academic achievement than those who do not possess this ability

(Andrade & Bunker, 2011; Dembo & Seli, 2008; Dembo et al., 2006; Zimmerman 1994; Zimmerman & Risemberg, 1997). This holds true across educational levels and contexts.

Both international and resident ESL students face many of the same types of challenges, depending on the length of time they have been in the United States and their previous schooling. Indeed, all learners benefit from controlling the factors and conditions that affect their learning. Institutions and faculty members must understand and address the diversity of expectations and approaches represented by ESL students. Cultural approaches to learning differ and affect learners' abilities to be self-regulated and, therefore, successful in achieving their educational goals. These factors must be addressed in higher education contexts. Many of the learning challenges faced by ESL learners are related to cultural values, educational practices, and approaches to learning.

Cultural Values and Educational Practices

When one of the authors of this chapter was giving his advanced-level ESL students a lesson on time management, he encouraged them to identify how they used their time in a typical day and isolate habits and pastimes that prevented them from completing and submitting assignments on time and coming to class prepared. These learners were enrolled in an intensive English program in an institution of higher education, and the majority desired to obtain a degree in the United States. The instructor talked about the concepts of prioritization and procrastination. One student indicated that in his language there was no word for procrastination. This provided insight into why students from that linguistic background had been unconcerned with deadlines. It also pointed to the fact that many of these students would have a difficult time being successful in future courses unless they understood this cultural difference and adjusted their frames of reference.

As this example demonstrates, in a university course, students' cultural practices may be at odds with behaviors that most faculty members would consider standard practice. Similarly, faculty members may not be aware of why students' actions depart from this norm. Limited understanding on both sides contributes to putting the student at risk of failure or, at the very least, causing a disconnect between students and faculty members and engendering negative feelings. Cultural disconnects occur regularly in higher education classrooms. And these classrooms are becoming more and more diverse.

In institutions of higher education in the United States, the percentages of students categorized as *minority* is increasing. For example, from 1976 to 2011, Hispanic student enrollments increased from 4% to 14% and Black student enrollments from 10% to 15% (National Center for Education Statistics, 2014). Additionally, 3.5% of higher education enrollments are international students (Institute of International Education, 2011). Although official figures are not available to indicate the percentage of students who speak English as a second language, estimates for international students, based on the largest sending countries (see Chapter 1), is 95%. Clearly language and cultural diversity are becoming a significant facet of the higher educational landscape in the United States. Such changes in the demographics of higher education demand curricular changes that will facilitate these students' success.

Any institutional change in programming aimed to help students develop as self-regulated learners must necessarily be preceded by an understanding of the students' educational and cultural backgrounds. As noted in Chapter 1, international students come to U.S. institutions with varying ideas of what it means to be successful and how to achieve that success. These students often have the concept that they must perform well, which they interpret as attaining high grades (see Dweck, 2000). Students may also be trying to please family members and others by getting good grades. One way students attempt to get good grades is by not taking on anything that is too challenging. This focus on performance does not mesh well with learning a language, which requires taking risks, making mistakes, and acknowledging weaknesses and limitations. Similarly, it does not integrate well with the principles and dimensions of self-regulated learning (SRL), which will be discussed in more detail later in this chapter.

Another cultural factor that may limit international students' abilities to develop SRL practices and improve their performance in classes includes their concept of teacher and student roles. Anyone who has taught international students understands the high level of respect many cultures extend to teachers. It is not uncommon for international students to view teachers as absolute authorities in their academic domains. Students' respect for this authority is manifest in their classroom behavior. Questioning a teacher might be seen as a matter of disrespect, so students do not ask questions. For similar reasons, students may deem it disrespectful to participate or offer their opinions and ideas when the teacher is present. Group work can be seen by international students as a waste of time. From the student's perspective, what could a group of students possibly know that a teacher could not more expertly present? While this respect for a teacher is admirable, it may limit a student's views of self-abilities, as we will illustrate.

A student's performance or lack thereof may be rooted in more than individual characteristics; culture can also impact performance (Barmeyer, 2004; Hofstede, 1980; Simy & Kolb, 2009). As such, individual and institutional adjustments must be implemented to maximize a student's performance in higher education institutions. With the understanding that cultural factors may limit international students' abilities and willingness to adapt to SRL principles, we next discuss ways to implement change in higher education institutions and offer theoretical frameworks for identifying solutions to cultural barriers.

Students and Faculty: Changing Perspectives and Practices

We do not intend to convey the idea that only students need to change. Institutions and those within them must also change to meet the needs of the diverse ESL populations. Institutions who admit underprepared, nontraditional, first-generation, or culturally and linguistically diverse students have an obligation to provide the requisite resources and opportunities to enable their success (Seidman, 2006). In this section, we address strategies for facilitating change in order to support students' learning-strategy development.

Higher education institutions are typically slow to change due to their loosely coupled organizational structure. They are separated into somewhat independent units, such as discipline-based departments and administrative divisions (e.g., student affairs and academic affairs). Decision making is decentralized and the faculty largely autonomous. Change may be administratively driven, although it typically involves forming committees to consider issues and make recommendations.

Resisting change is more typical than embracing it. Understanding the three essential elements that foster comprehensive change in higher education is vital. These elements include the reason for change (why), the substance of change (what or how much), and the process of change (who and how) (Eckel, Green, Hill, & Mallon, 1999). First, people must believe that the status quo is unsatisfactory and that change is beneficial. Reasons for the change, consequences of not changing, mission alignment, costs and risks, institutional climate, and core effects on functions, such as teaching, learning, and scholarship, must be considered.

Next, the extent of the change needed must be examined. This involves considering the "depth and pervasiveness" (Eckel et al., 1999, p. 14) of the problems or needed improvements. The source of the pressure to change and the degree of pressure determine the desired amount of change. Change can range from minor adjustments in limited areas to institution-wide transformation.

The third change factor focuses on whom to involve and how. Leaders must consider who might resist and why, how to address various responses and garner support, and how to encourage people to see beyond their own areas of responsibility. This may entail opportunities for debate and exploration, restructuring, training, and incentives. Finally, evaluation must occur to determine if change has been effective.

Effective organizational change must be based on the "assumption that people, like all life, are creative and good at change" (Wheatley, 2005, p. 76). As such, people need to be involved in creating it. Leaders should assume that organizations possess the expertise needed to determine new directions and implement change; the role of the leader is to provide connections across the organization and appropriate structures to enable this.

Most, if not all, of the ideas in this chapter involve change; therefore, leaders, whether those with a formal leadership role or those advocating on behalf of ESL learners, must review their current practices related to ESL-learner success, determine if and where change is needed, communicate the need for change, structure the change process, and empower others to exercise their creativity in determining solutions.

Implementing an SRL approach within classrooms, and thus within individual learners, requires faculty members and students to rethink their roles. Discussions of how to respect the cultural and educational backgrounds of ESL students, yet facilitate their successful transition into higher education in an English-speaking institution, need to be widespread for shared goals and common vision to be formed. With this common vision in place, stakeholders can use their creativity to determine how to accomplish the vision.

Theoretical Perspectives

Although all students benefit from improved learning practices, ESL learners have specific challenges due to their lack of English proficiency and possible cultural dissonance. The acquisition of effective learning practices supports development of linguistic ability. The two areas are complementary—strategies for language learning have been a central topic since the 1970s (Rubin, 2008). These strategies extend to all areas of learning. Although some students enter higher education with effective learning practices, others do not. All students experience a transition that can be mitigated by taking greater responsibility for the factors affecting their learning. In this section, we explore how SRL addresses this need.

SRL: Categories, Dimensions, Principles, Strategies

As we noted at the outset of this chapter, self-regulated learners understand that they have the ability to control the factors and conditions that affect their learning (Dembo et al., 2006). As a result they have higher levels of academic achievement than those who do not possess this ability. Furthermore, research tells us that self-regulation can be taught and learned (Dembo & Eaton, 2000; Dembo et al., 2006; Dweck, 2000). A significant way to help ESL learners succeed is to teach SRL strategies that will support them in the many academic and linguistic challenges they face in what is often an entirely new learning environment.

Self-regulation is divided into four general categories of learning: metacognitive (planning, setting goals, monitoring), motivation (developing self-efficacy and the ability to self-motivate), cognitive (understanding and remembering information), and behavior (seeking help and creating a positive learning environment) (Dembo et al., 2006; Wernke et al., 2011; Zimmerman

& Risemberg, 1997). From these four categories, we draw six dimensions of SRL: motive, methods of learning, time, physical environment, social environment, and performance (Andrade & Evans, 2013; Zimmerman & Risemberg, 1997). Each of these dimensions can be associated with "w/h" questions: why, how, when, where, with whom, and what.

Basic principles of learning stem from each of these six dimensions, and using these principles as guidelines, specific learning strategies can be created. We define a principle as a general guideline that directs specific behaviors or actions (Andrade & Evans, 2013). For example, time management, procrastination avoidance, and task prioritization are each principles related to the dimension of time. From these principles, we can create specific strategies that can help individuals develop as self-regulated learners. For instance, the dimension of time has the associated principle of time management, from which we can develop such strategies as using a planner, holding daily planning sessions, or setting time limits on tasks.

Dimensions and Principles

Motive, or motivation, is related to reasons for learning; it answers the question *why*. Values, beliefs, and expectations are related to the dimension of motive (Andrade & Evans, 2013; Dembo & Seli, 2008). Motivated learners can encourage themselves through difficult tasks even when they do not feel like completing them. In this dimension, learners are guided by principles such as knowing their values, beginning with an end in mind, and having a clear vision of how current expectations and tasks will lead them to where they ultimately wish to be. As is the case with each of the six SRL dimensions, motive is not an innate characteristic that some have and others do not. It can be taught and learned.

Methods of learning relate to *how* learners learn. In other words, this dimension pertains to the strategies and techniques used to accomplish tasks (Dembo & Eaton, 2000). Self-regulated learners must be aware of the methods of learning that help them improve, and they must know how to modify methods to their learning styles. This dimension is closely related to the other five dimensions in that it draws principles from each. For instance, setting goals (motive), managing time (time), or studying in a learning-conducive setting (physical environment) are principles that apply to this dimension. Research suggests that learners with a wide array of learning strategies achieve more than those with limited strategies (Zimmerman & Martinez-Pons, 1986). Again, it is important to remember that "inherent ability is beyond one's control, but familiarity with learning strategies is not" (Andrade & Evans, 2013, p. 48).

The dimension of *time* addresses the questions of *when* and for *how long* learners apply themselves to tasks (Dembo & Seli, 2008; Zimmerman, 1990; Zimmerman & Kitsantas, 1997). Knowing what time of day is best for certain tasks and gauging how long a task will take are central to this dimension. Related principles include prioritizing tasks, managing time, dividing tasks into manageable components, avoiding procrastination, and studying at optimum times. The dimension of time is noticeably related to motive. For example, when one has a clear goal in mind, time and task management are logical strategies for achieving goals.

Physical environment relates to *where* the learning takes place. A successful learner must understand that physical surroundings can contribute to or distract from learning (Dembo & Seli, 2008; Zimmerman, 1998). These factors are typically associated with external variables like sights, sounds, smells, and temperature. However, certain internal factors that can impact learning are also related to the physical environment. These consist of such things as not feeling well, being sleepy, or experiencing high anxiety. The associated principles are being aware of and avoiding external and internal distractions.

Social environment determines *with whom* one associates to improve learning (Zimmerman & Risemberg, 1997). This can include teachers, classmates, tutors, and peers. Principles derived from this dimension consist of associating with others who have similar academic aims; asking questions when you don't understand; using your teacher as a resource; surrounding yourself with human, print, and electronic resources; and getting involved with learning communities, such as study groups, lab sessions, and tutoring sessions.

Performance answers such questions as: What have I accomplished? What needs to be improved? And what are my strengths and weaknesses? Zimmerman (2002) states that performance should be thought of in terms of self-observation and self-control. Related principles include knowing yourself as a learner, always being aware of your status in class (grades, attendance, participation), and analyzing to improve. In many ways *performance* is the process of monitoring progress on each of the SRL dimensions with the aim of adjusting performance to achieve maximum learning outcomes.

SRL Strategies

With an understanding of the six dimensions and associated guiding principles, one can then begin to develop strategies from those principles. We define strategy as a specific action or technique that will lead to the desired outcome. In terms of learning a language, Griffiths (2008) defines strategy as "activities consciously chosen by learners for the purpose of regulating their own language learning" (p. 87). The words *activities* and *consciously* are meaningful here. First, activity in the plural form suggests that no single activity or strategy will do. Grabe and Stoller (2006) define strategic readers as those who "make use of a wide repertoire of strategies in combination rather than in isolated applications" (p. 195). When it comes to strategies, more is better. Furthermore, a self-regulated learner "consciously" selects the strategies that will best meet the tasks at hand.

As dimensions, principles, and strategies are used to improve performance, it is important to remember that a dimension stems from a broad category of learning and that a principle related to a dimension is a general guideline that determines what specific strategy to use to improve learning performance. It is also important to recognize that dimensions overlap with principles, which intersect with strategies. It may be helpful to think of these elements in terms of their level of abstraction. Categories are the most abstract. Dimensions are less abstract than categories but are more abstract than principles, which are more theoretical than strategies.

Imagination is the only limitation to the nature of a strategy. A teacher or tutor helping a student develop as a self-regulated learner can use principles drawn from the dimensions to help shape specific strategies. Table 8.1 provides a small sampling of strategies for each of the six SRL dimensions (see Andrade & Evans, 2013 for more examples of strategies).

Figure 8.1 demonstrates how the six dimensions of SRL interact to increase not only ESL learners' language proficiency but also their mastery of content (Andrade, 2012; Andrade & Bunker, 2009, 2011). As learners recognize strengths and weaknesses, set goals, adopt study methods, address time-management issues, and monitor their performance, they will develop greater responsibility for controlling the factors and conditions that affect their success. The arrows in the model imply continuation of the process as learners enroll in subsequent courses and apply the components of SRL either on their own or while facilitated by instructors.

The six dimensions of SRL help educators establish a holistic network for ESL students in higher education. The model can be adopted in ESL courses, developmental reading and writing programs, English courses, learning-assistance centers, workshops, and faculty training. SRL helps students move from an entity theory of intelligence to an incremental theory, or the belief that

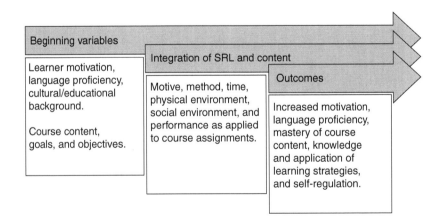

FIGURE 8.1 Integrating SRL and Content.

TABLE 8.1 Self-Regulated Learning Strategies

Dimensions	Principles	Strategies
Motive	• Know your values • Begin with an end in mind • Think positively	• Set SMART goals (specific, measurable, attainable, relevant, timely) • Define what motivates you • Identify de-motivators • Engage in positive self-talk
Method of Learning	• Know what strategies work for you • Customize strategies to your learning style • Seek better ways to learn specific material (e.g., vocabulary, content)	• Take notes • Ask questions • Use vocabulary flashcards • Use graphic organizers (draw pictures) • Use tutors when needed
Time	• Manage time • Be aware of time • Prioritize tasks	• Hold daily self-planning sessions • Buy a planner and use it • Determine when you study best • Label daily tasks using an "urgent and important" distinction • Follow the 80/20 rule (find tasks that yield the greatest result and make them priorities)
Physical Environment	• Avoid external and internal distractions	• Determine where you study best • Identify key distracters • Surround yourself with positive reminders • Study where resources are readily available
Social Environment	• Recognize that many people can help you learn; associate with them (teachers, tutors, classmates, librarians) • Access resources (libraries, study centers, internet)	• Be involved in group study sessions • Meet with your teacher or tutors for clarifications • Surround yourself with resources (classmates, library, internet)
Performance	• Keep track of key performance indicators (test scores, attendance, participation) • Learn from your errors • Seek feedback from others	• Monitor your performance using tables or graphs • Identify your strengths and weaknesses • Always be aware of your class standing/grade • Adjust goals based on performance

intelligence can be changed (Dweck, 2000). Such students are willing to take on challenges in order to extend their learning rather than ensuring success by choosing easy tasks. Through practicing the strategies associated with SRL, learners begin to understand that they can address weaknesses and improve their learning. They have the tools to be successful at challenging tasks, and their confidence increases.

Students' views of intelligence also affect the SRL dimension of motivation. Learners who focus on grades as a source of motivation (i.e., those who possess an entity or fixed theory of intelligence) are not concerned with learning—only with appearing that they are doing well. Thus, they may give up when they get a low score rather than examine what they can do to improve. Learners with an incremental theory of intelligence are motivated by learning itself and view errors as learning opportunities. SRL supports the belief that intelligence can be changed.

Implications and Applications

This chapter began with a vignette about Erica, an ESL student who implemented SRL practices to be successful in an online English language course and prepare for study at a higher education institution in the United States. Such preparation is dependent on institutional stakeholders being familiar with ESL students' needs and implementing programs and policies that address these needs. Many students go through their entire educational experience without understanding the basic lessons of SRL that Erica learned. Because of this, we next focus on why it is important to institutionalize SRL, how SRL might be implemented, and at what levels pedagogy and practice for ESL learners must be changed.

Student Reactions

Perhaps the best way to explain why implementing SRL into a curriculum is important is to hear the voices of students who have been positively impacted by SRL in their own study habits. As evidenced by Erica's story, shared at the beginning of the chapter, SRL can make a difference in a student's outlook and ultimate success. The following excerpts highlight various aspects of success related to the inclusion of SRL in an ESL writing course, as expressed in the students' own words. In addition to increased levels of SRL, the students' quotations and our own evaluations of their work demonstrate that students have applied SRL strategies. They have noticeably improved their academic skills, such as paragraph organization, unity and coherence, vocabulary use, grammatical accuracy, and reading comprehension, as they have set goals, identified and implemented appropriate strategies, and evaluated their performance.

Motive

The following student journal excerpts show evidence of various components of motive, such as increased confidence, recognition of strengths and weaknesses, and the value of goal-setting:

> I like one of the activity is analysis myself that tell me what my study style and what my values on studying English and what my motivation. Also I will find my weakness I can improve it.

> I should set very specific, achievable, realistic and measurable goal. That way I can achieve my goals better. For example, if I set too high goals, I might give up, so goals must be very realistic and achievable. Also, goals must be very specific because specific goals let us stay well organized and focused.

Methods

Methods of learning related to improving reading, writing, vocabulary, grammar, and overall study skills are evident in the following entries:

> I got to make it a habit to preview and review the studying materials every day. This has helped me to study more effectively. For example, previewing helped me better prepared for the tutor time and to have a better understanding for the materials to be covered the next day. And reviewing helped me remember the things I learned better.

> The learning skills I learned from this class have helped me a lot because I could apply these skills to other subjects too.

Time

Course activities helped learners improve their time-management skills as follows:

> I must do it [writing assignments] before the deadline. Prioritizing is very important. If we don't prioritize well, we will spend our precious time not useful.

> Before I started taking this course, my good life was moving slowly without deadline. My first questions were what the meaning of deadline, assignment and submission. Therefore it was good to have this [SRL] activities to be aware my learning habits and tips of improvement for my writing. I could deal with many things unlike before. That's because of Time Management activities.

Social Environment

Effective use of the social environment enabled learners to seek help and improve their communication skills:

> The most important thing is to plan and prepare for the tutor session. For example, I should read my tutor session instructions several days before the tutor session so that I might talk to my tutor about the assignment very well. Also, I should make notes of what I don't understand or I should write down list of questions that I want to ask.

> The learning activities helped me to speak and explain better in my daily lives when I needed to write emails or talk to other people. I could think more logically and explain better.

Physical Environment

Students considered factors that impacted their study in various locations and made conscious choices about where to study and how to control their environments:

> In my house, there is a corner where I have a table and a chair. This is my place that I use to study or do my work. I do not have much space in my house, but the corner that I use for study and work is quiet enough for me to be concentrated. With the place that I have for study I can start to study immediately, I can work without getting interrupt, I can find my study materials and they are available, I can take breaks and then return to my studying and sometimes I can manage my time while I am there.

Performance

Learners demonstrated the ability to apply SRL strategies, monitor their performance, revise their goals, and set new goals:

> I review the goals I set for the course to see if I am making progress. I think, I need to make some changes, for what I have done before to what I have put in now in order to get better grades. These are new set goals for the second half: first, try to distinguish between important things and unimportant things. Second, try to improve part of speed and the last one is improve on finding ideas.

> There are several new goals I set in half of this semester. First of all, I set a goal to use a small amount of time. For example, I can read my textbook during lunch time, read my vocabularies when I travel, and I will get up

at 5:30. Sometimes I have so many things to do that I am against the clock always in my life. However, I will have more time to study, and I can become a better student because of the goal.

Implementation

It is important to remember that these quotations represent learners enrolled in English language courses with embedded SRL activities. Students can learn to be self-regulated, but that learning will require instruction. Where and how that instruction can be included is our next topic of discussion.

Where

SRL can be included in a curriculum at various levels and in a number of ways. The most obvious levels of implementation include class, course, program, and institution. At the class level, a single teacher may choose to incorporate SRL into the existing curriculum, be that writing, grammar, biology, or economics. Course implementation would consist of multiple sections of the same class. For example, all the first-year writing teachers would include SRL as part of their common curriculum. Implementing SRL in a program would consist of all courses within a department including SRL as part of their curriculum. We are familiar with an intensive English program that teaches SRL to all students in the program. Materials are modified for language proficiency at the various levels within the program.

Finally, institutional implementation would consist of an entire school adopting SRL as part of what they teach their students. Implementing at this level obviously presents challenges. Foremost is the size of the institution. The larger the school, the more difficult implementation would be. In some cases, a department at a large school has more students than an entire small college or university. The possibilities of institutional implementation, regardless of size, tie back to our discussion of recognizing the need for institutional change. With administrative buy-in and delegation, it is possible to implement SRL at the institution level. For example, a university administrator might assign a department that oversees certain first-year courses, such as composition, to include SRL in the curriculum. In addition, faculty workshops could be used to inform faculty members about how students are being taught to be self-regulated learners. Faculty members could then build on this framework as they see appropriate in the various contexts of their disciplines.

How

Just as there are various levels for implementation, multiple methods are also possible. As noted, contexts vary, and each institution must determine how SRL will be implemented to best meet the institutional structure and students' needs. We suggest three possible approaches: concentrated, gradual, and selected reinforcement (Andrade & Evans, 2013). A concentrated implementation consists of SRL being taught all at once as a unit in a class. The unit may span from a single class session to multiple consecutive class sessions. A workshop setting could also be an appropriate venue to present SRL in a concentrated manner. A gradual implementation involves breaking the concepts of SRL into component parts (overview, dimensions, principles, strategies, etc.) and teaching each part at some length over the span of the course. A selected-reinforcement model consists of introducing and providing an overview of SRL, then allowing students to customize their own SRL plans. The teacher can then adjust and adapt SRL lessons both in terms of content and length based on demonstrated learner needs.

Conclusion

Self-regulated learning (SRL) is the ability of learners to control the factors or conditions that affect their learning. SRL is viewed both as a set of teachable skills and as a developmental process that emerges from experience (Dembo & Eaton, 2000; Dembo et al., 2006; Dweck, 2000). These perspectives are not mutually exclusive. Both support the idea that educators can help learners become more effective. In this chapter we have demonstrated that both the learner and the institution must embrace the need for change in the way things are taught and learned for SRL to have an impact. From our own and our students' experiences, SRL can make a positive difference in an ESL learner's ability as a reader, writer, and student in general.

Summary

- Students who accept the fact that they can control their performance as learners, indeed who become self-regulated learners, perform better than learners who do not. Furthermore, SRL can be taught and learned.
- Students' cultural and educational background can impact learning styles. Both students and educators must understand this concept.
- SRL offers a sound pedagogical approach to help ESL learners succeed as language learners and students in their various major disciplines. The SRL framework can be used to inform instruction and shape support services.
- Institutions can help students develop as self-regulated learners by adapting curricular and service-center components to follow the SRL model. This will require, in many cases, willingness to change on an institutional level.
- SRL can be considered in three components: dimension, principle, and strategy. Principles derived from dimensions can be used to design specific strategies for learning improvement.

• SRL can be implemented at various levels depending on institutional context: class, course, program, or institution. Furthermore, it can be implemented in varying degrees: concentrated, gradual, and selected reinforcement.

Discussion Questions

1. Culture has been presented as a possible barrier to students' ability to develop as self-regulated learners. From your experiences with ESL learners, what factors beyond those presented in this chapter might deter students' development as self-regulated learners? Do any of the six dimensions seem to be more limited by cultural factors than others?

2. Change is a central element to successful implementation of SRL. Both individuals and institutions must make changes. Divide a piece of paper into four columns. Label column 1 as *Individual Barriers*, column 2 as *Possible Solutions*, column 3 as *Institutional Barriers*, and column 4 as *Possible Solutions*. Using your current context, identify as many barriers as you can that would limit the implementation of SRL. Then, on a separate sheet of paper, identify possible solutions to those barriers.

3. Table 8.1 presents a few possible strategies that would help learners succeed. Identify learning strategies that have helped you succeed as a learner. Can you associate those strategies with particular SRL dimensions?

4. In your current position, or in a position you anticipate holding in the future, how would you implement SRL? What steps would be needed? Outline a plan for implementing SRL at the course, section, or institutional level. What types of training and support would be needed for students, faculty, and administrators? Could SRL be part of an institutional learning model? If so, how could such a model be identified and implemented?

Further Reading

Andrade, M. S., & Evans, N. W. (2013). *Principles and practices for response to second language writing: Developing self-regulated learners*. New York, NY: Routledge.

Dembo, M. H., & Seli, H. (2008). *Motivation and learning strategies for college success: A self-management approach* (3rd ed.). New York, NY: Erlbaum.

Zimmerman, B. J. (1994). Dimensions of academic self-regulation: A conceptual framework for education. In D. H. Schunk & B. J. Zimmerman (Eds.), *Self-regulation of learning and performance* (pp. 3–21). Hillsdale, NJ: Erlbaum.

References

Andrade, M. S. (2012). Self-regulated learning activities: Supporting success in online courses. In J. S. Moore (Ed.), *Distance learning* (pp. 111–132). Rijeka, Croatia: InTech. Retrieved February 10, 2015, from www.intechopen.com/articles/show/title/self-regulated-learning-activities-supporting-success-in-online-courses.

Andrade, M. S., & Bunker, E. L. (2009). Language learning from a distance: A new model for success. *Distance Education, 30*(1), 47–61.

Andrade, M. S., & Bunker, E. L. (2011). The role of SRL and TELEs in distance education: Narrowing the gap. In G. Dettori & D. Persico (Eds.), *Fostering self-regulated learning through ICTs* (pp. 105–121). Hershey, PA: IGI Global.

Andrade, M. S., & Evans, N. W. (2013). *Principles and practices for response to second language writing: Developing self-regulated learners.* New York, NY: Routledge.

Barmeyer, C. I. (2004). Learning styles and their impact on cross-cultural training: An international comparison in France, Germany, and Quebec. *International Journal of Intercultural Relations, 28*, 577–594.

Dembo, M. H., & Eaton, M. J. (2000). Self-regulation of academic learning in middle-level schools. *The Elementary School Journal, 100*(5), 473–490.

Dembo, M. H., Junge, L. G., & Lynch, R. (2006). Becoming a self-regulated learner: Implications for web-based education. In H. F. O'Neil & R. S. Perez (Eds.), *Web-based learning: Theory, research, and practice* (pp. 185–202). Mahwah, NJ: Erlbaum.

Dembo, M. H., & Seli, H. (2008). *Motivation and learning strategies for college success: A self-management approach* (3rd ed.). New York, NY: Erlbaum.

Dweck, C. S. (2000). *Self-theories: Their role in motivation, personality, and development.* Philadelphia, PA: Psychology Press.

Eckel, P., Green, M., Hill, B., & Mallon, W. (1999). *On change III. Taking charge of change: A primer for colleges and universities.* Washington, DC: American Council on Education. Retrieved February 10, 2015, from www.acenet.edu/Search/Pages/results.aspx?k=Eckel.

Grabe, W., & Stoller, F. (2006). Reading for academic purposes: Guidelines for ESL/EFL teachers. In M. Celce-Murcia (Ed.), *Teaching English as a second or foreign language* (3rd ed.) (pp. 187–203). Boston, MA: Heinle & Heinle.

Griffiths, C. (Ed.). (2008). *Lessons from good language learners.* Cambridge: Cambridge University Press.

Hofstede, G. (1980). *Culture's consequences: International differences in work-related values.* Beverly Hills, CA: Sage.

Institute of International Education. (2011). *Top 25 institutions hosting international students, 2010/11.* Open doors report on international educational exchange. Retrieved February 10, 2015, from www.iie.org/Research-and-Publications/Open-Doors/Data/International-Students/Leading-Institutions/2010-11.

National Center for Education Statistics. (2014). *Fast facts.* Retrieved February 10, 2015, from http://nces.ed.gov/fastfacts/display.asp?id=98.

Rubin, J. (2008). Reflections. In C. Griffiths (Ed.), *Lessons from good language learners* (pp. 10–15). Cambridge: Cambridge University Press.

Seidman, A. (2006). A retention formula for student success. Retrieved February 10, 2015, from www.google.com/url?sa=t&rct=j&q=&esrc=s&source=web&cd=2&ved=0CCc QFjAB&url=http%3A%2F%2Fwww.cscsr.org%2Fdocs%2FRetentionFormulaUpdateFo rWeb2006.pdf&ei=gUzqU5jUO9LboAT14IDwAw&usg=AFQjCNHS6EBx_dQNo5YIRxiL-af7h0ni7w&sig2=XWXyjfx4MNYLlAgr1jl8jA&bvm=bv.72938740,d.cGU.

Simy, J., & Kolb, D. A. (2009). Are there cultural differences in learning style? *International Journal of Intercultural Relations, 33*, 69–85.

Wernke, S., Wagener, U., Anschuetz, A., & Moschner, B. (2011). Assessing cognitive and metacognitive learning strategies in school children: Construct validity and arising questions. *The International Journal of Research and Review, 6*(2), 19–38.

Wheatley, M. J. (2005). *Finding our way: Leadership for an uncertain time.* San Francisco, CA: Berrett-Koehler Publishers, Inc.

Zimmerman, B. J. (1990). Self-regulated learning and academic achievement: An overview. *Educational Psychologist, 25*(1), 3–17.

Zimmerman, B. J. (1994). Dimensions of academic self-regulation: A conceptual framework for education. In D. H. Schunk & B. J. Zimmerman (Eds.), *Self-regulation of learning and performance* (pp. 3–21). Hillsdale, NJ: Erlbaum.

Zimmerman, B. J. (1998). Academic study and the development of personal skill: A self-regulatory perspective. *Educational Psychologist, 33*(2/3), 73–86.

Zimmerman, B. J. (2002). Becoming a self-regulated learner: An overview. *Theory into Practice, 41,* 64–142.

Zimmerman, B. J., & Kitsantas, A. (1997). Developmental phases in self-regulation: Shifting from process goals to outcome goals. *Journal of Educational Psychology, 89*(1), 29–36.

Zimmerman, B. J., & Martinez-Pons, M. (1986). Development of a structured interview for assessing student use of SRL strategies. *American Educational Research Journal, 23*(4), 614–628.

Zimmerman, B. J., & Risemberg, R. (1997). Self-regulatory dimensions of academic learning and motivation. In G. D. Phye (Ed.), *Handbook of academic learning: Construction of knowledge* (pp. 105–125). San Diego, CA: Academic Press.

9

THE RESEARCH–INSTRUCTION CYCLE IN SECOND LANGUAGE READING

William Grabe and Xiangying Jiang

Vignette

Armando is an ESL reading teacher. As a reading teacher, he knows that research says that strategy instruction is very important. But the textbook he uses has a strategy activity at the end of each of the 10 chapters (scanning, finding the main idea, summarizing, distinguishing fact from opinion, recognizing cause and effect, guessing words from context, using a dictionary effectively, recognizing problem and solution organization, etc.). He doesn't think that the disconnected strategy lessons once every 10 days is a useful way to help students become strategic in understanding challenging texts. As the teacher, he wonders how students can become more strategic through effective instruction and include enough practice in using strategies to make a difference in students' reading abilities. This is just one of several puzzles that reading teachers face when they try to connect research and teaching.

Beyond the above specific vignette, other disconnects between researchers and teachers could include students having to build a very large recognition vocabulary but teachers not having any clear way to do this based on the textbooks used. Another challenge is students needing to become aware of how discourse is organized in texts as a way to improve comprehension, but teachers not seeing a clear and obvious way to accomplish this with the textbooks used. A third example could be the teachers needing to use meaningful, coherent content as a way to develop academic reading skills, but not having an obvious way to move beyond the two to three thematic readings around a general concept so common in reading textbooks.

Introduction and Overview to the Challenges

If you are a researcher in the field of second language (L2) reading, you may have been wondering why so many good research findings in reading do not seem to make their way into effective and consistent instructional practices. On the other hand, if you are a language teacher who is teaching L2 reading, you may have been wondering why teaching constraints in real everyday classrooms are often not taken into account by researchers when they carry out their research studies under controlled situations. The relationship between teaching and research is often assumed or ignored, and the gulf between the two can at times seem large. In this chapter we would like to conceptualize the relationship between research and instruction in L2 reading as a cyclic process that can eventually lead to improved student learning outcomes. In developing the research–instruction interaction as an iterative cycle, we hope to demonstrate what support reading research has to offer to L2 reading instruction, but also, in turn, what evidence language instruction in the classroom can provide to researchers.

The Research–Instruction Cycle

Reading is a complex and dynamic process that involves the ability to extract meaning from a text. To explain how reading works, many groups of researchers have contributed to the development of theories about reading comprehension abilities. Several key component skills of reading comprehension abilities have been identified in current reading research; these skills work together in a complex, finely coordinated set of processes (Grabe, 2004, 2009; Koda, 2005). The key issue is how to translate this research into instruction that is both effective and feasible for teachers to carry out on a consistent basis. We will explain this translation and implementation issue with a research–instruction cycle. We divide the cycle into six stages (see Figure 9.1). The first three stages depict the main steps in research: theory development (stage 1), verification of theory (stage 2), and feasibility for implementation (stage 3). Stages 4 and 5 describe the implementation of research findings in effective instructional environments and the assessment of learning outcomes in instruction. Finally, stage 6 connects the research–instruction cycle by providing recommendations for research, rethinking theories, and implications.

Stage 1: Research on Theory Development

The processes of theory building draw on multiple sets of findings and the work of many groups of researchers. It is fairly straightforward to imagine groups of researchers working on the development of theories about reading comprehension abilities. They begin with two basic questions: What is reading comprehension, and how does it develop? They then read both earlier and more recent research studies on component abilities that other researchers have identified as important for reading abilities (e.g., expanding vocabulary knowledge, identifying main ideas). They observe different groups of readers reading. They develop many ways to assess reading abilities. Based on the data they collect,

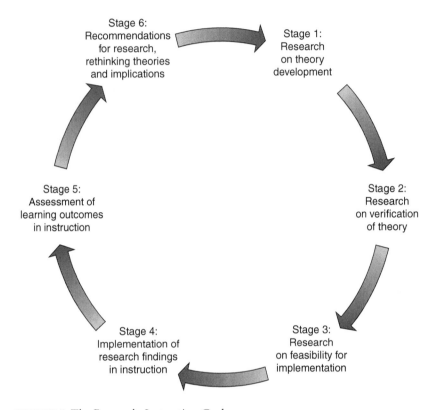

FIGURE 9.1 The Research–Instruction Cycle.

they co-relate their data to see which skills and cognitive resources work together to provide positive results with respect to reading skills. They use many statistical procedures to identify the most important abilities, they do further research to identify the contributions of each ability to reading comprehension, they explore which component abilities are causal, and they do additional studies to see if these skills can be improved through training (and then see if reading comprehension improves as well). At some point, they write up their results (and the results of other researchers), and they propose theories of reading comprehension.

In the field of L2 reading, then, a more general recognition emerges of what contributes to reading comprehension (and, in effect, defines reading comprehension). At this stage, a number of specific skills take on major roles in interpreting reading comprehension abilities because of extensive research findings. Such skills include efficient word recognition, a large recognition vocabulary, strong sentence and discourse processing skills, and the ability to use reading strategies. This component-skills approach to reading comprehension has become the most important approach to research in L2 reading.

Stage 2: Research on Verification of Theory

The initial findings on the specific skills have to be replicated to some extent for different groups of students learning to read, including various groups of L2 students. A goal of this research is usually to demonstrate the impact of a component skill on reading abilities. This research usually involves the teaching of a specific skill in a controlled experimental or quasiexperimental context, requiring pre- and post-assessment and a control group. Results of this research, assuming sufficient controls and treatment fidelity, sufficient time, and sufficient treatment intensity, will allow the research to argue for the immediate and direct impact of a component skill (or component skills) on the improvement of reading abilities for a given group of students.

Many studies have trained groups of students to improve in various component reading abilities, and even combinations of abilities, to identify resulting reading comprehension benefits. In many cases, the experiments and the treatments are very quick, often just a single set of training tasks over a short period of time, perhaps lasting from a few days to a week or two, and the intensity of repeated tasks might be a few times per week. In other studies, groups of students receive extended training in a set of tasks repeated many times. This type of longitudinal experimental instructional study, or quasiexperimental instructional study, enables researchers to see if the relevant implications from research can be integrated into a set of instructional practices that can be carried out in an extended fashion and in a real classroom context. The instructional practices might someday form the core of a new reading curriculum, although the research has priority over curriculum development at this stage. The question moves more to the potential application in a fairly realistic setting. This stage also reinforces implications from research for instruction.

Longitudinal experimental (or quasiexperimental) instructional studies are a difficult type of study to carry out because they are expensive, time consuming, easily derailed, and require much cooperation. However, this is the level of research that L2 reading research efforts should be pursuing. Results of these studies, if replicated sufficiently, provide lasting evidence for stronger claims about the development of L2 reading abilities. Over time, based on these efforts, certain processing skills, linguistic resources, and related cognitive resources emerge as important for reading development, and as a result, a set of implications for teaching emerge.

For example, it is now evident that a large recognition vocabulary is essential for fluent EAP reading skills. Not only is this a consensus among reading researchers, but it is also a strong consensus among teachers and materials writers. If we collect any large set of EAP reading textbooks, there will be activities on vocabulary building in each chapter. Perhaps we can call this a successful outcome of the research–instruction cycle.

Stage 3: Research on Feasibility for Implementation

However, at this stage, even though the research says "Try it, you'll like it, and so will your students," the application in real everyday classrooms usually does not happen. What is needed is a stage for piloting, materials development, and teacher training. In a sense, there needs to be feasibility research to persuade the various decision makers that the new teaching ideas are feasible in regular classroom contexts, that the new ideas can be fairly easily implemented either with training and/or appropriate support resources, and that the new ideas can be integrated with existing practices that do not create major disruptions to the curriculum. In particular, pilot instructional research with a smaller student group, fewer teachers, and fewer outcome measures is an important way to persuade others of the benefits of the new applications. However, many interesting research findings cannot survive the translation into wider teaching environments. We need to know which research results can be translated widely into instructional practices. As Pearson (2009) states for strategy instruction:

> It is one thing to implement strategy instruction for a certain number of minutes each day for ten weeks of a pedagogical experiment, but it is quite another to sustain a strategy emphasis over an entire school year. In short, it is easy to teach strategies in short spurts, but it is hard to curricularize them.
>
> *p. 22*

There is relatively little feasibility research of this type in L2 settings. It requires knowledgeable researchers and an informed program administration and teachers, effective assessment instruments, an ability to develop effective teaching resources and curricula, and the implementation of multiple longitudinal studies. Some feasibility studies can begin more simply from teacher action-research inquiry (e.g., Grabe & Stoller, 2011). In large-scale L1 research, when feasibility research does happen, it usually begins from adopting school districts or schools that are willing to experiment and innovate. There is usually a pilot program for school or district to demonstrate effectiveness and then gradual expansion. The full process can be a multi-year undertaking. But successful outcomes can provide "translational" research on reading with real practical outcomes (e.g., Guthrie, Mason-Singh & Coddington, 2012).

Stage 4: Implementation of Research Findings in Instruction

When the research findings show practical implications and potential for classroom application, the next stage in the research–instruction cycle will be instruction, i.e., the implementation of research findings in instruction. This stage aims to address the following question: If these new ideas are implemented in real everyday classrooms with real teachers (in nonexperimental situations), will they work to improve students' reading comprehension abilities as compared to what students might do otherwise within the same amount of instructional time? Many different activities need to take place in this stage, including materials development, teacher and institutional buy-in, teacher training, appropriate and fair assessment instruments and procedures, engagement (by someone) in data collection and multimethod analysis of data, and responsible interpretations. The outcomes of this stage in the research–instruction cycle have a major impact on institutions, teachers, and, most importantly, students. One example of this stage (and perhaps the only good L2 example) is the large-scale research studies by Elley (2000) over the course of more than 20 years, showing that extensive reading and book-flood programs can make a real difference in student reading outcomes in real school contexts (see also Krashen, 2004; Lightbown, Halter, White, & Horst, 2002).

Stage 5: Assessment of Learning Outcomes in Instruction

Assessment of instructional outcomes leads to a cycle of adoption, adaptation, and/or revision if these new ideas are to continue in the curriculum, or leads to the end of the specific research–instruction cycle if the results are not encouraging at all. Assuming that the new instructional ideas fared no worse, and perhaps a bit better, than already existing teaching practices, groups of researchers, administrators, and teachers might want to make adaptations or larger revisions to the new instructional practices, or find different ways to integrate the new instructional ideas. Action research projects, teacher interviews, student interviews, new materials, more teacher training—all might be suggested for improving a second cycle of large-scale implementation, possibly leading to the production of new types of textbooks. These new ideas, having demonstrated successful outcomes, will likely become common in newer textbooks over time.

Stage 6: Recommendations for Research: Rethinking Theories and Implications

The data and the student learning outcomes from the instruction stage lead to the final stage in the cycle. In the theory review stage, students, teachers, and administrators explain their views on the problems, strengths, benefits, limitations, and possibilities of the new instructional ideas. Although it is difficult to change established research theories or longstanding implications from research, it is at this stage that researchers have the opportunity to take feedback and suggestions from the implementers and assessors. Researchers are then able to determine whether the theory needs revising, if they have missed some key factors in their theories (such as motivation, amount of prior exposure to print, or proficiency level), if the instructional implications and implementations are valid, or if problems at other stages in the research–instruction cycle led to less than impressive outcomes. Sadly, this last stage rarely happens with well-established instructional practices, popular textbooks, and commonly accepted curricular designs.

Challenges to the Research–Instruction Cycle

We've presented the research–instruction cycle, but not because it is complete, or because it addresses all of the major research design issues, or because the cycle really is so linear. In fact, much of the research–instruction cycle is iterative at each stage. However, the cycle is a way to sort through much of the reading research in L1 and L2 contexts, consider what issues still need much more research development, and understand what might be done to integrate researchers, teachers, administrators, and materials writers more productively. Though the power of the research–instruction cycle is the ability to see how research and instruction can be mutually supportive, it is also a major challenge because it is so difficult to complete the cycle as a principled way to improve learning. In the following sections, we would like to develop these issues further through reviewing the types of reading research implications that should drive reading instruction, suggesting ways that teachers can achieve these pedagogical goals, and finally, discussing how the research–instruction cycle can be strengthened.

The most commonly accepted way for researchers to explain reading comprehension is to identify the key component abilities and skills that allow reading comprehension to develop. Reading comprehension involves abilities to recognize words rapidly and efficiently, develop and use a very large recognition vocabulary, process sentences in order to build comprehension, engage a range of strategic processes and underlying cognitive skills (e.g., setting goals, changing goals flexibly, monitoring comprehension), interpret meaning in relation to background knowledge, interpret and evaluate texts in line with reader goals and purposes, and process texts fluently over an extended period of time. These processes and knowledge resources allow the reader to generate text comprehension to the level required by a given task (or goal).

In this section we briefly review research evidence that supports a number of implications for reading instruction. Grabe (2007) noted 12 such implications and stated that students need to develop all of the following abilities to become fluent L2 readers:

1. automatic word recognition skills;
2. a large recognition vocabulary;
3. a reasonably efficient process for syntactic parsing;
4. discourse structure awareness;
5. metalinguistic awareness;
6. comprehension abilities to develop a text model of comprehension;

7. the appropriate use of background knowledge;
8. strategic processing;
9. reading independently for extended time periods;
10. reading fluency;
11. extensive reading;
12. motivation to read.

However, due to chapter length limits, we will address research developments of only three of these implications and address how these research implications can be translated into empirically supported classroom practices.

Building a Large Recognition Vocabulary

Research on English L1 vocabulary knowledge has demonstrated that fluent readers have very large recognition vocabulary knowledge resources. The most widely accepted figure is that high school graduates know on average 40,000 words (not counting inflectional differences in word suffixes) as fluent L1 readers (Stahl & Nagy, 2006). This is a very large number of words to learn, and most accounts suggest that many of these words are learned by repeated exposure to new words through continual reading practice. Research on L2 vocabulary knowledge has also highlighted the relationship between vocabulary knowledge and reading comprehension and has shown that vocabulary is correlated with L2 reading comprehension. Laufer (1992) reported correlations of .50 to .75 between vocabulary knowledge and reading performance. Qian (2002) reported correlations from .73 to .82. Schmitt (2008) notes that L2 readers will require approximately 35,000 different word forms as well if they are going to read a range of English reading materials independently and fluently. L2 students are never going to be taught 35,000 words in English (or, for Schmitt, 2008, and Nation, 2014, 8,000–9,000 different word families). So, over time, a lot of words need to be learned incidentally through reading exposure (i.e., through extensive reading).

There is good evidence that 10–15% of words encountered for the first time while reading an appropriate text will be learned to some measurable extent (L1 and L2). There is some evidence that encountering words frequently while reading a given text will improve the rate of new word learning (from 16–20% of new words after one reading of a text all the way to 42%; see Horst, 2009). There is also good evidence that 10–12 encounters (as a benchmark minimum) with a word will lead to successful learning of that word (for both L1 and L2; see Rott, 2007). Perhaps more importantly, the more a person reads, the more vocabulary will be learned, and learned better over extended time (Pulido & Hambrick, 2008).

If students are to become good readers with a wide range of texts (see Anderson in this volume), they need to recognize at least 95% of the words they might encounter in these texts, and fluency generally occurs when a reader can recognize 98–99% of the words in a given text (95% coverage usually reflects a challenging reading experience). The number of words that would be needed for 95% coverage of most texts seems to lie somewhere between 10,000 and 15,000 words; 98–99% coverage of words probably requires a recognition vocabulary of about 40,000 words (Stahl & Nagy, 2006). The real goal for more advanced L2 reading is an L2 recognition vocabulary level anywhere above 10,000 words. At the same time, the need to know the first 2,000 words still retains its force as a key argument for vocabulary instruction.

Translating this research to an active vocabulary development framework in the L2 curriculum, a carefully designed framework for instructional activities must be built around the following nine goals:

1. a framework for understanding vocabulary learning in the classroom;
2. procedures for selecting words to focus on;
3. techniques for introducing new words;
4. ways to practice using words;
5. activities to build word learning strategies;
6. a vocabulary-rich environment to support learning;
7. activities to help students collect words;
8. ways to build motivation for word learning;
9. activities that recycle texts and vocabulary.

There are a number of good resources for exploring each of these principles. In L1 settings, useful ideas are outlined by Beck, McKeown, and Kucan (2013) and Stahl and Nagy (2006). Good L2 vocabulary instruction ideas can be found in Anderson (2008, 2013–2014) and Nation (2014). The vocabulary research–instruction cycle has typically extended through stages 1–4 in the research–instruction cycle, but not through stages 5 and 6. Much current vocabulary instruction remains fairly traditional in real everyday (nonexperimental) classrooms.

Building Discourse Structure Awareness

Discourse knowledge is strongly related to reading comprehension (Meyer & Poon, 2001; Perfetti, Landi, & Oakhill, 2005; Trabasso & Bouchard, 2002). Research on discourse knowledge points to the importance of recognizing discourse signaling mechanisms, organization patterns and text structures in texts, and lexically signaled relations both within and across clauses and sentences. Meyer and Poon (2001) have demonstrated that students with a better awareness of higher-level text structuring recall more information from the texts and recall more top-level, main idea information. Both Meyer and Poon (2001) and Lorch and Lorch (1995) have shown that lexical signaling contributes directly to reading comprehension with multiple types of discourse patterns. In L2 research on the role of discourse knowledge, Jiang (2012) and Jiang and Grabe (2007) have shown that discourse structure knowledge relates strongly with reading comprehension. Chung (2000) has shown that L2 students, overall, improved their reading comprehension when supported by lexical signaling words. This finding was especially true for less skilled readers.

Teaching students to become more aware of text structure is a further critical aspect of reading instruction and curriculum planning. Teachers need to be aware that texts have larger units of structure that achieve writers' purposes. Moreover, writers' goals and task requirements determine basic discourse organization, and the specific information that a writer presents has a major impact on how a text is organized (see Stoller in this volume). A teacher with some knowledge of text organization and discourse signaling markers can help students build their knowledge of text structure and discourse organization. Eight specific activities are noted, though many more could be incorporated into a reading curriculum (see also Almasi & Fullerton, 2012):

1. Preview texts and highlight key words that signal text structure.
2. Highlight a paragraph in a text and decide its function in the text.
3. Fill in an outline of the text and determine main units of the text. Decide what makes each unit identifiable as a separate unit.
4. Fill in a table, chart, graph, timeline, tree, etc. How was the information that was taken from the text signaled so that it fits in the given place in a graphic organizer?
5. Find patterns of discourse organization in a text (cause and effect, comparison and contrast, problem and solution, etc.) and generate very simple graphic displays.
6. Reorganize scrambled paragraphs and sentences to reassemble a text or to make a good summary.
7. Remove a wrong sentence from a summary or a paragraph.
8. Match main ideas and supporting information across two columns.

Much like other types of knowledge and skills to be learned, there are some key principles for text structure instruction. First and foremost, this type of instruction must be consistent and continual. Second, teachers must also use the texts that they are reading for other purposes so that students see the pervasiveness of discourse structure—students shouldn't be provided with special texts to show the discourse structure. Finally, students need to explain to teachers and classmates how texts are structured and how discourse structure is signaled. The research–instruction cycle is more limited for text structure awareness. Stages 1–3 are well represented, but the general translation into instructional practice in real classrooms (as opposed to experimental settings) is very limited. Few reading textbooks focus intensely on raising students' text structure awareness (cf. Pakenham, 2004).

Promoting Strategic Reading (Becoming a Strategic Reader)

Reading comprehension is strongly influenced by reading instruction that emphasizes the coordinated use of multiple strategies while students actively seek to comprehend texts (Almasi & Fullerton, 2012; Guthrie, McRae, & Klauda, 2007; Klingner, Vaughn, Boardman, & Swanson, 2012; Pressley, 2006). Strategy instruction is best seen as the development of more complex sets of strategic routines (combinations of strategies) to build better text comprehension. The complex ability to apply multiple appropriate strategies in combination when reading difficulties are encountered is strategic processing, something that is regularly carried out by strategic readers. Appropriate strategy combinations are determined by text and task difficulty and by a student's motivation to persist and learn.

Many L1 studies have demonstrated a causal impact of intense strategy instruction on reading comprehension. Overall, a number of effective strategies have been identified in instructional research, though combinations of strategic responses to texts appear to be more effective in supporting comprehension (Baker & Beall, 2008; Grabe, 2009). For L2 students, relatively little research has been done on strategic reading development (cf. Cohen, 1998; Janzen, 2001; Klingner & Vaughn, 2000). There is relatively little research on strategy instruction embedded within a reading comprehension curriculum, and there are few efforts to explore the impact of multiple-strategy instruction on reading development (cf. Almasi & Fullerton, 2012; Macaro & Erler, 2008; Taylor, Stevens, & Asher, 2006).

Strategies for reading comprehension build on the linguistic resources (words, phrases, and structures) and support the basic comprehension model developed by the reader. When good readers read for careful comprehension, usually with challenging texts, they actively engage academic texts through multiple strategies and a heightened level of metacognitive awareness. Combinations of strategies are used by strategic readers from among those shown in Table 9.1.

These strategies and associated goals, as well as a few other strategies, are often applied in combinations that support each other to achieve comprehension. Among good readers, these strategies are often applied initially without a lot of conscious thought. It is only when the initial set of strategies does not lead to successful understanding that a much more conscious problem-solving mode of attention is activated.

Three major instructional approaches in L1 contexts that center on building strategic readers are Transactional Strategies Instruction (TSI; Pressley, 2006), Concept-Oriented Reading Instruction (CORI; Guthrie et al., 2004; Guthrie, Mason-Singh, & Coddington, 2012), and Collaborative Strategic Reading (CSR; Hitchcock, Dimino, Kurki, Wilkins, & Gersten, 2011; Klingner et al., 2012). All three require that strategy development be given a high priority throughout the curriculum and that strategy instruction be seen as a long-term

TABLE 9.1 Strategies Used by Strategic Readers

1. Planning and forming goals for reading	12. Summarizing and paraphrasing
2. Reading selectively according to goals	13. Making inferences
3. Previewing	14. Using discourse markers to see discourse relationship
4. Forming predictions	
5. Confirming, rejecting, or modifying predictions	15. Creating mental images
	16. Guessing word meanings from context
6. Posing questions	17. Monitoring main idea comprehension
7. Answering questions	18. Identifying reading difficulties
8. Connecting text to background information	19. Taking steps to repair faulty comprehension
9. Identifying important information/ main ideas	20. Rereading
	21. Translating mentally
10. Paying attention to text structure	22. Synthesizing information across parts of the text
11. Raising genre awareness	

Note
Adapted from Grabe and Stoller (2011, p. 226).

goal. Strategies are developed in the course of instruction and interaction, with teachers providing direct teaching of strategies while students are reading the course texts.

Teaching for strategic reading involves consistent modeling, scaffolding, extensive practice, and eventually independent use of the strategies by students. Discussions centered on text comprehension are the most important way to introduce and practice strategies (Almasi & Fullerton, 2012; Wilkinson & Son, 2011), and comprehension monitoring is a regular feature of instruction. In this way, strategy instruction is seen as part of everyday reading instruction and not as separate lessons. A long-range goal is to automatize strategy use for more fluent reading. Teaching students to become more strategic readers is central to comprehension instruction and deserves greater instructional attention. The research is very persuasive with respect to training students to become more strategic readers. However, this research has not extended beyond stage 4 to widespread adoption in real classrooms by real teachers (e.g., Hitchcock et al., 2011; Klingner, Vaughn, Arguelles, Hughes, & Leftwich, 2004; cf. Pressley, Gaskins, Solic, & Collins, 2006). This is a serious problem because so much of academic text comprehension depends on students becoming strategic readers.

Closing the Research–Instruction Cycle

To this point, we have sought to establish that several important implications from research are reasonably well supported and can be implemented in classroom reading instruction (and additional examples can be readily provided). The goal for reading instruction, at a general level, is to incorporate the development of key component skills and knowledge into an effective reading curriculum.

A priority in building a reading curriculum is to consider which goals will have a high priority and how to combine all of the priority goals into a coherent overall educational plan. Any careful consideration of academic reading development has to take into consideration the various component skills.

We have also learned that some interesting theoretical ideas and research findings do not seem, at this point, to translate readily into efficient and effective instructional practices even though it is fairly easy to state the implication from research for instruction. Some implications seem counterintuitive for teachers, and the teachers resist. Some activities and practices are too involved for and demanding on teachers and curriculum developers to implement consistently and easily over an extended time (e.g., see Klingner et al., 2004). Some implications and teaching resources are too expensive, or take too much teacher training time, or go beyond normal levels of teacher training to be used well. Finally, some implications, once in a curriculum, strongly limit other good ideas for teaching reading that are also based on a strong set of research evidence.

Perhaps most importantly, reading instruction that becomes stabilized as a core component of popular reading textbooks are not usually assessed for their effectiveness in relation to alternative instructional approaches or alternative task combinations. But this is precisely what needs to be assessed as research inquiry by both researchers and teachers. Usually, textbooks are changed when a seemingly better version, or a more appropriate version, is identified. Textbooks are almost never changed because research was carried out to assess the overall effectiveness of the lessons provided. Such research would be a key part of closing the research–instruction cycle (even though publishers would probably not want to encourage research that might impact future sales). Constraints on this final stage in the cycle represent perhaps the largest obstacle to having teaching inform researchers (or collaborate with researchers) when the "implications from research" do not seem to work as expected. If such feedback were provided to researchers, perhaps our ability to enhance student learning over time would accelerate.

Summary

- Research implications are often not transferred to the regular instructional curriculum because researchers often do not carry out research to close the research–instruction cycle.
- Evidence-based reading instruction, to be most relevant and useful, needs to draw on research across the full range of the research–instruction cycle, even though this is a fairly demanding criterion to ask for.
- Research supporting L1 instructional practices may not automatically be applicable to L2 instructional contexts. It is important to examine L2 experimental research that demonstrates that specific reading skills improve L2 reading comprehension.

- Long-term experimental training studies in L2 reading are needed to identify whether or not instruction in specific skills will lead to better reading comprehension. When cases demonstrate positive results, the next step is to identify the best ways to teach students so that the skills are learned efficiently and reading comprehension is most improved.

Discussion Questions

1. In order to bridge the gap between research and instruction, efforts need to be made to promote understanding of the research–instruction cycle among researchers, teachers, teacher educators, and administrators. What do you think can specifically promote understanding of the research–instruction cycle?
2. A lot of reading research that L2 teachers and researchers have access to has been conducted in the field of L1 reading. Due to the differences between L1 and L2 reading contexts, we cannot assume that research supporting L1 instructional practices will automatically be applicable to L2 instructional contexts. Can you think of some examples of instructional practices that only work for an L1 or L2 context but not both?
3. You may have noticed that many teaching materials are used consistently without a high level of research support to justify their use. Can you think of some examples of exercises or practices used in reading textbooks that are not supported by research findings?
4. One approach to building a coherent and effective reading curriculum would be to combine an emphasis on content learning as well as language learning (and language skill use), often labeled as content-based instruction. What do you think are the benefits of combined content and language learning in academic L2 reading development?

Further Reading

Farrell, T. (2009). *Teaching reading to English language learners: A reflective guide.* Thousand Oaks, CA: Corwin Press.

Grabe, W. (2009). *Reading in a second language: Moving from theory to practice.* New York, NY: Cambridge University Press.

Grabe, W., & Stoller, F. (2011). *Teaching and researching reading* (2nd ed.). New York, NY: Longman.

Han, Z., & Anderson, N. (Eds.). (2009). *Second language reading research and instruction: Crossing the boundaries.* Ann Arbor, MI: University of Michigan Press.

Hedgcock, J., & Ferris, D. (2009). *Teaching readers of English: Students, texts, and contexts.* New York, NY: Routledge.

Pressley, M. (2006). *Reading instruction that works* (3rd ed.). New York, NY: Guilford Press.

References

Almasi, J., & Fullerton, S. (2012). *Teaching strategic processes in reading* (2nd ed.). New York, NY: Guilford Press.

Anderson, N. (2008). *Practical English language teaching: Reading.* New York, NY: McGraw-Hill.

Anderson, N. (2013–2014). *Active skills for reading* (3rd ed., Vols. 1–4). New York, NY: Heinle & Heinle.

Baker, L., & Beall, L. C. (2008). Metacognitive processes and reading comprehension. In S. Israel & G. Duffy (Eds.), *Handbook of research on reading comprehension* (pp. 373–388). New York, NY: Routledge.

Beck, I., McKeown, M., & Kucan, L. (2013). *Bringing words to life: Robust vocabulary instruction* (2nd ed.). New York, NY: Guilford Press.

Chung, J. (2000). Signals and reading comprehension: Theory and practice. *System, 28,* 247–259.

Cohen, A. D. (1998). *Strategies in learning and using a second language.* New York, NY: Longman.

Elley, W. (2000). The potential of book flooding for raising literacy levels. *International Review of Education, 46,* 233–255.

Grabe, W. (2004). Research on teaching reading. *Annual Review of Applied Linguistics, 24,* 44–69.

Grabe, W. (2007). What every teacher needs to know about L2 reading. In Y.-N. Leung (Ed.), *Selected papers from the sixteenth international symposium and book fair on English teaching* (pp. 31–46). Taipei: English Teaching Association.

Grabe, W. (2009). *Reading in a second language: Moving from theory to practice.* New York, NY: Cambridge University Press.

Grabe, W., & Stoller, F. (2011). *Teaching and researching reading* (2nd ed.). New York, NY: Longman.

Guthrie, J., Mason-Singh, A., & Coddington, C. (2012). Instructional effects of Concept-Oriented Reading Instruction on motivation for reading information text in middle school. In J. Guthrie, A. Wigfield, & S. Klauda (Eds.), *Adolescents' engagement in academic literacy.* Retrieved July 22, 2014, from www.corilearning.com/research-publications/2012_adolescents_engagement_ebook.pdf.

Guthrie, J., McRae, A., & Klauda, S. (2007). Contributions of concept-oriented reading instruction to knowledge about interventions for motivations in reading. *Educational Psychologist, 42,* 237–250.

Guthrie, J., Wigfield, A., Barbosa, P., Perencevich, K., Taboada, A., Davis, M., Scafiddi, N., & Tonks, S. (2004). Increasing reading comprehension and engagement through concept-oriented reading instruction. *Journal of Educational Psychology, 96,* 403–423.

Hitchcock, J., Dimino, J., Kurki, A., Wilkins, C., & Gersten, R. (2011). *The impact of collaborative strategic reading on the reading comprehension of grade 5 students in linguistically diverse schools.* (NCEE 2011-4001). Washington, DC: National Center for Educational Evaluation and Regional Assistance, Institute of Educational Sciences, U.S. Department of Education. Retrieved July 21, 2014, from http://ncee.ed.gov.

Horst, M. (2009). Developing definitional vocabulary knowledge and lexical access speed through extensive reading. In Z. Han & N. Anderson (Eds.), *Second language reading research and instruction: Crossing the boundaries* (pp. 40–64). Ann Arbor, MI: University of Michigan Press.

Janzen, J. (2001). Strategic reading on a sustained content theme. In J. Murphy & P. Byrd (Eds.), *Understanding the courses we teach: Local perspectives on English language teaching* (pp. 369–389). Ann Arbor, MI: University of Michigan Press.

Jiang, X. (2012). Effects of discourse structure graphic organizers on EFL reading comprehension. *Reading in a Foreign Language, 24*, 84–105.

Jiang, X., & Grabe, W. (2007). Graphic organizers in reading instruction: Research findings and issues. *Reading in a Foreign Language, 19*, 34–55.

Klingner, J., & Vaughn, S. (2000). The helping behaviors of fifth graders while using collaborative strategic reading during ESL content classes. *TESOL Quarterly, 34*, 69–98.

Klingner, J., Vaughn, S., Arguelles, M., Hughes, M., & Leftwich, S. (2004). Collaborative strategic reading: "Real-world" lessons from classroom teachers. *Remedial and Special Education, 25*, 291–302.

Klingner, J., Vaughn, S., Boardman, A., & Swanson, E. (2012). *Now we get it! Boosting comprehension with collaborative strategic reading.* San Francisco, CA: Jossey-Bass.

Koda, K. (2005). *Insights into second language reading.* New York, NY: Cambridge University Press.

Krashen, S. (2004). *The power of reading* (2nd ed.). Portsmouth, NH: Heinemann.

Laufer, B. (1992). Reading in a foreign language: How does L2 lexical knowledge interact with the reader's general academic ability? *Journal of Research in Reading, 15*, 95–103.

Lightbown, P., Halter, R., White, J., & Horst, M. (2002). Comprehension-based learning: The limits of "do it yourself." *Canadian Modern Languages Review, 58*, 427–464.

Lorch, R., & Lorch, E. (1995). Effects of organizational signals on text-processing strategies. *Journal of Educational Psychology, 87*, 537–544.

Macaro, E., & Erler, L. (2008). Raising the achievement of young-beginner readers of French through strategy instruction. *Applied Linguistics, 29*, 90–119.

Meyer, B., & Poon, L. (2001). Effects of structure strategy training and signaling on recall of texts. *Journal of Educational Psychology, 93*, 141–159.

Nation, I. S. P. (2014). *Learning vocabulary in another language* (2nd ed.). New York, NY: Cambridge University Press.

Pakenham, K. (2004). *Making connections: High intermediate* (2nd ed.). New York, NY: Cambridge University Press.

Pearson, P. D. (2009). The roots of reading comprehension instruction. In S. Israel & G. Duffy (Eds.), *Handbook of research on reading comprehension* (pp. 3–31). New York, NY: Routledge.

Perfetti, C., Landi, N., Oakhill, J. (2005). The acquisition of reading comprehension skill. In M. Snowling & C. Hulme (Eds.), *The science of reading* (pp. 227–247). Malden, MA: Blackwell.

Pressley, M. (2006). *Reading instruction that works* (3rd ed.). New York, NY: Guilford Press.

Pressley, M., Gaskins, I., Solic, K., & Collins, S. (2006). A portrait of benchmark school: How a school produces high achievement in students who previously failed. *Journal of Educational Psychology, 98*, 282–306.

Pulido, D., & Hambrick, D. (2008). The virtuous circle: Modeling individual differences in L2 reading and vocabulary development. *Reading in a Foreign Language, 20*, 164–190.

Qian, D. (2002). Investigating the relationship between vocabulary knowledge and academic reading performance: An assessment perspective. *Language Learning, 52*, 513–536.

Rott, S. (2007). The effect of frequency of input-enhancements on word learning and text comprehension. *Language Learning, 57,* 165–199.

Schmitt, N. (2008). Instructed second language vocabulary learning. *Language Teaching Research, 12,* 329–363.

Stahl, S., & Nagy, W. (2006). *Teaching word meanings.* Mahwah, NJ: Erlbaum.

Taylor, A., Stevens, J., & Asher, J. W. (2006). The effects of explicit reading strategy training on L2 reading comprehension. In J. Norris & L. Ortega (Eds.), *Synthesizing research on language learning and teaching* (pp. 213–244). Philadelphia, PA: J. Benjamins.

Trabasso, T., & Bouchard, E. (2002). Teaching readers how to comprehend texts strategically. In C. Block & M. Pressley (Eds.), *Comprehension instruction: Research-based best practices* (pp. 176–200). New York, NY: Guilford Press.

Wilkinson, I. A. G., & Son, E. Y. (2011). A dialogic turn in research on learning and teaching to comprehend. In M. L. Kamil, P. D. Pearson, E. B. Moje, & P. P Afflerbach (Eds.), *Handbook of reading research* (Vol. IV, pp. 359–387). New York, NY: Routledge.

10

SUPPORTING MULTILINGUAL WRITERS THROUGH THE CHALLENGES OF ACADEMIC LITERACY

Principles of English for Academic Purposes and Composition Instruction

Dana Ferris

Vignette

"Sunny" was an international student at a large state university in California. She had come to the United States from China to pursue a master's degree in social work. Unfortunately, she failed the university's writing proficiency examination upon entrance and was required to take a remedial writing course for multilingual students who had failed the exam. Some weeks into the course, she was asked to write an in-class midterm on the topic of "single-sex schools," based upon a newspaper article the class had read.

In some ways, Sunny's writing is competent for a college writer. Her essay is well structured at the macro level and her opinion is supported with quotes from the source and personal examples. The errors in her writing typically associated with English as a second language (ESL) students are not frequent or especially serious and do not interfere with the comprehensibility of the message. However, her word choice is repetitious and her sentence structure is simplistic. She attempts few complex sentences, and when she does, the syntax usually breaks down. Sunny's writing style is unsophisticated, and while it might have gotten her through a developmental writing course for freshmen, it is unlikely to be adequate for her graduate-level written work. Indeed, she was at risk of failing the remedial writing course that she was taking when she wrote this essay.

How does this happen? How does a hardworking student like Sunny, who had studied English for many years and had already graduated from college, arrive in a U.S. master's program so underprepared for the requirements of academic literacy in her field? What can an academic department and institution do to help students like Sunny be more successful?

While the answers to these questions are complex and variable, depending upon the backgrounds of individual students and their prior educational experiences, research in second language (L2) reading and writing offers some suggestions, both as to the causes of students' struggles and the ways to help these students. This chapter examines the challenges of L2 academic literacy, identifying five major areas of struggle and possible goals or emphases for classroom instruction. The bulk of the chapter focuses on specific strategies that programs and instructors—especially in English for academic purposes (EAP) literacy courses and writing/composition courses—can and should explore and adopt for maximum student success.

Challenges of L2 Academic Literacy

U.S. colleges and universities are enrolling increasing numbers of multilingual students from a wide range of backgrounds (see Chapters 1 and 3; Ferris & Hedgcock, 2014; Harklau, Losey, & Siegal, 1999; Roberge, Siegal, & Losey, 2009). Though these growing and diverse groups of multilingual college students differ from one another in many ways, most have several characteristics in common:

1. They are simultaneously acquiring the L2 itself (at least its academic features) and general academic literacy skills (like all other college students).
2. On a relative scale, they have had less exposure to the patterns of the English language (both oral and written) than have their monolingual English-speaking peers.
3. Depending upon their educational pathways, and especially their previous English language instruction, their prior experience in writing (and reading) in English may be extremely limited.

While again there is tremendous variation within and across different subgroups of multilingual students (see Chapters 1, 3, and 6; Ferris, 2009; Roberge, 2002, 2009), these general descriptors may lead these students to experience some or all of the following challenges in coping with postsecondary-level, academic literacy demands:

*   Because such students may have never read extensively in English, they may struggle with completing lengthy reading assignments in their college classes.
*   They also may have limited experience with written fluency in the L2, and requirements such as "a 1,200-word paper" may seem overwhelming to them (Silva, 1993).
*   Many or most students lack native intuitions about how the L2 works, leading to errors in writing and to an inability to self-monitor or self-correct errors that are called to their attention (Bitchener & Ferris, 2012; Ferris, 1999; Ferris, Liu, Sinha, & Senna, 2013; Silva, 1993).

- A limited L2 vocabulary base may affect their reading comprehension, their perceived writing competence (as with the above example of Sunny), and even their ability to avoid plagiarism (see Folse, 2008, for a cogent discussion of this point).
- Depending upon their cultural and rhetorical background knowledge, they may have trouble anticipating the needs of a target audience, developing a convincing argument, or structuring a text at both the macro- and micro-levels in ways that are expected by an American academic audience (see Chapter 13; Ferris & Hedgcock, 2014).
- Considering the sum of all of these issues, L2 college/university students may have a substantial confidence gap, relative to their L1 peers, about their ability to succeed in U.S. academic settings (see Eskey, 1986).

Academic literacy requirements are challenging for many new undergraduate students (and graduate students pursuing more advanced studies in a specialized field). Even monolingual English speakers have a learning curve with regard to adjusting to reading demands, coping with unfamiliar vocabulary, and writing in various genres and to different audiences. L2 college students face all of these challenges and more, given their (relatively) late start in learning English and fewer opportunities to listen to and read, write, and speak in English. Thus, they and their EAP/writing instructors must work strategically and quickly to address these preparation and experience gaps and to develop their skills for coping with a range of literacy demands (see also Chapter 8). This strategic competence will, in turn, benefit students' overall confidence in their ability to meet the academic challenges they will face. The next section of this chapter focuses on ways that EAP programs, writing programs, and instructors can equip multilingual students (particularly newly arrived international students) for their present and future academic literacy needs.

Strategic Support for Academic Literacy Development

There are various books for teachers that present comprehensive approaches for teaching L2 reading (e.g., Aebersold & Field, 1997; Grabe, 2009; Grabe & Stoller, 2011; Hedgcock & Ferris, 2009; see also Chapters 9 and 11), L2 writing (e.g., Ferris & Hedgcock, 2014), L2 vocabulary (e.g., Coxhead, 2006; Folse, 2004; Zimmerman, 2008; see also Chapter 12), and accuracy in L2 writing (e.g., Bitchener & Ferris, 2012; Ferris, 2011). For the purposes of this chapter, however, I will condense the advice from these (and other) sources into five general subtopics:

1. Build extensive and intensive reading skills.
2. Build receptive and productive vocabulary.
3. Improve fluency and accuracy in writing.

4. Develop transferable strategies.
5. Improve student confidence.

Discussion and suggestions around these subtopics, taken together, should provide EAP/writing instructors with practical strategies for supporting their L2 students who are preparing to grapple with the challenges of academic literacy throughout their college/university studies and beyond.

Build Extensive and Intensive Reading Skills

Extensive Reading: Benefits and Approaches

As noted by Hedgcock and Ferris (2009),

> Rarely in language education do we find a teaching approach that is so universally hailed as beneficial, important, and necessary—truly an approach that has *no* detractors and many fervent advocates—yet is so underutilized and even ignored in curricula, course/lesson design, and materials development.
>
> *p. 208*

Extensive reading is defined by Day and Bamford (1998) as "the teaching of reading through reading ... the best way for students to learn to read is by reading a great deal of comprehensible material" (p. xi). In addition to its most obvious benefit—improved skill and confidence in reading itself—extensive reading has been shown to provide many other advantages to L2 acquirers: it builds vocabulary and grammar knowledge, it enhances background knowledge (of both content and text structure in the L2), it improves L2 production (especially writing), and it motivates students and builds their confidence. These advantages, which are well established in existing research (see Chapter 9; Day & Bamford, 1998; Grabe, 2009; Hedgcock & Ferris, 2009; Krashen, 2004), hold for both L1 and L2 readers.

This discussion raises the obvious question: "Why isn't everyone doing it?" (Grabe, n.d., cited in Day & Bamford, 1998, p. 41). At the college/university level, the reasons for the neglect of extensive reading are likely much more practical than philosophical (Hedgcock & Ferris, 2009). In busy, tightly scheduled EAP or composition courses, asking students to read extensively in or out of class (from self-selected texts that they enjoy) may appear to be a luxury that neither instructors nor their students can afford. It also may seem difficult to justify such activities or assignments to students, who likely have their own opinions about how they should spend their study time. Further, it can be difficult to decide how to measure or assess extensive reading activities when calculating a course grade or evaluating the effects of such reading.

These barriers to utilizing extensive reading in college-level EAP or writing courses are not insurmountable. Students can be asked to complete certain amounts of extensive reading as part of their course homework, and it can be measured in time spent, number and types of texts read, or number of pages. They will need at least two types of preparation for these assignments: instructors should (1) justify the activity by sharing/discussing the benefits for students' overall language/literacy development; and (2) support students in finding extensive reading materials that are appropriate for their interests and reading/language levels. Students can be asked to share what they have read (for grading purposes) in a reading journal, a summary/response paper, or an oral presentation to the whole class or in reading groups. Other examples of how to implement extensive reading in L2 classes can be found in Day and Bamford (1998) and Hedgcock and Ferris (2009), but the main point is that extensive reading is an extremely powerful tool that *can and should* be utilized in EAP settings.

Intensive Reading: Approaches

With that said, the intentional development of *intensive* reading skills is also extremely important for academic literacy courses. Intensive reading instruction is defined by Aebersold and Field (1997) as follows: "Each text is read carefully and thoroughly for maximum comprehension. Teachers provide direction and help before, sometimes during, and after reading. Students do many exercises that require them to work in depth with various selected aspects of the text" (p. 45). While students do need to develop their "fluency muscles"—reading for quantity in the L2—there are many academic tasks (exams, writing assignments, lecture comprehension, seminar discussions) for which they must also read carefully and with great accuracy and understanding. Such reading requirements can be extremely challenging for L2 college students, so EAP instructors must build skills and strategies that can provide ongoing support for these crucial literacy tasks (see also Chapter 11).

Space does not permit me to detail all of the stages of intensive reading instruction and all of the many lesson options that instructors have (but see, for example, Aebersold & Field, 1997; Grabe, 2009; Hedgcock & Ferris, 2009; Seymour & Walsh, 2006; and Chapters 9 and 11), so I will simply list several important strategic areas that teachers might want to highlight in their course designs and lesson planning:

- previewing a text before reading it closely;
- using active reading strategies such as highlighting and annotating a text;
- grappling with unfamiliar vocabulary in the text;
- comprehending main ideas and key supporting details (and recording them through answers to guiding questions and/or outlining them in graphic organizers);

- summarizing, responding to, and critically analyzing the ideas/arguments in a text;
- analyzing the language (word choices, tone, style, and syntax) of a text that has already been carefully read for content;
- making reading/writing connections by incorporating ideas into students' own texts using summary, paraphrase, and quotation.

In an integrated multi-skills EAP course or a composition course, an instructor might not be able to spend as much time on intensive reading activities as in a class that focuses exclusively on reading. However, some or all of the above skills and stages should be incorporated systematically and recursively into classroom work on any assigned reading text. Students will have many other classes in the future in which their instructors will simply assume that they can and will read their assignments competently. The EAP class is one setting where effective intensive reading strategies can be explicitly presented, modeled, and practiced, and doing so is arguably one of the most important goals of such a course.

Build Receptive and Productive Vocabulary

Inadequate vocabulary can create challenges for multilingual students in both reading and writing tasks. Lack of both specific content vocabulary and general academic vocabulary (Coxhead, 2000) can impede reading comprehension (as well as comprehension of lecture material or class discussion). Inadequate vocabulary control in writing can lead to lexical errors or to an immature writing style due to a lack of variety and precision in expression (as we saw with Sunny above). Further, it can be difficult for students to paraphrase and summarize sources well if they do not possess a large enough vocabulary to compose alternate versions of these texts (Folse, 2008; Schuemann, 2008).

Most multilingual students (and, indeed, college students in general) are painfully aware of their gaps in lexical knowledge, but EAP and composition instructors do not always perceive vocabulary development as part of their job (Folse, 2008) and/or do not know how to effectively and authentically integrate vocabulary development into other L2 literacy activities. This section presents several principles and suggestions for instructors to consider (see also Chapter 12).

Receptive Vocabulary/Reading Comprehension

Developing vocabulary awareness and vocabulary learning strategies can and should be an integral part of intensive reading instruction. This can be approached in a variety of ways (see Hedgcock & Ferris, 2009, especially chapters 5 and 8):

- When teachers are *selecting* texts for course syllabi/lessons, they should analyze how much vocabulary in the reading might be unfamiliar to students. If a digital version of the text is available, instructors can use online text analyzers such as the Vocabulary Profiler (www.lextutor.ca) or the AWL (Academic Word List) Highlighter (www.nottingham.ac.uk/alzsh3/acvocab/awlhighlighter.htm). Such tools can help teachers determine whether a text might be too difficult for students and/or what vocabulary items they might want to emphasize or help students with.

- Teachers may wish to *preview*, *preteach*, or *gloss* the key vocabulary in assigned readings that they want students to pay special attention to and/or that they think might cause reading comprehension difficulties. Glosses can be provided in a separate document or in the margins of the text (if feasible given the format).

- As part of the intensive reading process (for homework or in-class activities), students can be asked to *identify, analyze, research,* and *record* new or unfamiliar vocabulary in an assigned text, not only to learn the new words themselves and facilitate reading comprehension, but also to heighten their awareness of lexical choices that authors make in constructing texts (see Ferris, 2011, 2014; Ferris & Hedgcock, 2014).

- Once students have read a text for content/ideas and have analyzed their own unfamiliar vocabulary items, a follow-up class discussion can help them pay attention to how the author uses lexical choices to emphasize key arguments or convey tone (anger, humor, irony/sarcasm, etc.).

- Students can be asked, as part of assigned extensive/intensive reading assignments, to maintain a vocabulary log so that they can consciously practice vocabulary-learning strategies (identify/analyze/research/record) while reading.

Productive Vocabulary

It can be even more challenging for instructors to know how to help students achieve greater lexical variety and precision in their own writing. However, doing so is very important because (1) an underdeveloped vocabulary can undermine writing quality, (2 lexical errors can impede comprehensibility of student texts, and (3) a lack of effective paraphrasing strategies can lead to charges of student plagiarism. There are several authentic ways that students' active vocabulary development can be supported:[1]

1. Help students notice how writers use precise and compelling word choice to convey meaning and add variety and interest to a text.
2. Help students identify useful vocabulary for a specific writing task. When students receive a writing assignment, whether for an EAP/writing class or for a course in the disciplines, they must generate content by reading

sources carefully, collecting other types of data, or generating relevant personal experiences or observations. Similarly, students should be encouraged to generate key vocabulary for a specific piece of writing.

3. Once students have drafted and revised a text, they can be led through editing workshops (as in-class activities or for homework) to examine their own texts (or those of peers) for accurate, effective, and varied word choice. They can be directed to examine their texts-in-progress for repetitive word choice (some is good for cohesion; too much can seem simplistic or dull), especially action or reporting verbs such as *suggest, claim, note, argue,* etc. They can also be taught to look for words that can inflate claims (*very, extremely, always*) or create vagueness or ambiguity (*this, it*). Appropriate usage of word-processing and online analysis tools can be very beneficial at this stage of self-editing (see also Chapters 12 and 13).

4. Teachers should also help students avoid common errors that can arise from students trying to achieve lexical variety without having adequate control of the vocabulary forms. For example, students sometimes inadvertently plagiarize because they are trying to add variation or sound more academic. Also, students should be trained to watch out for "thesaurus errors," which can include grammatical gaffes (caused by not understanding the syntactic constraints of synonyms), inaccurate substitutions, and ineffective register choices.

For many students, being encouraged to notice lexical choices in other authors' texts and to self-evaluate their own vocabulary usage, while being provided with some practical tools for doing so, can make a substantial short-term difference in their ability to read course texts accurately and to write more effectively. While substantive vocabulary growth takes time (and extensive exposure to written texts), instructors should not give up on helping students develop sustainable and transferable vocabulary-learning strategies that they can use right away (see also Chapter 12).

Improve Fluency and Accuracy in Writing

Fluency

Many multilingual students, depending upon their primary and secondary educational pathways, may have had limited experience with writing at length in English. First-year composition courses with word requirements such as 6,000 words in a 10-week quarter or 8,000 words in a 15-week semester may appear extremely daunting to students with little or no experience in that quantity of text production.

EAP instructors preparing students for such challenging requirements can support the development of students' written fluency in a variety of ways:

1. *Ask students to write frequently in class.* Students should write in class, if not daily, very consistently. Such writing can consist of a variety of low-stakes tasks such as freewrites on course content, reflections on class activities, and prewriting exercises for a longer paper. While such activities have other goals as well, the key point here is to help students become more comfortable with writing often and *especially* without worrying in that moment about perfection/accuracy.
2. *Consider speed/timed writing as a regular class activity.* I mentioned freewrites in the previous item; the scope of these exercises can be formalized, if desired, so that students regularly write for the same amount of time (say 5, 10, or 15 minutes), and then count and chart their word production to see if they can generate more text through repeated practice.
3. *Have students keep a journal as a homework assignment.* Journaling or blogging is one way for students to practice writing in English in a low-stress and enjoyable way. Students and instructors can decide whether such activities should be private (between the student and instructor only), for the class (class discussion board, wiki, or blog), or public (a blog on a platform such as Word Press). Besides giving students writing practice to develop fluency, such activities can also be an effective way to discuss target audiences.
4. *Ensure that students have appropriate scaffolding to generate content for formal writing assignments.* Beginning college students, regardless of language background, may struggle with assignments such as "write a 1,500-word paper on…" for two distinct but related reasons: (a) they do not allot enough time for the task, and (b) they do not adequately generate content (from texts or other sources) to have enough to write about. A well-planned assignment will walk students through prewriting and drafting stages on a carefully designed timeline that will allow and require students to read carefully, generate ideas, plan their papers, and write and revise drafts. If students have adequate time and enough content, they should be able to meet the word counts for assigned papers.

The common element in the above suggestions is that students should be asked to write regularly for a variety of situations and purposes—but in low-risk situations where they do not feel pressure to be perfect on their first attempts. Many college writers, especially multilingual students, associate school-based writing with high-stakes testing (see Chapter 15). Helping them see, through experience, that writing can and should be a perfectly normal, everyday activity will defuse anxiety and build confidence.

Accuracy

While helping students build fluency, lower anxiety, and raise confidence and self-esteem about their writing are extremely important goals for EAP writing courses, it is also crucial to help students learn transferable strategies for monitoring and self-editing their written work and for making accurate and effective language choices in their writing for a range of rhetorical situations (see Chapter 8). The question of whether instructors' feedback on students' language errors is beneficial or harmful to their writing development has been a controversial one over the past 20 years, but recent lines of research suggest that, carefully implemented, error treatment (Ferris, 2011; Hendrickson, 1980) can facilitate more accurate written production and facilitate ongoing second language acquisition (see van Beuningen, de Jong, & Kuiken, 2012; Bitchener & Ferris, 2012; Ferris et al., 2013; Hartshorn et al., 2010). According to the most current research findings, error feedback and other classroom support can help students improve their written accuracy and develop self-editing strategies under several important conditions:

- Feedback on student papers should generally be *selective* rather than comprehensive so that students can focus on a few errors at a time.
- Feedback should be *focused* (on specific patterns of error) rather than unfocused (simply marking whatever error/problem the teacher notices).
- Feedback should include *explicit metalinguistic information* about the error so that the student writer learns more about the L2 from the feedback. (This can take a variety of forms, such as explanations in the margins or in an endnote, links to handbook explanations, etc.).
- Feedback should primarily focus on *"treatable" patterns of error* (i.e., issues about which students can study/learn rules) rather than idiosyncratic issues (e.g., preposition errors).
- Feedback should be *followed up* with opportunities for students to ask questions about their errors (in class or in a conference with a teacher or tutor), to revise or rewrite their texts based upon the corrections, and to reflect upon or analyze what they have learned about their own error patterns.
- In addition to receiving error feedback from the teacher, students should receive *explicit strategy training* on finding and correcting their own errors so that they can move towards greater autonomy and control in this area (see Ferris, 2011; Ferris & Hedgcock, 2014; also see Chapter 8 for an extended discussion of this point).
- Students may also benefit from a procedure known as *dynamic written corrective feedback* (DWCF; see Hartshorn et al., 2010), in which they write short texts frequently (even daily), receive immediate correction, revise the texts until they are error-free, and chart their progress. DWCF allows students to focus consistently on a smaller piece of text (a paragraph or so) so that they can attend to and analyze their own language errors more effectively.
- Teachers can provide classroom *mini-lessons* targeted to the students' needs (common errors that the teacher has noticed and/or language forms that students may need for a particular writing task). These lessons should not

only present rules but also give students focused opportunities to apply new language knowledge to in-progress or completed texts of their own. Such lessons can be a useful complement to individualized error feedback (see Ferris, 2011, 2014; Ferris & Hedgcock, 2014).

- In-class *peer- and self-editing workshops* can be useful ways for students to practice self-editing strategies that they can use in the future (for more guidelines on using such workshops successfully, see Ferris, 2011; Ferris & Hedgcock, 2014).

Addressing accuracy and facilitating ongoing second language acquisition in student writing is a challenging endeavor that requires thoughtful planning to do well. Haphazard, decontextualized grammar exercises will not bear much fruit, nor will excessive but unfocused correction/line-editing of student texts. However, it can be done, and student success in academic literacy development depends, in part, upon programs' and teachers' effective implementation of strategies to foster accuracy in students' writing.

Develop Transferable Strategies

In the above three sections, the word "strategies" has been used frequently—intensive reading strategies, vocabulary learning strategies, and self-editing strategies. The job of both EAP and composition courses is to provide students with both skills and metacognitive/metalinguistic awareness of the productive and proactive steps that they can take to be successful in a variety of general education and major courses in the future (see also Chapter 8). In addition to improving their strategies in the three areas (reading, vocabulary, and editing) already discussed, students should learn *rhetorical analysis strategies*—the ability to engage in a broad range of academic and professional writing contexts and respond successfully to the genre and audience expectations within a given task or writing activity (see Carroll, 2010). They should also develop effective *collaboration strategies*—learning to work with peers on jointly constructed, written texts—and *digital/multimodal strategies*—at minimum, using computer-based (word-processor) tools and online tools to facilitate reading and writing development and to build research skills (see also Chapter 14).

Entire books could be written about such strategy/skill areas and how to facilitate the development of each, but for the purposes of this section, I will simply discuss some common principles for strategy training of different types, specifically for the purpose of developing transferable knowledge and skills. First, strategy training must be *explicit*. Rather than, for example, teachers just providing reading or vocabulary exercises and hoping that students will induce some strategies from the practice, teachers must present strategies to students in very transparent ways. (For instance: "In this course, we are going to practice the following strategies for learning and applying new vocabulary in your reading and writing for school: [list of strategies].") The students should be reminded early and often that these are not just activities to pass the time in their EAP or writing class; these activities can be applied to all of their other coursework. Ideally, they could even be assigned to practice the newly learned strategies with assignments for other courses in other disciplines.

Second, strategy training should be *individualized*. Most students have different strengths and weaknesses in reading, in vocabulary learning, and in monitoring their own written production for errors. Instructors should allot time at the beginning of EAP/writing courses to diagnose student needs and to ask students to self-identify what they should work on and set goals. Third, strategy development should be *measured*. Once students' individual needs in different strategic areas have been identified, the students should keep track of their progress. Depending on the type of strategy, this can be done through checklists, questionnaires, charts, or responses to reflection questions. Finally, strategy learning should be *transferable*. Research in composition (e.g., Beaufort, 2007; Downs & Wardle, 2007) has highlighted several variables that appear to facilitate skills transfer: *reflection* (metacognition) and *mastery of key terms* (metalanguage). Students who finish EAP/writing courses should be able to articulate specifically what they have learned about reading, writing, and vocabulary development—ideally using important terms that were explicitly presented and practiced throughout the course (e.g., *genre, cohesion*, etc.)—and to discuss how they will use the strategies that they have learned in the future.

Improve Confidence

As discussed in the opening sections, multilingual students pursuing degrees at U.S. universities face daunting academic challenges. Most also face external pressures such as finances (needing to work part-time or loading up on classes to graduate quickly and save their parents money), parental expectations, and the social/emotional adjustments that all young adults face in college, but these external pressures are often exacerbated for L2 students because they are members of a minority group or because they feel isolated/unwanted as international students. EAP/writing instructors cannot address all of these problems, but they can be sensitive to them and not make matters worse for students. Instead, they should support students by thoughtfully and intentionally boosting their confidence.

Many of the specific suggestions in the previous sections will work towards building students' self-esteem. In addition, instructors can build morale and confidence in other important ways, such as how they assess students, what types of tasks they assign, and how they provide feedback. EAP and writing classes should bias for best rather than promoting a culture of failure. Among other things, "bias for best" means assessing their proficiency as readers and writers through multiple measures (see Chapter 15; CCCC, 2009; Crusan,

2010; Ferris, 2009) taken at different times and under different conditions rather than grading solely or primarily on stressful, high-stakes timed writing examinations. Adversarial testing environments demoralize and demotivate students—not just at the end of the course but throughout the term as their anxiety and fear of failure increase. Such environments certainly do not build confidence, and in an academic environment where L2 students already face daunting challenges on multiple levels, their EAP/writing class should be a supportive space, not a hostile one.

Instructors can also build confidence by giving students opportunities to grapple with a wide range of reading and writing tasks that become progressively more challenging as the term proceeds and/or as students reach higher levels of instruction. Many EAP or multilingual writing courses simply ask students to write the same type of generic expository/persuasive essay repeatedly on different topics. Similarly, instructors often select reading texts that are short and simple so that students are not overwhelmed and/or so that they are engaged or interested. It can be difficult for teachers to design a range of writing assignments and to select and scaffold reading tasks so that students make progress. However, students will actually gain more confidence through completing a variety of tasks with gradually increased difficulty than through completing simple, repetitive tasks.

Third, teachers should give feedback to students, whether oral or written, very carefully. Some instructors are too harsh or too critical with students, and a paper covered with pen marks or tracked changes can undermine students' confidence even if the teacher does not say anything unkind. Other teachers are too nice or too hands-off, not wanting to discourage students or "take over" the writing process (see Reid, 1994). Students need expert support and feedback to develop and improve their academic literacy skills, and the EAP/writing class is the place for them to receive that support. In short, building confidence should be a conscious objective for classroom teachers, as every type of instructional decision and interaction with students can either develop students' self-esteem or tear it down.

Summary

This chapter has discussed the challenges of academic literacy faced by multilingual writers at U.S. colleges and universities and has discussed five principles that programs and instructors should consider for supporting these students' continued literacy development. Specifically:

• Multilingual college writers face the dual challenge of ongoing second language acquisition and developing college-level literacy skills. Because of differing educational pathways (from each other and from monolingual English-speaking peers), they may have gaps in fluency (the ability to read and write lengthy texts), in reading and vocabulary learning strategies, and in linguistic control of their writing (accuracy and style). These various gaps may also lower their confidence, leading to anxiety and self-esteem issues.

- Teachers and programs should give students practice in both extensive and intensive reading. Extensive reading builds students' fluency, vocabulary, and a range of other language/literacy benefits. Intensive reading builds students' effective skills and strategies for grappling with the academic texts that they will have to read carefully and critically.

- EAP and writing classes should support students in developing strategies for building their receptive vocabulary through reading. Teachers should also be intentional about helping students apply vocabulary knowledge accurately and effectively to their own writing.

- EAP/writing courses should be designed to help students build both fluency and accuracy in their writing. Fluency can be promoted by asking students to write frequently in low-risk, intrinsically motivating situations. Accuracy can be improved through effective teacher feedback strategies, through strategy training, and through carefully designed language mini-lessons.

- Programs should prioritize student development of transferable strategies that will carry them through and beyond the EAP and composition program into other classes and professional settings. Strategy training should include explicit instruction, individual goal setting, evaluation of progress, and development of metacognitive- and metalinguistic-awareness strategies. Most importantly, this training should emphasize how such strategies could be applied elsewhere.

- Promoting and developing students' confidence should be a conscious goal of programs and courses designed to support students in facing the challenges of academic literacy. Confidence can be built through a range of teacher/program choices about assessment strategies, reading and writing tasks, and feedback strategies. The keys to building student morale are both understanding and empathizing with the challenges that multilingual students face and also developing positive and strategic approaches to help them succeed.

The challenges these students face are daunting when one stops to consider them, but a thoughtful and carefully designed approach to their academic literacy development that considers the suggestions presented here will go a long way towards equipping ESL students for short- and long-term success in their studies.

Discussion Questions

1. Consider the opening anecdote about Sunny and the ways in which her writing may fall short of meeting her academic goals. Have you had students similar to Sunny? From your own experience and observation, can you think of other stories and other challenges that such students face?

2. The section on the challenges of academic literacy outlines the specific ways in which multilingual writers may face even greater barriers to success than other students (monolingual/native English speakers) face in college. Do you disagree with any of these? Would you add anything, and if so, what?

3. The support section outlines five specific ways that programs and teachers can help multilingual students prepare for the challenges of academic literacy. Were any of these new to you or a surprise to you? Are there any suggestions you disagree with, and if so, why? Are there ideas that you would like to learn more about?

4. While the first three support topics (on reading, vocabulary, and fluency/accuracy in writing) are fairly typical ones, what about the final two (on transferable strategies and confidence)? Are these ideas that you have explicitly considered before? Do you agree with the emphasis placed on these two issues? Why or why not?

5. As an application activity for this chapter, obtain a copy of either a course syllabus/description for an EAP literacy course and/or a commonly used textbook for such a course. Look through it and evaluate to what extent the syllabus or textbook addresses the suggestions in this chapter. You can use the chart below to take notes.

TASK 10.1

Topic	Extensive and Intensive Reading	Receptive and Productive Vocabulary	Fluency and Accuracy in Writing	Transferable Strategies	Building Student Confidence
How does this syllabus or text address this issue? (Write "none" if it doesn't or include notes/page numbers if it does.)					

Note

1. The suggestions in this section are adapted from Ferris and Hedgcock (2014, pp. 328–335). See also tutorials 4, 6, 12, and 13 in Ferris (2014).

Further Reading

Andrade, M. S., & Evans, N. W. (2012). *Principles and practices for response in second language writing: Developing self-regulated learners.* New York, NY: Routledge.
Beaufort, A. (2007). *College writing and beyond: A new framework for university writing instruction.* Logan, UT: Utah State University Press.
Ferris, D. (2009). *Teaching college writing to diverse student populations.* Ann Arbor, MI: University of Michigan Press.
Grabe, W., & Stoller, F. (2011). *Teaching and researching reading* (2nd ed.). Harlow: Longman/Pearson Education.
Reid, J. M. (Ed.) (2008). *Writing myths: Applying second language research to classroom teaching.* Ann Arbor, MI: University of Michigan Press.
Zimmerman, C. B. (2008). *Word knowledge: A vocabulary teacher's handbook.* Oxford: Oxford University Press.

References

Aebersold, J., & Field, M. (1997). *From reader to reading teacher: Issues and strategies for second language classrooms.* Cambridge, MA: Cambridge University Press.
Beaufort, A. (2007). *College writing and beyond: A new framework for university writing instruction.* Logan, UT: Utah State University Press.
van Beuningen, C., de Jong, N. H., & Kuiken, F. (2012). Evidence on the effectiveness of comprehensive error correction in second language writing. *Language Learning, 62*(1), 1–41.
Bitchener, J., & Ferris, D. (2012). *Written corrective feedback in second language acquisition and writing.* New York, NY: Routledge.
Carroll, L. B. (2010). Backpacks vs. briefcases: Steps toward rhetorical analysis. In C. Lowe & P. Zemliansky (Eds.), *Writing spaces: Readings on writing* (Vol. 1, pp. 45–58). Retrieved April 23, 2014, from www.parlorpress.com/pdf/carroll-backpacks-vs-briefcases.pdf.
Conference on College Composition and Communication (CCCC). (2009). *Statement on second language writing and writers.* Retrieved April 23, 2014, from www.ncte.org/cccc/resources/positions/secondlangwriting.
Coxhead, A. (2000). A new academic word list. *TESOL Quarterly, 34*(2), 213–238.
Coxhead, A. (2006). *Essentials of teaching academic vocabulary.* Boston, MA: Houghton Mifflin.
Crusan, D. (2010). *Assessment in the second language writing classroom.* Ann Arbor, MI: University of Michigan Press.
Day, R. R., & Bamford, J. (1998). *Extensive reading in the second language classroom.* New York, NY: Cambridge University Press.
Downs, D., & Wardle, E. (2007). Teaching about writing, righting misconceptions: (Re)envisioning "first-year composition" as "introduction to writing studies." *College Composition and Communication, 58*, 552–584.
Eskey, D. E. (1986). Theoretical foundations. In F. Dubin, D. E. Eskey, & W. Grabe (Eds.), *Teaching second language reading for academic purposes* (pp. 3–23). Reading, MA: Addison-Wesley.
Ferris, D. R. (1999). One size does not fit all: Response and revision issues for immigrant student writers. In L. Harklau, K. Losey, & M. Siegal (Eds.), *Generation 1.5 meets college composition* (pp. 143–157). Mahwah, NJ: Erlbaum.

Ferris, D. R. (2009). *Teaching college writing to diverse student populations.* Ann Arbor, MI: University of Michigan Press.

Ferris, D. R. (2011). *Treatment of error in second language student writing* (2nd ed.). Ann Arbor, MI: University of Michigan Press.

Ferris, D. R. (2014). *Language power: Tutorials for writers.* Boston, MA: Bedford/St. Martin's.

Ferris, D. R., & Hedgcock, J. S. (2014). *Teaching L2 composition: Purpose, process, and practice* (3rd ed.). New York, NY: Routledge.

Ferris, D. R., Liu, H., Sinha, A., & Senna, M. (2013). Written corrective feedback and individual L2 writers. *Journal of Second Language Writing, 22,* 428–429.

Folse, K. S. (2004). *Vocabulary myths.* Ann Arbor, MI: University of Michigan Press.

Folse, K. S. (2008). Myth 1: Teaching vocabulary is not the writing teacher's job. In J. Reid (Ed.), *Writing myths: Applying second language research to classroom teaching* (pp. 1–17). Ann Arbor, MI: University of Michigan Press.

Grabe, W. (2009). *Reading in a second language: Moving from theory to practice.* Cambridge: Cambridge University Press.

Grabe, W., & Stoller, F. (2011). *Teaching and researching reading* (2nd ed.). Harlow: Longman/Pearson Education.

Harklau, L., Losey, K. & Siegal, M. (Eds.) (1999). *Generation 1.5 meets college composition: Issues in the teaching of writing to U.S.-educated learners of ESL.* Mahwah, NJ: Lawrence Erlbaum Associates.

Hartshorn, J. K., Evans, N. W., Merrill, P. F., Sudweeks, R. R., Strong-Krause, D., & Anderson, N. J. (2010). The effects of dynamic corrective feedback on ESL writing accuracy. *TESOL Quarterly, 44*(1), 84–109.

Hedgcock, J., & Ferris, D. (2009). *Teaching readers of English: Students, texts, and contexts.* New York, NY: Routledge.

Hendrickson, J. M. (1980). The treatment of error in written work. *Modern Language Journal, 64,* 216–221.

Krashen, S. D. (2004). *The power of reading: Insights from the research* (2nd ed.). Portsmouth, NH: Heinemann.

Reid, J. (1994). Responding to ESL students' texts: The myths of appropriation. *TESOL Quarterly, 28*(2), 273–292.

Roberge, M. M. (2002). California's Generation 1.5 immigrants: What experiences, characteristics, and needs do they bring to our English classes? *CATESOL Journal, 14*(1), 107–129.

Roberge, M. M. (2009). A teacher's perspective on Generation 1.5. In M. M. Roberge, M. Siegal, & L. Harklau (Eds.), *Generation 1.5 in college composition* (pp. 3–24). New York, NY: Routledge.

Roberge, M. M., Siegal, M., & Losey, K. (Eds.) (2009). *Generation 1.5 in college composition.* New York, NY: Routledge.

Schuemann, C. M. (2008). Myth 2: Teaching citation is someone else's job. In J. Reid (Ed.), *Writing myths: Applying second language research to classroom teaching* (pp. 18–40). Ann Arbor, MI: University of Michigan Press.

Seymour, S., & Walsh, L. (2006). *Essentials of teaching academic reading.* Boston, MA: Houghton Mifflin.

Silva, T. (1993). Toward an understanding of the distinct nature of L2 writing: The ESL research and its implications. *TESOL Quarterly, 27*(4), 657–677.

Zimmerman, C. B. (2008). *Word knowledge: A vocabulary teacher's handbook.* Oxford: Oxford University Press.

11

ASSISTING ESP STUDENTS IN READING AND WRITING DISCIPLINARY GENRES

Fredricka L. Stoller and Marin S. Robinson

Vignette

Consider an English as a second language (ESL) student who is a chemistry major and who has successfully completed her first two years of college, aided by introductory text-books and lab manuals. As she begins her third year, imagine her surprise when she is faced with a text like this:

> **Reagents and Materials.** *The PCB congeners, 2,4,4'-trichlorobiphenyl (PCB-28), 2,2',5,5'-tetrachlorobiphenyl (PCB-52), 2,2',4,5,5'-pentachlorobiphenyl (PCB-101), 2,3,3',4,4'-pentachlorobiphenyl (PCB-105), 2,3',4,4',5-pentachlorobiphenyl (PCB-118), 2,2',3,4,4',5'-hexachlorobiphenyl (PCB-138), 2,2',3,4,4',5'-hexachlorobiphenyl (PCB-153), 2,3,3',4,4',5'-hexachlorobiphenyl (PCB-156), and 2,2',3,4,4',5,5'-heptachlorobiphenyl (PCB-180) (PCB numbering according to IUPAC) were supplied by Ultra Scientific (North Kings-town, RI).*
>
> Llompart, Pazos, Landín, & Cela, 2001, p. 5859

This "surprise" is not unique to chemistry majors; it occurs in all disciplines as students transition from introductory coursework to more advanced classes in their majors. Navigating this academic juncture is difficult for all students, but particularly for ESL learners whose reading abilities make it challenging for them to access, learn, apply, and critique course content. Moreover, they have trouble writing for their disciplines because they lack awareness of the linguistic and nonlinguistic conventions that must coalesce for their written work to be effective.

Introduction and Overview of the Challenges

ESL students encounter numerous challenges as they navigate through their studies. These students' trials and tribulations often begin well before they enter college, when, for example, they are high-school students seeking advice from college counselors, taking standardized college-entrance exams (e.g., SAT, TOEFL), and completing college-application materials (Hafernik & Wiant, 2012; Kanno & Harklau, 2012). Additional challenges arise as students transition from high school to college (Bunch & Endris, 2012; Harklau, 2000; Johns, 1997; see also Evans & Morrison, 2011), from introductory to discipline-specific courses (Johns, 2007; Karukstis & Elgren, 2007; Leki, 2007), and from undergraduate to graduate programs (Swales & Feak, 2012). As students progress in their studies, they will need to read and write more strategically. Furthermore, they will (1) encounter new written and spoken genres, (2) complete more challenging tasks, (3) display and/or apply what they have learned in diverse ways, and (4) find that their instructors' expectations become more demanding. All tertiary-level students (native and nonnative speakers) experience the shifting demands of the college experience, but ESL students experience added pressures associated with less fluent reading and writing, limited vocabulary, the need to coordinate listening with note taking, and varied interpretations of classroom experiences that stem from their different educational and cultural backgrounds (Andrade, 2006).

Many of these challenges are exacerbated by institutional policies and practices (or their absence). For example, student-learning centers do not always have tutors trained to work with nonnative English speakers. Faculty who find themselves with increasing numbers of nonnative speakers in their classes may not recognize (or accept) the responsibility to adjust their teaching and assessment practices to reach these students (Horning, 2013; Snow & Kamhi-Stein, 2002). Furthermore, explicit literacy-skills instruction is oftentimes confined to students' early college semesters (e.g., first-year composition). Such is the case in the sciences where literacy-skills development is typically not part of doing and learning science (Learning to speak and write, 2001). The lack of institutional attention to students' evolving literacy needs (cf. institutions with a commitment to Writing Across the Curriculum) puts all students, including ESL students, at a disadvantage (Hyland, 2004a, 2004b).

Despite these institutional "deficiencies," efforts are being made by professionals in applied linguistics and other disciplines to address the challenges that students face as they transition from general English to English for academic purposes (EAP) and English for specific purposes (ESP). Research in the following areas is particularly pertinent:

- EAP and ESP (Belcher, 2009; Belcher, Johns, & Paltridge, 2011; de Chazal, 2014; Paltridge & Starfield, 2013; Tang, 2012);

- disciplinary genres and genre-based writing (Cheng, 2006; Hyland & Bondi, 2006; Nesi & Gardner, 2012; Paltridge, 2001; Robinson, Stoller, Costanza-Robinson, & Jones, 2008; Swales, 1990, 2004; Swales & Feak, 2011; Tardy, 2009; Wingate, 2012);
- reading–writing relations (Grabe & Zhang, 2013a, 2013b; Hirvela, 2004; Horning & Kraemer, 2013); and
- scientific literacy (Moskovitz & Kellog, 2011; Norris & Phillips, 2003).

In this chapter we focus on students' transition from general academic literacy skills to discipline-specific reading and writing. This shift typically occurs in the junior (third) year, as students complete introductory coursework and declare their majors, and again when students enter graduate school. It is at these two academic junctures that students encounter disciplinary genres that require ESP. How can we support students who are in need of ESP? Here, we explore a *read–analyze and write* instructional approach as a viable form of assistance for students making these vital transitions. We conclude with an examination of challenges that ESP educators often face and suggest solutions that involve collaboration with professionals from target discourse communities.

Read–Analyze and Write as Instructional Support

Students who are transitioning from general academic English to ESP benefit from recognizing the defining characteristics of key disciplinary genres. For instance, students in engineering need to develop reading and writing skills associated with design reports, whereas students in the sciences need to develop reading and writing skills associated with research genres (e.g., posters, proposals, journal articles). ESP students often learn to read and write for their disciplines through trial and error by reading material from target genres and then figuring out on their own how to write them. Although most students succeed with this read-to-write approach, it is inefficient (not to mention frustrating). In its place, we propose an iterative read–analyze and write approach, which we describe in the following sections with examples from chemistry, although parallels can certainly be drawn to other disciplines.

This iterative read–analyze and write approach was developed for the Write Like a Chemist project (Robinson et al., 2008).[1] This straightforward approach combines the reading of authentic passages from target genres (entire texts, full sections, excerpts, and textual elements, such as figures and tables) with analyses; in this way, students gain a better understanding of the defining linguistic, non-linguistic, and organizational features of the target genres (in our context, journal articles, proposals, conference abstracts, and posters). Specifically, students are guided in their analyses by five essential writing components: audience and purpose, organization, field-specific writing conventions, grammar and mechanics, and content. By analyzing writing across these five dimensions (as discussed in more detail below), students learn to identify and appreciate the different aspects of writing that are required for their work to meet disciplinary expectations. Instructionally, these five components offer students (and instructors) a manageable way to break down larger analytic tasks into smaller, more achievable goals.

After reading and analyzing multiple examples of the target genre (and its parts), students begin to write, with teacher and peer feedback, using excerpts as models. While writing, students will likely return to the sample texts for additional rounds of reading and analysis to check and verify disciplinary practices or to seek further insights into the genre that they are trying to emulate. By means of this iterative cycle (depicted in Figure 11.1)—accompanied by explicit instruction, discussion, practice, feedback, and time—students develop the skills needed for access to and control of the genres that will be important for them (Tardy, 2009).

Scaffolding the Approach

Before engaging students in the read–analyze and write approach with target-genre texts, it is helpful to ease students into the process with familiar genres (e.g., menus, used-car ads). Students analyze these "everyday" genres by considering audience and purpose, organization, language, and content. Such tasks are designed to raise students' consciousness about the read–analyze process and help them begin examining written work through new eyes. After reading and analyzing everyday genres, students read and analyze writing on familiar yet discipline-specific topics (perhaps encountered in first- or second-year courses). To accomplish this, two articles on the same topic can be juxtaposed, one written by a science writer for a general audience, the other by chemists for an expert audience. Students read and analyze both texts, iteratively, while

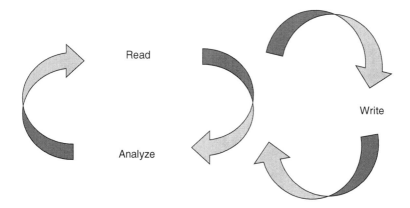

FIGURE 11.1 Depiction of the Read–Analyze and Write Approach.

considering audience and purpose, organization, language, and content. The instructor guides students to discover linguistic and nonlinguistic features that distinguish the two papers. After a class discussion of differences (e.g., experts would be surprised to see a catchy title and direct quotations in a journal article) and similarities, students better understand the need to learn to write for the discipline. This strategy of juxtaposing excerpts written for different audiences also has value later in students' training (as the sample tasks below illustrate).

Such scaffolding prepares students to tackle more intimidating chemistry texts (as shown in the vignette above). Initially, students are asked to scan an entire text of the target genre to notice, for example, standard sections (e.g., Introduction, Methods, Results, and Discussion sections in journal articles) and the formatting of section headings (e.g., bolded). From there, students read and analyze distinct parts of the target genre (e.g., title, abstract, and introduction) to discover how they differ across the five essential writing components. As students become more familiar with the expectations of the discipline, they are prompted to write sections of the genre using the analyzed excerpts as models.

As another form of scaffolding, read–analyze and write activities can be sequenced to parallel authors' (not readers') practices. Unlike readers, writers do not always start at the beginning. Thus, with the journal-article genre, instructors can begin with excerpts from the Methods (M) section, followed by excerpts from Results (R), Discussion (D), and Introduction (I) sections, paralleling a typical (chemistry) author's path. In line with this thinking, students can be guided in analyzing abstracts and titles last because they are often written last. There are numerous reasons for starting with the Methods section, as suggested here, including the following: (1) Methods sections are often the most formulaic and, hence, the easiest for students to grasp; (2) many chemists (as we have learned through interviews) begin writing their papers with this section; and (3) in writing their own mock journal articles, students are most familiar with their own research methods. Thus, this is the section that they are most prepared to write first.

Reading and Analyzing for Five Essential Elements of Writing

The five essential elements of writing that guide students' genre analyses are identified in Table 11.1. Our refinement of the components is based on analyses of our students' writing needs, disciplinary expectations as set forth in the American Chemical Society's *ACS Style Guide* (Coghill & Garson, 2006), and extensive analyses (including corpus and move analyses) of target genres. Each component is described in more detail below, using tasks adapted from Robinson et al. (2008) to illustrate effective practices.

TABLE 11.1 Five Essential Components of Writing, with Focal Points for Chemistry Students

Audience and Purpose	Organization	Writing Conventions	Grammar and Mechanics	Science Content
Conciseness	Broad structure	Abbreviations and	Parallelism	Graphics
Level of detail	Fine structures	acronyms	Punctuation	Text
Level of formality	(i.e., moves)	Formatting	Subject–verb	
Word choice		Verb tense	agreement	
		Voice	Word usage	

Source: Adaptation of Table 1.1 in *Write Like a Chemist: A Guide and Resource* (Robinson et al., 2008, p. 7). By permission of Oxford University Press, USA.

Audience and Purpose

To write effectively, students must know for whom they are writing. In our courses, we instruct students to write for an expert audience (when writing a mock journal article) and a scientific audience (when writing a research proposal, conference abstract, or poster). Guided by results from needs assessments and corpus analyses, we have identified areas of writing that will improve students' ability to write for these audiences: conciseness, detail, formality, and word choice. For example, chemistry students often include too much detail in their writing (e.g., they describe how to weigh a sample) or too little (e.g., they omit compound purity). Thus, we ask students to examine target-genre excerpts for level of detail (Task 11.1) and to indicate what details are appropriate for a journal article's Methods section (Task 11.2). We ask students to repeat the latter task before and after they have read and analyzed several Methods sections.

Our needs analysis also revealed that chemistry students frequently use imperatives in their writing (e.g., "Reflux the mixture for 30 min.") rather than the more formal language appropriate for a journal article (e.g., "The mixture was refluxed for 30 min."). Thus, students can be asked to rewrite a list of procedures, written with imperatives, in a more formal style. Similarly, we ask students to substitute everyday words (e.g., see, find out) used in sentences adapted from the target genre with more formal (and scientific) words (e.g., monitor, analyze, investigate).

Task 11.1: Compare the following three excerpts that describe X. The first is adapted from an undergraduate lab manual. The other two, written for expert audiences, are from the *Journal of Organic Chemistry*. What details are included for the expert audience? What details are excluded?

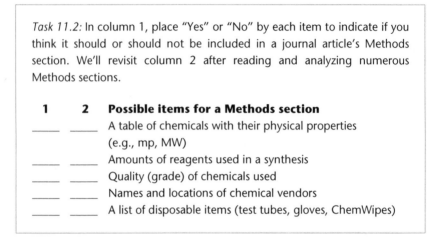

Task 11.2: In column 1, place "Yes" or "No" by each item to indicate if you think it should or should not be included in a journal article's Methods section. We'll revisit column 2 after reading and analyzing numerous Methods sections.

1	2	**Possible items for a Methods section**
____	____	A table of chemicals with their physical properties (e.g., mp, MW)
____	____	Amounts of reagents used in a synthesis
____	____	Quality (grade) of chemicals used
____	____	Names and locations of chemical vendors
____	____	A list of disposable items (test tubes, gloves, ChemWipes)

After students learn to identify audience and purpose in the target genre, they can be asked to determine which section (I, M, R, or D) a sample passage comes from. Students can be guided to identify distinctions based on audience (e.g., the level of detail included in a textbook passage versus a journal article; see Task 11.3) or purpose (e.g., to *describe* data in a Results section or *interpret* data in a Discussion section; see Task 11.4).

With activities such as these, ESP students notice how authors write to reach their intended audiences, achieve the overall purpose of the genre, and attain the more specific purposes (and even slightly different audiences) of the sections within them.

Task 11.3: Each of the following passages is about X. Four are from journal articles (two from Introduction sections and two from Discussion sections), and one is from a textbook. Based on your understanding of the purpose and intended audience of each section and genre, read each passage and decide where it came from. Explain what information you used to make your decisions.

Task 11.4: The following statements are taken from a combined Results and Discussion section of an article that reports on a study of X. For each sentence, decide whether its primary purpose is to describe, interpret, or both.

Organization

Clear organization is indispensable for effective writing. In our classes, we teach and reinforce organization in two ways. First, we emphasize the *broad* organization of texts, often indicated by identifiable sections such as I, M, R, D or I, M, [R&D], the latter indicating a combined Results and Discussion section. Second, we introduce the *fine* organization of texts (or *moves*, following Swales, 1990, 2004) as revealed by typical patterns of organization within paragraphs, between paragraphs, and within sections.

The broad organization is relatively transparent, especially when identifiable (and oftentimes bolded) headings are used. The fine structure is more challenging to discern. To assist students, we introduce easy-to-consult visual representations (i.e., move structures) of the organization of each target-genre section (see Figure 11.2; see also Robinson et al., 2008). Of course, the use of such pedagogical tools requires that ESP instructors analyze target genres to generate move structures that capture common patterns (Stoller & Robinson, 2013). When students recognize broad and fine organizational structures, they become better prepared to read and write the target genre.

Students' grasp of organizational conventions can be reinforced by a variety of pedagogical tasks, including the reordering of jumbled sentences or the activities such as those in Tasks 11.5 and 11.6 (see also Stoller & Robinson, 2014).

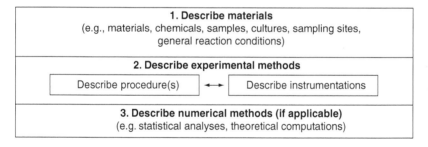

FIGURE 11.2 Move Structure of a Typical Chemistry Journal Article's Methods Section. The two-way arrow in Move 2 signals variable sequencing. *Source:* Fig: 3.1 from *Write Like a Chemist: A Guide and Resource* (Robinson et al., 2008, p. 62). By permission of Oxford University Press, USA.

Task 11.5: Consider the following excerpt. How well does the excerpt adhere to the move structure represented in Figure X? How do the authors use subheadings to help the reader locate the moves? Can you equate each subheading with one of the moves? Are any moves left out? If so, which one(s)?

Task 11.6: Consider the following sentences taken from journal articles' Discussion sections. Although the sentences are presented out of context, specify which submove you think is accomplished in each.

Students can apply the same principles to their analyses of other elements of a written genre, such as journal article titles. What students discover through analyses is that titles follow a pattern similar to that displayed in Table 11.2.

Writing Conventions

Every discipline has its own writing conventions. In applied linguistics, for example, authors typically adhere to conventions detailed in the *Publication Manual of the American Psychological Association* (2010). Chemistry, too, has its own conventions, most notably those presented in *The ACS Style Guide* (Coghill & Garson, 2006). In our classes, students are introduced to writing conventions that are common in chemistry, such as the preferred uses of acronyms, numbers and units, capitalization, passive and active voice,[2] and present and past tense. Writing conventions also dictate how graphics (tables and figures), bibliographical references, and in-line citations are formatted.

Students often view such conventions as trivial, but the lack of adherence to these expectations is an indicator of a novice writer (and is often a pet peeve for instructors). This is true even when no grammatical errors have been committed. For example, it is grammatically correct to write "To the mixture was

TABLE 11.2 The X of Y by Z Pattern in Chemistry Journal Articles' Titles

X *(optional)*		Y *(required)*		Z *(optional)*
A nominalization (e.g., Determination, Investigation, Analysis, Measurement)	of in for to …	What was studied	on in via by using at from …	Target of Y or what was impacted by Y Method used (or detail of method used) to study Y
A phrase that refers to, describes, or modifies Y				
[a] Preparation	of	5-substituted 1*H*-tetrazoles	from	nitriles in water

Source: Adaptation of Table: 7.1 in *Write Like a Chemist: A Guide and Resource* (Robinson et al., 2008, pp. 246–247). By permission of Oxford University Press, USA.

Note
a From Demko and Sharpless (2001, p. 7945).

added ten milliliters of Ethanol," but most chemists expect "To the mixture was added 10 mL of ethanol." The good news is that writing conventions are relatively easy to teach through text analyses and discipline-specific style manual consultation.

Grammar and Mechanics

Target-genre excerpts can be analyzed for grammatical constructions and mechanics (e.g., punctuation). Emphases are most appropriately placed on problems seen in students' written work, such as subject–verb agreement (e.g., the data *suggest*, not suggests), easily confused words (e.g., effect and affect), and the uses of commas, semicolons, and colons. In tandem with text analyses, students can complete instructor-designed exercises with discipline-specific content that will bring these issues to students' attention. Cloze exercises, using target-genre excerpts, are easy to create and useful for consciousness raising and practice.

Content

In chemistry, as in most disciplines, content is expressed in two forms: text (prose) and graphics (e.g., tables, graphs, figures). Effective writers learn to weave back and forth between these two forms in a way that effectively tells a story of scientific discovery. Although the writing skills needed to succeed in this task are complex, read–analyze tasks are helpful. For example, in Task 11.7, students learn, through reading and analysis, that content should not be repeated in the text and graphics, that only *representative* data (not all data) need be shared, that the content ("story") need not be told chronologically (because of false starts and detours), and that conclusions should lead logically from key results.

After students have read and analyzed text samples for the five essential elements of writing, they are ready to begin writing, as described in the next section.

Task 11.7: Read and analyze Excerpt *X* and the accompanying graph. What trends in the graph are highlighted in the text? Are any results repeated in the text and graph? Explain why the authors include only three of seven samples in Figure *X*. How likely is it that these results are in chronological order? What conclusion do you think the authors will draw from these findings?

Writing (after Reading and Analyzing)

No ESP curriculum with writing goals is complete without writing assignments. Such assignments often involve drafting, revising, editing, peer reviewing, and, when needed, returning to model texts for rereading and continued analyses. It is key, of course, for students to have something robust and appropriate to write about. In our classes, students write either about their own undergraduate research projects or a "canned" research project (which is created for students who are not engaged in undergraduate research).

Our approach to writing is also scaffolded, first asking students to remember what they learned during read–analyze tasks and then encouraging them to read and analyze model texts again in light of the writing assignment. Writing tasks are divided into manageable steps—move by move and section by section, along with revisions, peer reviews, continued revisions, and editing. Writing tasks are best linked to observations made during reading and analyzing, as illustrated in Tasks 11.8 and 11.9.

We find it useful to engage students in simulated peer reviews (with mock student texts manipulated by us to highlight writing elements covered and discovered during read–analysis tasks), followed by authentic peer reviews that are guided by peer-evaluation forms.[3] Reinforcing the value of having a new set of eyes review one's written work is important. Asking students to then fine-tune their written work, after receiving feedback from peers and the teacher, rounds out the cycle. To guide final revisions of each section of the genre, we provide students with support in the form of questions about the five essential components of writing. Task 11.10 showcases some of the questions we pose for students' Methods sections.

Task 11.8: Which chemicals, samples, and/or general conditions do you plan to describe in your Methods section? Prepare a list of these items, including information such as vendor, grade, and/or purity. Convert your list into prose, thereby writing the first move (Describe Methods) of your Methods section. Be sure to include an appropriate bolded subheading for this section (e.g., **Chemicals**, **Materials**, or **Samples**).

Task 11.9: In preparation for describing your procedures, create a flow chart outlining the steps that you followed. Cross out steps that are too basic for an expert audience. Organize the remaining steps into a concisely written paragraph, using the sequencing of your sentences to convey the appropriate order. Repeat this process for each procedure. Follow standard conventions for expressing numbers and units.

Task 11.10: Revise your methods section, where appropriate, considering the questions below.

1. **Audience and purpose**. Are you writing for an expert audience, leaving out unnecessary details? Try to find at least three sentences that can be written more concisely. Check for information that should be placed inside parentheses.

2. **Organization**. Check your overall organizational structure. Did you follow the move structure in Figure 11.2 and include appropriate sub-headings? Do your experimental procedures clearly convey the order followed in your work (without using ordinal language)?

3. **Writing conventions**. Check to be sure that you have used voice (mostly passive) and tense (mostly past tense) correctly. Check your formatting of units and numbers, use of abbreviations and acronyms, and capitalization of compounds and vendors.

4. **Grammar and mechanics**. Check your spelling, subject–verb agreement (e.g., the data suggest, not suggests), punctuation, and word usage (e.g., effect vs. affect).

5. **Content**. Have you correctly conveyed the science in your work? Have you used words and units correctly? If asked, could you define all of the words that you have used? Do you understand how the instruments described in your methods section work?

Although space does not permit a full description of how we guide students through the read–analyze and write approach, we hope that this snapshot demonstrates how instructors can provide ESP students with support as they transition from general academic English to disciplinary reading and writing. Although students do not write like professionals at the end of a single course, we have observed measurable improvements and, importantly, raised students' consciousness about (1) the language and genres of their discipline and (2) the skills needed to read and analyze texts to guide their subsequent reading and writing.

Challenges and Solutions for ESP Instructors

The challenges that ESP instructors face, regardless of their instructional approaches, are often linked to their lack of familiarity with (1) students' areas of study, (2) the genres associated with those fields, and (3) students' disciplinary knowledge base. What helped us achieve our aims was having chemists and language professionals working side by side (for more details, see Horn, Stoller, & Robinson, 2008). Our interdisciplinary collaboration allowed us to combine our different knowledge resources to (1) identify and analyze target genres, (2) create instruments (pretests and posttests) to assess student learning, and (3) design instructional materials to be accessible (in terms of language, content, and format) to our target audience. We recommend that ESP instructors seek out professionals in the target discipline to do the same. The combined knowledge resources (i.e., our knowledge of language and language teaching and our colleagues' disciplinary content knowledge) can result in ESP instruction that meets students' present and future needs.

Summary

- ESL students transitioning from general academic English to the discipline-specific English of their majors benefit from ESP instruction.
- An iterative read–analyze and write approach to ESP instruction is effective in giving students access to and control over the genres that they will need to read and write as they progress in their studies.
- ESP instructors are encouraged to collaborate with disciplinary experts to combine knowledge resources to (1) identify key disciplinary genres, (2) analyze them for their defining linguistic and nonlinguistic features, and (3) create instructional materials.
- Even if we cannot predict exactly what students will be reading and writing in their futures, the read–analyze and write approach provides students with analytic tools that will help them determine the disciplinary expectations that must coalesce to produce successful written communication (Johns, 1997, 2007).

Discussion Questions

1. The authors introduce a read–analyze and write approach to ESP instruction using examples from their work with chemistry students. In what ways might the approach have to be modified for students in other disciplines or classes with students from multiple disciplines?
2. Think about what you know about reading and writing. What can you apply from your background knowledge to enhance the read–analyze and write approach introduced in this chapter?
3. If you were to build linkages with professionals in another discipline to enhance your teaching of an ESP class, what would be the ideal characteristics of that interdisciplinary relationship?
4. How have you learned the disciplinary conventions of your field of study? What can you use from your own experience to support your students?

Notes

1. The Write Like a Chemist project was supported by the U.S. National Science Foundation (NSF), with CCLI grants DUE 0087570 and 0230913. The views expressed here are those of the authors and do not necessarily reflect NSF views.
2. ESP students who are prepared to tackle disciplinary genres have typically been introduced to passive and active constructions and know how to "produce" them. But they may not know *when* to use them in target genres. Thus, at this level, tense and voice become a writing-convention issue rather than a grammatical one.
3. See http://global.oup.com/us/companion.websites/9780195305074/student_resources/forms/ for sample peer-review forms.

Further Reading

Grabe, W., & Zhang, C. (2013). Reading and writing together: A critical component of English for academic purposes teaching and learning. *TESOL Journal, 4*(1), 9–24.

Lin, L., & Evans, S. (2012). Structural patterns in empirical research articles: A cross-disciplinary study. *English for Specific Purposes, 3*, 150–160.

Paltridge, B. (2013). Genre and English for specific purposes. In B. Paltridge & S. Starfield (Eds.), *The Handbook of English for Specific Purposes* (pp. 347–366). Malden, MA: Wiley-Blackwell.

References

American Psychological Association. (2010). *Publication manual of the American Psychological Association* (6th ed.). Washington, DC: Author.

Andrade, M. S. (2006). International students in English-speaking universities: Adjustment factors. *Journal of Research in International Education, 5*(2), 131–154.

Belcher, D. (Ed.). (2009). *English for specific purposes in theory and practice.* Ann Arbor, MI: University of Michigan Press.

Belcher, D., Johns, A. M., & Paltridge, B. (Eds.). (2011). *New directions in English for specific purposes research.* Ann Arbor, MI: University of Michigan Press.

Bunch, G. C., & Endris, A. K. (2012). Navigating "open access" community colleges: Matriculation policies and practices for U.S.-educated linguistic minority students. In Y. Kanno & L. Harklau (Eds.), *Linguistic minority students go to college: Preparation, access, and persistence* (pp. 165–183). New York, NY: Routledge.

Cheng, A. (2006). Understanding learners and learning in ESP genre-based writing instruction. *English for Specific Purposes, 25*, 76–89.

Coghill, A. M., & Garson, L. R. (Eds.). (2006). *The ACS style guide: Effective communication of scientific information.* New York, NY: Oxford University Press.

de Chazal, E. (2014). *English for academic purposes.* Oxford: Oxford University Press.

Demko, Z. P., & Sharpless, K. B. (2001). Preparation of 5-substituted $1H$-tetrazoles from nitriles in water. *Journal of Organic Chemistry, 66*, 7945–7950.

Evans, S., & Morrison, B. (2011). Meeting the challenges of English-medium higher education: The first-year experience in Hong Kong. *English for Specific Purposes, 30*, 198–208.

Grabe, W., & Zhang, C. (2013a). Reading and writing together: A critical component of English for academic purposes teaching and learning. *TESOL Journal, 4*(1), 9–24.

Grabe, W., & Zhang, C. (2013b). Second language reading–writing relations. In A. S. Horning & E. W. Kraemer (Eds.), *Reconnecting reading and writing* (pp. 108–133). Anderson, SC: Parlor Press/WAC Clearinghouse.

Hafernik, J. J., & Wiant, F. M. (2012). *Integrating multilingual students into college classrooms: Practical advice for faculty.* Bristol: Multilingual Matters.

Harklau, L. (2000). From the "good kids" to the "worst": Representations of English language learners across educational settings. *TESOL Quarterly, 34*(1), 35–67.

Hirvela, A. (2004). *Connecting reading and writing.* Ann Arbor, MI: University of Michigan Press.

Horn, B., Stoller, F. L., & Robinson, M. S. (2008). Interdisciplinary collaboration: Two heads are better than one. *English Teaching Forum, 42*(2), 2–13.

Horning, A. S. (2013). Writing and reading across the curriculum: Best practices and practical guidelines. In A. S. Horning & E. W. Kraemer (Eds.), *Reconnecting reading and writing* (pp. 71–88). Anderson, SC: Parlor Press/WAC Clearinghouse.

Horning, A. S., & Kraemer, E. W. (Eds.). (2013). *Reconnecting reading and writing.* Anderson, SC: Parlor Press/WAC Clearinghouse.

Hyland, K. (2004a). *Disciplinary discourses: Social interactions in academic writing.* Ann Arbor, MI: University of Michigan Press.

Hyland, K. (2004b). *Genre and second language writing.* Ann Arbor, MI: University of Michigan Press.

Hyland, K., & Bondi, M. (Eds.). (2006). *Academic discourse across disciplines.* New York, NY: Peter Lang.

Johns, A. M. (1997). *Text, role, and context: Developing academic literacies.* New York, NY: Cambridge University Press.

Johns, A. M. (2007). Genre awareness for the novice academic student: An ongoing quest. *Language Teaching, 41*, 237–252.

Kanno, Y., & Harklau, L. (Eds.). (2012). *Linguistic minority students go to college: Preparation, access, and persistence.* New York, NY: Routledge.

Karukstis, K. K. & Elgren, T. E. (Eds.). (2007). *Designing and sustaining a research-supportive curriculum: A compendium of successful practices.* Washington, DC: Council on Undergraduate Research.

Learning to speak and write. (2001). *Nature, 411*(6833), 1.

Leki, I. (2007). *Undergraduates in a second language: Challenges and complexities of academic literacy development.* New York, NY: Lawrence Erlbaum.

Llompart, M., Pazos, M., Landín, P., & Cela, R. (2001). Determination of polychlorinated biphenyls in milk samples by saponification: Solid-phase microextraction. *Analytical Chemistry, 73*, 5858–5865.

Moskovitz, C., & Kellogg, D. (2011). Inquiry-based writing in the laboratory course. *Science, 332*, 919–920.

Nesi, H., & Gardner, S. (2012). *Genres across the disciplines: Student writing in higher education.* Cambridge: Cambridge University Press.

Norris, S. P., & Phillips, L. M. (2003). How literacy in its fundamental sense is central to scientific literacy. *Science Education, 87*, 224–240.

Paltridge, B. (2001). *Genre and the language learning classroom.* Ann Arbor, MI: University of Michigan Press.

Paltridge, B., & Starfield, S. (Eds.). (2013). *The handbook of English for specific purposes.* Malden, MA: Wiley-Blackwell.

Robinson, M. S., Stoller, F. L., Costanza-Robinson, M., & Jones, J. K. (2008). *Write like a chemist: A guide and resource.* New York, NY: Oxford University Press.

Snow, M. A., & Kamhi-Stein, L. D. (2002). Teaching and learning academic literacy through Project LEAP. In J. Crandall & D. Kaufmann (Eds.), *Content-based instruction in higher education settings* (pp. 169–181). Alexandria, VA: TESOL International Association.

Stoller, F. L., & Robinson, M. S. (2013). Chemistry journal articles: An interdisciplinary approach to move analysis with pedagogical aims. *English for Specific Purposes, 32,* 45–57.

Stoller, F. L., & Robinson, M. S. (2014). An interdisciplinary textbook project: Charting the paths taken. In N. Harwood (Ed.), *English language teaching textbooks: Content, consumption, production* (pp. 262–298). London: Palgrave Macmillan.

Swales, J. M. (1990). *Genre analysis: English in academic and research settings.* Cambridge: Cambridge University Press.

Swales, J. M. (2004). *Research genres: Exploration and applications.* Cambridge: Cambridge University Press.

Swales, J. M., & Feak, C. B. (2011). *Navigating academia: Writing supporting genres.* Ann Arbor, MI: University of Michigan Press.

Swales, J. M., & Feak, C. B. (2012). *Academic writing for graduate students: Essential tasks and skills* (3rd ed.). Ann Arbor, MI: University of Michigan Press.

Tang, R. (Ed.). (2012). *Academic writing in a second or foreign language: Issues and challenges facing ESL/EFL academic writers in high education contexts.* London: Continuum.

Tardy, C. M. (2009). *Building genre knowledge.* West Lafayette, IN: Parlor Press.

Wingate, U. (2012). Using academic literacies and genre-based models for academic writing instruction: A "literacy" journey. *Journal of English for Academic Purposes, 11,* 26–37.

12

CORPUS-BASED VOCABULARY SUPPORT FOR UNIVERSITY READING AND WRITING

Mark Davies and Dee Gardner

Vignette

Imagine that you are Susana Meléndez, a nonnative speaker from Peru, who is enrolled in an advanced writing course at a university in the United States. As you write a paper for your class, you have the following questions: Which is more common—potent argument or powerful argument? How about utter despair or sheer despair? What verb should I use with havoc—make, wreak, or produce? Which sounds better in academic English—brainy or knowledgeable? Is (urban) sprawl a good thing or a bad thing? Does scheme have a different meaning in American and British English? Do I use excel in or excel at? Would informal writing use should talk or must talk in American English (and what about British English)? Is it have strived or have striven in American English? Assuming your dictionary and thesaurus can't answer these questions, where can you go to get quick answers as you write your paper?

Introduction and Overview of the Challenges

Academic vocabulary knowledge has been identified as a key component of academic literacy skills (Biemiller, 1999; Corson, 1997), which, in turn, have been strongly correlated with academic success, economic opportunity, and societal wellbeing (Goldenberg, 2008; Jacobs, 2008). It is also widely recognized in English-speaking countries like Great Britain, the United States, Australia, Canada, and New Zealand that higher education students from non-English-speaking backgrounds face a formidable challenge in trying to acquire adequate levels of English academic literacy (Henry & Roseberry, 2007). The complex demands placed on such learners has sparked a number of important technological innovations, one of these being the use of electronic corpora to support academic literacy needs.

The advent of high-powered technology and searchable electronic corpora has recently inspired a host of data-driven resources for teaching and learning English. Examples of the range of corpus applications include (1) large megacorpora such as the Corpus of Contemporary American English (COCA) and the British National Corpus (BNC); (2) corpora dealing with language change over time (e.g., the Corpus of Historical American English [COHA]—Davies, 2012); (3) corpora based on actual learner language, or Learner Corpora (e.g., Gilquin, Granger, & Paquot, 2007); (4) corpora used to determine core academic words and phrases (e.g., Gardner & Davies, 2014; Simpson-Vlach & Ellis, 2010); and (5) specialized corpora such as those used to investigate the language of engineering (e.g., Mudraya, 2006), agriculture (Martínez, Beck, & Panza, 2009), biochemistry (Kanoksilapatham, 2005), business (e.g., Blanpain, Heyvaert, & Laffut, 2008; Nelson, 2006), history (Cortes, 2004), medicine (Wang, Liang, & Ge, 2008), law (Hafner & Candlin, 2007), and many other areas of academic literacy. All of these corpus applications attest to the fact that data-driven methodologies have found a home in contexts where academic English is being studied.

The appeal of corpora for language training is that they represent the way people really write or talk, rather than the textbook examples we often find in traditional course materials, or explanations about language usage based on our intuitions, which are often inaccurate (Hunston, 2002). While corpus-based vocabulary resources such as word lists have been with us for nearly 80 years—thanks to tedious manual calculations and rudimentary computer analyses in the early days of linguistic computing—the recent introduction of machine-searchable corpora and the availability of powerful personal computers, smartphones, and other electronic devices has also made it possible to bring data-based applications directly to classrooms and individual learners (Aijmer, 2009; Bennett, 2010; Gardner, 2012; Granger, Hung, & Petch-Tyson, 2002; Reppen, 2010).

However, Bernardini (2004) makes an important distinction between "uses of corpora as sources of descriptive insights relevant to language teaching/learning and uses of corpora that directly affect the learning and teaching process(es)" (p. 15). While the line between these two uses of corpora may be blurred at times, it is perhaps helpful to think of the distinction as "resources" versus "methods." The purpose of this chapter is to show how COCA and its online interface, WordAndPhrase.info, can be used as a "resource" to support the academic literacy needs of English language learners in higher education, particularly in terms of vocabulary usage (both words and phrases), understanding of genre (Flowerdew, 2005), and knowledge of grammatical/syntactical patterns (Hunston, 2002). Actual corpus-based classroom methods that have been shown to directly affect learning and teaching will not be discussed, as such methods are in their relative infancy and lack an adequate body of empirical support (Aijmer, 2009; Bennett, 2010). However, it is hoped that our discussions and examples in this chapter will encourage advanced language learners and their teachers to begin to see the possibilities for learning and teaching that corpus searches can provide.

Implications and Applications

Consider again the many different challenges faced by our hypothetical university student, as posed in the vignette at the beginning of this chapter. Where could she go to get answers to these questions—a dictionary, or perhaps a thesaurus? Actually, very few of these questions could be answered with either type of resource. What she needs is the ability to quickly search millions of words of text from different styles and genres of English to determine what sounds the most natural.

A corpus can provide this type of insight. Since the 1980s, there have been available a number of corpora—such as the BNC and the Bank of English—which allow language learners to see what is "really happening" in the language. Unfortunately, neither of these two corpora is currently being updated, and neither corpus focuses on American English. Since 2008, however, the 450 million-word COCA (see Davies 2009, 2011) has been available, and it can help advanced ESL students and their teachers to answer the kinds of questions most English language learners face.

In addition to the regular COCA interface (corpus.byu.edu/coca), a number of other COCA-based resources—also very relevant for language learners—have also become available (see corpus.byu.edu). Perhaps the most useful of these is www.WordAndPhrase.info, which will also be discussed in this chapter. In the following sections, we will consider how all of these corpus-based resources can be used to answer many different types of questions that nonnative speakers of English and their teachers might have, as they deal with the literacy demands of academic English in higher education.

Using Collocates to Find the Meaning of Words

COCA allows language learners to quickly find the collocates (nearby words) of a given word or phrase, and these collocates can provide very useful insight into the meaning and usage of a word. For example, what is the meaning of *break*, or "what do we break"? In order to find out, users simply input the word, (optionally) specify the part of speech for the collocates, and then click to find the collocates. In less than two seconds, users can see a list of words like *law* (1,527 tokens near *break*), *heart* (1,454), *news* (1357), *record* (995), *rules* (943), *silence* (896), *ground* (804), *leg* (567), *barriers* (486), *cycle* (468), and *pieces* (445). Users can also choose to find collocates that occur much more frequently with *break* than their overall frequency in the corpus might suggest, which often indicates that the two words (*break* + collocate) have an idiomatic sense. For example, when users sort by "relevance," they find that the top collocates are *logjam* (83 occurrences), *deadlock* (127), *monotony* (71), *stranglehold* (48), *taboos* (46), *impasse* (75), *stalemate* (66), and *barrier* (398), most of which have a strongly idiomatic feel to them. (See Davies and Gardner 2010 for the most frequent collocates of the top 5,000 words in English.) Of course, obtaining such rich output so quickly does not guarantee that students will know how to quickly sort through the data to draw conclusions, so they will need plenty of practice (both teacher-directed and independent) to become comfortable with interpreting the results of corpus searches. They should also be encouraged to utilize the tutorials provided in the COCA interface to understand how to actually perform various searches.

So how could nonnative speakers use this information, as they develop advanced proficiency in reading or writing? The answer is that in many cases, the collocates provide insight into meaning and usage that can't be found in even the best of dictionaries. We will provide two quick examples. First, consider the word *brooding*. A typical dictionary entry might indicate that the word means "cast in subdued light so as to convey a somewhat threatening atmosphere" (dictionary.com). On the other hand, consider the collocates of this word in COCA: (noun) *dark, eyes, look, silence, presence, sky, sense, cloud, thought, mood, portrait, bird*; (misc.) *dark, over, sit, silent, heavy, gray, stare, handsome, mysterious, beneath, moody*. Most would agree that the collocates "paint a picture" of the sense of this word that is far beyond what a dictionary can produce.

Consider a second example: the collocates (and thus the meaning and usage) of the word *sprawl*. The site www.dictionary.com indicates that (as a noun) this word means "the act or an instance of sprawling" or "a sprawling posture," neither of which is overly insightful. COCA, on the other hand, provides the following collocates: (adjective) *urban, suburban, rural, industrial, metropolitan, vast, unchecked, surrounding, Southern, increasing*; (noun) *city, development, traffic, growth, pollution, congestion, land, town, farmland, county*; (verb) *create, encourage, stop, fight, reduce, curb, slow, threaten, limit, crawl*. As we can see, the collocates show that *sprawl* refers particularly to the growth of cities (*city, suburban, farmland*), that it may be more common in the *Southern* United States, that it is associated with *pollution* and *congestion*, and that people are trying to *reduce, stop*, and *fight* against it. In summary, collocates "paint a picture" of a word that is far beyond what virtually any dictionary can provide.

Using Collocates to Compare Synonyms

One of the most useful aspects of collocates is their ability to show "shades" of differences in meaning between two near synonyms and therefore help language learners to use the most appropriate of the two synonyms. And this information, which can be easily obtained from a corpus, is not the type of detail that would be found in a typical thesaurus, which simply provides lists of words that—in principle—could be substituted for each other.

For example, consider the two near synonyms *small* and *little*. For a student who is a native speaker of Spanish, these two words look quite interchangeable, and relate to the Spanish word *pequeño*. It would therefore be quite difficult for such a student to know which of the two English words are used with different collocates. But with the COCA interface, in a matter of three to four seconds, users can begin to observe that the following collocates are used primarily with *little*: *quantities, percentage, populations, amounts, sizes, fraction* (all of which refer in some way to quantities and ratios), whereas the following collocates are used primarily with *small*: *while, league, luck, sleep, fun, attention, sympathy, sister, doubt, sympathy, help* (most of which refer to abstract nouns). So a language learner who is struggling to find the right word—*little* or *small*—to use with a given collocate could find, with some practice, which of the two is more frequent. It is also important to note here that simply asking the teacher this same question is likely to be unproductive, as such information generally is not explicitly known by teachers, and is often not intuitive.

Consider a second example. A nonnative speaker of English wants to know whether you *rob food* or *steal* it. Do you *steal* or *rob* someone's *identity*? And do you *steal* from or *rob* someone at *gunpoint*, or *rob* or *steal* from someone *blind*? With the corpus, these are easy questions to answer. Collocates that occur much more frequently with *steal* are *money, food, cars, wallet, identity*, and *drugs* (where the noun is the thing that is directly taken). The collocates of *rob*, on the other hand, tend to refer to the person or institution from which things are stolen (*bank, store, victim, person, restaurant, children*), or they refer to the circumstance or way in which the item was taken (*gunpoint, sleep, blind, rape, place*).

Finally, consider a case like the near synonyms of *complete*: *total, sheer*, and *utter*. Again, if students were to consult a thesaurus, they would simply see a list of words, with little, if any, indication of what the differences between them might be that might help them select the most appropriate word in a given context. But a quick search in COCA shows quite nicely that the collocates of *sheer* (but not *utter*) are *number(s), volume, force, size, weight, scale, magnitude* (referring to quantity) as well as *luck*, and also *cliff(s), rock, face*, and *drop* (referring to a steep drop-off). The collocates of *utter* are perhaps even more interesting: *darkness, failure, destruction, disregard, contempt, fool, desolation, defeat, silence, absence, disbelief, hopelessness, disaster*, and *defeat*. All of these are very negative, reflecting the strong negative "prosody" of this word. When learners see such a list, they are able to understand that to use *utter* is to use a word that is very heavily loaded with a negative sense, which is something that shows up very nicely in a corpus, but which would likely not show up at all had they consulted only dictionaries or thesauri.

Comparing Synonyms Directly

In a simplistic thesaurus-based approach to synonyms, learners simply see a long list of words, with no sense of which synonyms are actually used in the "real world," and particularly in different styles of speech and writing. For example, learners might see that *perambulate* and *saunter* are "synonyms" of *walk* (verb), and therefore they might be tempted to write or say things like "So, when did you perambulate to class today," or "When I was young, I often sauntered to class by myself."

The COCA web interface is unique among corpora in that it allows users to quickly find the frequency and use of the synonyms of a given word, and also see how and how much they are used in different genres, a technique that avoids the problems of a simple thesaurus-based approach. For example, suppose that students want to see the synonyms of *precarious*. They would simply enter [=precarious] in the search form, and they would then see something like the results presented in Table 12.1, which shows the overall frequency of each synonym and its frequency in each genre. The fact that *precarious* is used only about one-tenth as much as *weak* or about one-sixth as much as *slight* could suggest to the learner that this word has a much narrower range of meanings and uses. (Note that on the corpus website there are 17 synonyms—only 10 are shown here—and the cells are colored to show relative frequency, whereas this is more difficult to see in the grayscale Table 12.1.)

One of the nice features of the interface is that students can "explore" a "chain" of meaning by simply clicking on the [S] after any synonym to see the synonyms of that word, and then clicking on another synonym in the new set, and so on. For example, if students click on *precarious*, they would then see *dangerous, uncertain, risky, hazardous, unstable, shaky,* and *unsafe* (among others), and they could then click on *shaky* to see *uncertain, trembling, questionable, unstable, dubious, doubtful, unreliable,* and so on. In this way, the students can follow through the chain of meaning, from one sense to another. And in each case, they could see the frequency of the synonyms and their distribution by genre to

TABLE 12.1 Synonyms of *Precarious* by Genre

Synonym	Total	SPOK	FIC	MAG	NEWS	ACAD
Weak [S]	16,176	2,190	3,816	3,266	2,820	4,084
Slight [S]	9,169	796	3,576	2,040	1,293	1,464
Delicate [S]	8,377	714	2,932	2,333	1,476	922
Fragile [S]	5,916	738	1,549	1,496	1,060	1,073
Unstable [S]	3,097	458	339	670	390	1,240
Shaky [S]	2,493	323	856	523	609	182
Frail [S]	1,986	188	898	347	244	309
Brittle [S]	1,679	79	730	491	234	145
Precarious [S]	1,612	182	299	334	280	517
Tenuous [S]	1,364	126	219	266	255	498

know whether a word has a more general and frequent use (or whether it is more specialized), and whether it is more informal or more formal.

The synonym feature is the most useful for learners when it is used in a particular context, like a writing assignment. For example, suppose that students are considering using the phrase *potent argument* in their papers but want to see whether there are better, more common ways to express this. The students would simply enter [=*potent*] *argument* into the search form, and they would then see *strong argument* (138 tokens), *powerful argument* (81), *convincing argument* (81), *persuasive argument* (63), *effective argument* (18), *vigorous argument* (7), *potent argument* (6), *influential argument* (5), and *forceful argument* (5)—all of which would probably suggest that there are better alternatives to *potent argument*. Of course, any number of examples like this could be given. The point is that the corpus can pinpoint just the right synonym to combine with a given word (and in a given genre), which is something that even the best thesauri cannot do.

The Importance of Genre

As we have seen, the appropriateness of a word is very much dependent on the genre in which it is used. If students are writing for an academic audience, then certainly they need to keep that in mind as they select from among the possible words and phrases they could use. Unfortunately, this type of genre-based information is typically not available in a dictionary, but, fortunately, it is quickly available via a corpus.

As a simple demonstration of this, in COCA it is possible to find all words that are more common in one genre than in another. For example, one simple search shows that the following verbs occur much more in fiction than in academic writing—*whimper, snore, waltz, squeal, slump, twirl, perk, snuggle, quiver, sob, claw, saddle,* and *croak*—while verbs that are much more common in academic than fiction writing include *operationalize, remediate, predominate, aggregate, reformulate, reconceptualize, abrogate, individualize, facilitate, marginalize,* and *reify*. And of course there are important differences in genre at the phrasal level as well. For example, a simple search shows that the following phrasal verbs are much more common in academic than in fiction writing: *bear out, contract out, phase out, emerge out, opt out, carry out, rule out, map out, separate out,* and *sketch out*. The search additionally shows that the following phrasal verbs are much more common in fiction: *stare out, freak out, scream out, pop out, make out, bust out, chill out,* and *chicken out*.

Learners can of course limit their search to just a specific set of words, such as synonyms of a given word. Suppose, for example, students want to see which synonyms of *strong* are used in different genres. With one simple search, they could see which synonyms of *strong* are much more common in an informal genre like fiction (e.g., *beefy, burly, strapping, spicy, pungent, brawny, well-built, biting, sturdy, dazzling*) and which are much more common in academic writing (e.g., *effective, deep-seated, clear-cut, durable, compelling, robust, persuasive, dedicated, potent, powerful*). This would hopefully serve as a clear reminder that students would not use the phrases *burly argument* or *spicy support* in an academic paper, or expect to see *deep-seated hands* or *compelling wind* in a short story.

Of course, many times learners simply want to know "Is this word an academic word, or not?" Such judgments are readily available to native speakers, but they are typically not for language learners. Therefore, it is very useful to simply input a given word or phrase and see how frequent that word or phrase is in different genres. For example, consider the frequency charts for *sustain* and *withstand* in Figure 12.1, which show that *sustain* is a much more academic word, whereas *withstand* is more evenly distributed across genres. (Note: the first row indicates the number of tokens in each genre per million words, and the second row shows the normalized frequency in each genre per million words.)

Learners can see the genre frequency of any single word or phrase or compare any two contrasting words (as in Figure 12.1). This can extend even to quasi-grammatical lexical choices, as in Figure 12.2, where we see that *have to* is relatively informal (e.g., *they have to leave*), *should* is more evenly distributed across all levels of formality (e.g., *they should leave*), and *must* is found primarily in formal, academic writing (e.g., *they must leave*). Again, native speakers can often "intuitively" sense such differences, but the corpus data can be invaluable to nonnative speakers to help them know which words are (in)formal and which ones are not.

Sustain

SPOKEN	FICTION	MAGAZINE	NEWSPAPER	ACADEMIC
1,412	882	2,658	1,940	5,022
14.78	9.75	27.82	21.15	55.15

Withstand

SPOKEN	FICTION	MAGAZINE	NEWSPAPER	ACADEMIC
461	348	1,028	632	706
4.82	3.85	10.76	6.89	7.75

FIGURE 12.1 Frequency of *Sustain* and *Withstand* in COCA, by Genre.

Have to

SPOKEN	FICTION	MAGAZINE	NEWSPAPER	ACADEMIC
96,221	47,166	40,008	41,096	15,386
1,006.86	521.58	418.67	448.07	168.95

Should

SPOKEN	FICTION	MAGAZINE	NEWSPAPER	ACADEMIC
88,828	55,890	67,961	59,607	81,919
929.50	618.05	711.20	649.90	899.55

Must

SPOKEN	FICTION	MAGAZINE	NEWSPAPER	ACADEMIC
21,909	44,586	35,694	28,865	59,801
229.26	493.05	373.53	314.72	656.68

FIGURE 12.2 Frequency of *Have to, Should,* and *Must* in COCA, by Genre.

Genre-based information can be particularly useful for language learners as they consider idioms, many of which are of course more common in the more informal genres, and are typically not as acceptable in formal, academic genres. Dictionaries typically do not indicate the highly informal nature of these idioms, but the charts from a balanced corpus can indicate this quite well. Consider, for example, the following three idioms with the word *head*: *use one's head* (e.g., *he told me to be careful and use my head*), *in over one's head* (e.g., *he was way in over his head on that project*), and *off the top of one's head* (e.g., *but off the top of my head, I can't imagine why*). In all cases, the idiom is much less frequent in formal or academic English, as can be seen in Figure 12.3.

Use one's head

SPOKEN	FICTION	MAGAZINE	NEWSPAPER	ACADEMIC
37	71	57	34	3
0.39	0.79	0.60	0.37	0.03

In over one's head

SPOKEN	FICTION	MAGAZINE	NEWSPAPER	ACADEMIC
37	71	57	34	3
0.39	0.79	0.60	0.37	0.03

Off the top of one's head

SPOKEN	FICTION	MAGAZINE	NEWSPAPER	ACADEMIC
90	46	21	25	6
0.94	0.51	0.22	0.27	0.07

FIGURE 12.3 Frequency of Several Idioms with *Head* in COCA, by Genre.

Notice also the importance of corpus size with idioms. If we just had a small 4–5 million word corpus, we could only have about one-hundredth of the number of tokens that we have in COCA (which is currently 450 million words in size), and so for each of these idioms we would have just two to three tokens—certainly not enough data to help learners.

COCA and its associated suite of corpus tools at corpus.byu.edu can also be used to investigate dialectal differences at the macro-register level—such as differences in vocabulary usage between British (BNC) and American (COCA) dialects of English—as well as historical issues, such as determining words and phrases that sound overly "new" or "old-fashioned." Space constraints in this chapter do not allow us to pursue these topics any further, but we encourage learners and their teachers to explore the possibilities of informing literacy practices that these resources provide.

Morphological and Syntactic Issues Related to the Lexicon

All of the discussion to this point has focused on the meaning and frequency of words and phrases. Words, of course, also have morphological and syntactic characteristics, and here again corpora can provide information that might not be readily available elsewhere.

Consider first the morphological characteristics of a word. For example, once students have determined that they want to use *strive*, should they use *have strived* or *have striven*? An online grammar guide may list both forms, but only a corpus can show the students what is really happening in the language, where we see that (perhaps surprisingly) *striven* is still used in the majority of the cases (about 59% of the total), with the highest use in academic texts (see Table 12.2). We also see, however (and probably not surprisingly), that the regular form *strived* is increasing over time—to nearly three times in the period 2010–2012 (labeled [10–12]) what it was just in the early 1990s (90–94).

To take just one more morphological phenomenon that nonnative speakers might face, we know that comparative adjectives can take either the *–er* suffix (e.g., *cleaner, faster*) or use *more* (e.g., *more wonderful, more considerate*). Unlike the adjectives just listed, however, many adjectives are divided between the two forms—for example, *purer/more pure*, or *unhappier/more unhappy*. Again, a corpus can easily show us what native speakers prefer. For example, the following forms prefer *–er*: *prettier* (98%), *simpler* (96%), *clearer* (90%), and *purer* (85%), while the following forms prefer *more* + adjective: *more unhappy* (65%), *more tender* (92%), *more sincere* (98%), and *more likely* (99%).

There are also phraseological and syntactic properties associated with words. To take just one example—which is more common—*different than, different to*, or *different from*? In this case, it depends on dialect, genre, and the time period. In terms of dialect, *different to* is definitely much more common in British than in American English. In terms of change over time, *different than* is clearly increasing in American English, but is still quite rare in British English. And in

TABLE 12.2 Word Forms: Have + Strived/Striven

	Total	SPOK	FIC	MAG	NEWS	ACAD	90–94	95–99	00–04	05–09	10–12
Striven	70	3	11	9	13	34	25	15	12	14	4
Strived	49	6	5	11	12	15	9	11	7	11	11
% Strived	0.41	0.67	0.31	0.55	0.48	0.31	0.26	0.42	0.37	0.44	0.73

terms of genre, *different from* is preferred to *different than* (the newer form) in (American) academic texts.

Of course, it is unreasonable to expect language learners to master the nuances of such variation, but even a quick corpus search would point out, for example, that *different from* is still the most common form in American English, and it would also point out the contrast between *different than* and *different to* in American and British English. And the fact is—based on the server log files of queries done with COCA and the other corpora—that thousands of people each week *do* use COCA primarily to look at fine-grained phraseological issues (such as which preposition to use with a particular verb or adjective), since this information is often not found in dictionaries or other online sources.

A New Learner-Friendly Interface: www.WordAndPhrase.info

As useful as the corpora are for the types of searches that we have described above, there are two problems in terms of how learners might use these resources. First, assuming that learners have a 500-to-600-word paper they have written, they would need to copy and paste many individual "snippets" from the paper (e.g., 1-to-5-word strings)—one after another, all of which is quite time consuming. Second, because there is a fair amount of "power under the hood" in terms of what the corpus can do, there is a learning curve in using the COCA corpus interface (even though there are many context-sensitive help files, with sample queries).

In order to make things easier for language learners, we recently created a new site, www.WordAndPhrase.info, that is based on COCA data, but which has a much more simplified interface. Most important, it allows users to enter and analyze entire texts, rather than requiring them to enter many individual words and phrases, as with the regular COCA interface. We will discuss the ability for users to enter entire texts below. First, however, we will briefly examine how the new WordAndPhrase interface provides information on individual words.

Via the WordAndPhrase interface, users simply enter the word that they are interested in, and they then see a wide range of useful information for that word (see Figure 12.4). This information includes (1) synonyms of the word, any of which can be clicked on to see the entry for the related words; (2) definitions of the word; (3) a chart showing the relative frequency of the word in each of the nine academic subgenres in COCA; (4) the top collocates of the word, which provide useful insights into meaning, usage, and phrasal possibilities; and (5) up to 200 sample concordance lines from COCA, which can be re-sorted to see the patterns in which the word occurs. In other words, rather than having to do separate searches for synonyms, and then collocates, and then concordance lines, and then frequency information (including by genre)—as with the regular COCA interface—all of this information is provided at one time at

SYNONYMS (click to see) [?]

consistent
2526	reasonable
4522	rational [1]
4612	logical
7112	coherent
6986	sound
16284	reasoned

intelligible
4522	rational
7112	coherent
12119	articulate
15827	lucid
18168	intelligible
20294	comprehensible

COHERENT j (#7112, ACAD FREQ 1919) (HELP)

	HIS	EDU	SOC	LAW	HUM	PHIL	SCI	MED	BUS
Click bar to limit									[3]
Per mill	1.4	0.9	0.8	1.4	1.7	1.3	1.0	0.2	0.1
See more	319	113	207	278	305	274	377	34	12

CONCORDANCE LINES

	DOMAIN		
1	SOC	[5]	social structure. It would have been difficult to present as
2	SCI		and transformed a confusion of facts into a singularly
3	SOC		1979) that also included an array of recommendations for a
4	MED		And the attempt is to grasp it -- to make life
5	MED		to account for PC's self-projection as the only humane and
6	SCI		deregulation has swept away the old rules without offering

DEFINITIONS (WORDNET) [2]   (BAD ENTRY?)

1. Marked by an orderly, logical, and aesthetically consistent relation of parts 2. sticking together 3. capable of thinking and expressing yourself in a clear and consistent manner [4]

COLLOCATES (click to see with COHERENT)

noun policy, strategy, whole, framework, theory, set, vision, identity, pattern, narrative, picture, lack

misc into, form, together, consistent, lack, single, clear, comprehensive, internally, theoretical, systematic, meaningful

CLICK WORD TO: ● SEARCH AS COLLOCATE ○ QUERY THAT WORD [?]

SORT	SORT	SORT
coherent	[a] [system] [which] combined a social structure forged by a	
coherent	[account] [of] [stellar] birth. Photograph SPANNING HALF A LIGHTYEAR	
coherent	[affirmative-action] [policy] [.] A grievance procedure was created	
coherent	[again] [.] I # When life feels out of control, spending time	
coherent	[alternative] [to] [economic] liberalism. This vision stems from	
coherent	[alternatives] [for] [who] should run the network and how they will gel	

FIGURE 12.4 Sample Display from WordAndPhrase for *Coherent*.

WordAndPhrase. Basically anything that COCA can tell users about a word is all displayed together, with extensive links from one word to another.

The second key feature of the site allows users to input a text of their choosing (perhaps a reading selection, or a paper that they have written) and then see frequency information for each word in that text. For example, in the sample passage in Figure 12.5 (a random news release from Science Daily, www.sciencedaily.com/releases/2012/09/120927144234.htm), users would see statistics showing that 60% of the words are in the top 500 words (lemmas) in COCA, with another 20% from words 501–3,000 in the core. A final 20% of the words are not in the top 3,000 lemmas in COCA. The interface also shows that about 8% of the words are "academic" words, meaning that the word occurs with at least twice the expected frequency (per million words) in COCA academic texts. (Note that in the printed grayscale version in Figure 12.5, it is difficult to distinguish core academic from subgenre-specific words, but the web interface allows us to use color-coding to make these distinctions much more transparent.)

At the most basic level, users can click on the different frequency bands (see the top of the figure: lemmas 1–500, lemmas 501–3,000, lemmas above 3,000, and also "academic"), to see the words from those lists. For example, by clicking on [>3,000], students would see the following words shown in Table 12.3, which provide a fairly nice summary of what the article is about.

Other sites, such as Tom Cobb's Compleat Lexical Tutor (www.lextutor.ca) offer similar functionality. But WordAndPhrase offers something quite useful, which is (to our knowledge) not available at any other site. This is the ability

SEE LISTS	FREQ RANGE 613 words	1-500 60%	501-3000 20%	>3000 20%	ACAD 8%	SAVE TEXT	HELP

The deserts of Utah and Nevada have not always been dry. Between 14,000 and 20,000 years ago, when large ice caps covered Canada during the last glacial cooling, valleys throughout the desert southwest filled with water to become large lakes, scientists have long surmised. At their maximum size, the desert lakes covered about a quarter of both Nevada and Utah. Now a team led by a Texas A&M University researcher has found a new water cycle connection between the U.S. southwest and the tropics, and understanding the processes that have brought precipitation to the western U.S. will help scientists better understand how the water cycle might be perturbed in the future.

FIGURE 12.5 Sample Display from WordAndPhrase, Showing Frequency Information.

TABLE 12.3 Keywords from Inputted Text

[5 tokens] glacial; [4 tokens] southwest, wet; [3 tokens] cycle, desert, intervals; [2 tokens] caps, inland, precipitation, sediments, shorelines, tropical, tropics; [1 token] altered, archaeological, archived, assembling, buried, coastal, cores, cycled, deer, deserts, enhancing, evaluated, geological, geologists latitude, marine, migration, monsoon, mystery, oceanography, paleoclimate, perturbed, pollen, profoundly, progression, radiocarbon, shelters, southeast, speculation, strengthen, surmised, synthesized, weak, wildfowl to click on any of the words in either of the customized lists (e.g., Table 12.3) or any of the words in the original text (e.g., Figure 12.5), and then see the full-featured entry for that word (e.g., Figure 12.4), including synonyms, definition, frequency information (including by genre), collocates, and concordances. In other words, users can click through the text, word by word, and get an incredible wealth of corpus-based information about any and all of these words.

Perhaps the most innovative (and hopefully useful) tool at WordAndPhrase is the ability to highlight selected phrases in the inputted text, and then have the interface suggest related phrases from COCA.

As an example, suppose that language learners had inputted the reading shown in Figure 12.6, and that they wanted to find other phrases related to *instructional methods*. The learners would simply click on these two words (*instructional* and *methods*), which are then inputted into the form below the inputted text, and they could then highlight *methods* and click [PART OF SPEECH] to find other phrases from COCA that are composed of *instructional* + NOUN: *instructional + strategies, materials, practices, time, methods, activities, program, techniques, programs, technology*.

In addition to [PART OF SPEECH], the users can select other ways to compare the phrase in their text to the 450 million words of text in COCA. For example, if the inputted text has the phrase *vintage cars*, the learners could then highlight this phrase in the text, select [SYNONYMS], and then see phrases like *old cars* (224 tokens), *classic cars* (86), or *antique cars* (52). Or—to return to an example shown above—if the students are writing a paper and they write the phrase *potent argument*, they could highlight that phrase in the paper, click on [SYNONYMS], and see the frequency of related phrases in COCA: *strong argument* (138 tokens), *powerful argument* (81), *convincing argument* (81), *persuasive argument* (63), *effective argument* (18), and so on.

The advantage of this interface over the regular COCA interface should be quite obvious. In COCA, the language learners have to input bits and pieces of the entire paper or article—phrase by phrase—and then see the related phrases for each one of these phrases—one by one. In the WordAndPhrase interface, on the other hand, they can input the entire text once. The students can then click on a phrase that they would like to explore and compare in COCA, then

educators were sent abroad to observe democratic citizenship education and study the instructional methods and materials in the established democracies. Those individuals were then asked to design new programs and new materials for use by Albanian teachers. The effort, however, has not been without difficulties; al though many forces are striving to en hance democratic citizenship education in Albania, many are endeavoring to in hibit its development.

1. SELECT WORD	instructional	methods				SEARCH	CLEAR
2. CHANGE TO	EXACT	WILDCARD	ALL FORMS	SYNONYMS	PART OF SPEECH	ANY WORD	REMOVE

HELP

FIGURE 12.6 Selecting Phrases from the Inputted Text.

select another one, and so on. It is much quicker and easier than using COCA, and it preserves the contextual integrity of the original text. And as we have mentioned, no other tool that is currently available allows language learners to use corpus data to this extent to analyze the words and phrases of a text.

Summary

- University-level learners of English face significant challenges in terms of learning vocabulary and using vocabulary appropriately in their writing. There are a number of types of variation that make it hard to find "just the right word":

  - Context is crucial and word choice is a function of the words that are nearby (collocates).
  - Learners have to choose between (near) synonyms.
  - "The right word" is often a function of genre (e.g., formal or informal).
  - "The right word" is often a function of dialect (e.g., British vs. American).
  - Word choice is also a function of language change—some words just sound too innovative or too "old-fashioned."

- There is no dictionary or thesaurus that provides the level of detail that learners need in order to address all of the issues mentioned above, and to have their writing sound more native-like. With a corpus like COCA (and COHA and the BNC), however, learners can quickly get information on all of these different factors.
- With tools like WordAndPhrase, which allow users to input entire texts and then focus on specific words and phrases in those texts (using corpus-based data), this is made even easier.

It is worth noting that most of these tools are very recent (i.e., COCA became available in 2008; COHA in 2010; and WordAndPhrase in 2012), which suggests that language learners today have access to a number of important resources that were not available to previous learners. It is our hope that these resources will become a more integral part of literacy training for nonnative students in higher education, and that effective methods will be developed to train learners to use them in the most productive ways.

Discussion Questions

1. What are some benefits of using corpus-based data to inform the writing decisions of nonnative English learners in higher education?
2. What vocabulary support is available through corpus searches that is not available through dictionaries and thesauri?

3. After reviewing the tutorials on corpus.byu.edu/coca, perform your own collocate, synonym, and genre-based searches. What possibilities for reading and writing support do you see from your own experience using the corpus? What potential limitations do you see? What training may be needed for nonnative English writers and readers to take advantage of these powerful tools?
4. Enter a short text on WordAndPhrase (perhaps a piece of your own writing) and utilize the word and phrase functionality. What potential writing support do you see when using this corpus-based tool? What training would be required for nonnative English learners to take advantage of this tool to support their English literacy needs?
5. How can corpus-based searches inform the intuitions of language teachers?

Further Reading

Aijmer, K. (Ed.). (2009). *Corpora and language teaching*. Amsterdam: John Benjamins.
Bennett, G. R. (2010). *Using corpora in the language learning classroom: Corpus linguistic for teachers*. Ann Arbor, MI: University of Michigan Press.
Granger, S., Hung, J., & Petch-Tyson, S. (Eds.). (2002). *Computer learner corpora, second language acquisition and foreign language teaching*. Amsterdam: John Benjamins.
Reppen, R. (2010). *Using corpora in the language classroom*. Cambridge: Cambridge University Press.

References

Aijmer, K. (Ed.). (2009). *Corpora and language teaching*. Amsterdam: John Benjamins.
Bennett, G. R. (2010). *Using corpora in the language learning classroom: Corpus linguistic for teachers*. Ann Arbor, MI: University of Michigan Press.
Bernardini, S. (2004). Corpora in the classroom: An overview and some reflections on future developments. In J. M. Sinclair (Ed.), *How to use corpora in language teaching* (pp. 15–36). Amsterdam: John Benjamins.
Biemiller, A. (1999). *Language and reading success*. Newton Upper Falls, MA: Brookline Books.
Blanpain, K., Heyvaert, L., & Laffut, A. (2008). Collex-Biz: A corpus-based lexical syllabus for business English. *ITL: International Journal of Applied Linguistics, 155*, 77–93.
Brooding. (n.d.). In *Dictionary.com's online dictionary*. Retrieved 2014 from http://dictionary. reference.com/browse/brooding?s=t.
Cobb, T. (n.d.). *The Compleat Lexical Tutor*. Retrieved 2014 from www.lextutor.ca.
Corson, D. (1997). The learning and use of academic English words. *Language Learning, 47*(4), 671–718.
Cortes V. (2004). Lexical bundles in published and student disciplinary writing: Examples from history and biology. *English for Specific Purposes, 23*, 397–423.
Davies, M. (2009). The 385+ million word Corpus of Contemporary American English (1990–2008+): Design, architecture, and linguistic insights. *International Journal of Corpus Linguistics, 14*, 159–190.
Davies, M. (2011). The Corpus of Contemporary American English as the first reliable monitor corpus of English. *Literary and Linguistic Computing, 25*, 447–465.

Davies, M. (2012). Expanding horizons in historical linguistics with the 400 million word Corpus of Historical American English. *Corpora, 7,* 121–157.

Davies, M., & Gardner, D. (2010) *A frequency dictionary of American English: Word sketches, collocates, and thematic lists.* London: Routledge.

Flowerdew, L. (2005). An integration of corpus-based and genre-based approaches to text analysis in EAP/ESP: Countering criticisms against corpus-based methodologies. *English for Specific Purposes, 24,* 321–332.

Gardner, D. (2012). Technology and usage-based teaching applications. In C. A. Chapelle (Ed.), *The Encyclopedia of Applied Linguistics* (pp. 1–7). Oxford: Wiley-Blackwell.

Gardner, D., & Davies, M. (2014). A new academic vocabulary list. *Applied Linguistics, 35*(3), 305–327.

Gilquin, G., Granger, S., & Paquot, M. (2007). Learner corpora: The missing link in EAP pedagogy. *Journal of English for Academic Purposes, 6,* 319–335.

Goldenberg, C. (2008). Teaching English language learners: What the research does—and does not—say. *American Educator,* (Summer), 8–44.

Granger, S., Hung, J., & Petch-Tyson, S. (Eds.). (2002). *Computer learner corpora, second language acquisition and foreign language teaching.* Amsterdam: John Benjamins.

Hafner, C. A., & Candlin, C. N. (2007). Corpus tools as an affordance to learning in professional legal education. *English for Academic Purposes, 6,* 303–318.

Henry, A., & Roseberry, R. L. (2007). Language errors in the genre-based writing of advanced academic ESL students. *RELC, 38*(2), 171–198.

Hunston, S. (2002). *Corpora in applied linguistics.* Cambridge: Cambridge University Press.

Jacobs, V. A. (2008). Adolescent literacy: Putting the crisis in context. *Harvard Educational Review, 78*(1), 7–39.

Kanoksilapatham, B. (2005). Rhetorical structure of biochemistry research articles. *English for Specific Purposes, 24,* 269–292.

Martínez, I. A., Beck, S. C., & Panza, C. B. (2009). Academic vocabulary in agriculture research articles: A corpus-based study. *English for Specific Purposes, 28,* 183–198.

Mudraya, O. (2006). Engineering English: A lexical frequency instructional model. *English for Specific Purposes, 25,* 235–257.

Nelson, M. (2006). Semantic associations in Business English: A corpus-based analysis. *English for Specific Purposes, 25,* 217–234.

Reppen, R. (2010). *Using corpora in the language classroom.* Cambridge: Cambridge University Press.

Simpson-Vlach, R., & Ellis, N. (2010) An academic formulas list: New methods in phraseology research. *Applied Linguistics, 31,* 487–512.

Sprawl. (n.d.). In *Dictionary.com's online dictionary.* Retrieved 2004 from http://dictionary.reference.com/browse/sprawl?s=t.

Wang, J., Liang, S., & Ge, G. (2008). Establishment of a medical academic word list. *English for Specific Purposes, 27,* 442–458.

13

WHEN EVERYTHING'S RIGHT, BUT IT'S STILL WRONG

Cultural Influences on Written Discourse

William G. Eggington

Vignette

Because of a two-year immersion experience in South Korea and in the Korean language as a young man, I chose to use Korean to fulfill one of my graduate school foreign language requirements. At that time, in the early 1980s, it was possible to test out of Korean classes by coming to some proficiency testing arrangement with a Korean language professor at my university. As such, he asked me to find an article in linguistics written in Korean and translate it into English. I dutifully scoured the library and found only one Korean language linguistics journal from which I randomly chose an article. About a month later, after spending weeks armed with an inadequate dictionary laboriously trying to drag meaning out of each sentence, I presented my finished translation to the professor with a copy of the original from which he would gauge the accuracy of my translation. I eventually met with him to hear his verdict.

Thankfully, he told me that I had passed. He said that my translation was adequate, but that it was unfortunate that I had chosen such a poorly written Korean article as my source text. I was mystified. I couldn't understand how the author of the article, a native Korean scholar with a PhD in linguistics from one of the major graduate linguistics programs in the United States could write poorly. My Korean professor then stated that I had chosen an article written by a Korean who had studied in the West, so even though he had written the article in Korean, he wrote it in a Western style, not in a traditional Korean style. In that sense, everything in the article was grammatically correct at the sentence level, but at the discourse level the article was "wrong" (using his word) at least from his point of view. Interestingly, from my orientation, the discourse structure of the article seemed logical and appropriate.

At about the same time, I took a class on "contrastive rhetoric" from Dr. Robert Kaplan. I used my Korean professor's evaluation of the Korean article as a first step in learning about the relationships between language, culture, and extended discourse. The paper I wrote for the class on that topic eventually became my first major publication (Eggington 1987). Since then, I have spent considerable time examining the phenomenon the field initially labeled as contrastive rhetoric (Kaplan 1966), and later as intercultural rhetoric (Connor 2002). Of course, the phenomenon is more frequently realized in reverse to my Korean translation experience in that ESL teachers evaluate English texts written by Koreans, or students from other cultures, as being mostly correct at the sentence level, but unclear, fuzzy, or "illogical" at the discourse level. In sum, everything's right, but it's still wrong.

The remainder of this chapter will briefly explore aspects of the intercultural rhetoric field culminating in ways that ESL reading and writing instructors can apply this knowledge to their teaching. I will begin with an explanation of the importance of intercultural rhetoric studies. I will then develop one line of reasoning that lies at the foundation of the field; namely, the relationships between language, culture, and discourse. These relationships will be further explored through the analysis of some exemplar texts. My involvement with Intercultural Rhetoric has centered around the relationships among English, Korean, and Korean English writers. This focus will be maintained throughout this chapter and serve as an example of other intercultural rhetorical relationships that exist among English and all English language learners. Finally, as noted, I will conclude by offering some ways that knowledge derived from intercultural rhetoric studies can be applied in the classroom. Because of extremely tight space restrictions, it is impossible to provide an in-depth overview of the field. Consequently, I beg readers' forgiveness as I provide a selective slice in order to accomplish my rhetorical purposes. The references section, as well as the myriad exceptional databases that are currently available online, will satisfy readers who want to pursue the topic further.

Introduction and Overview of Challenges

As my reference to information databases at the conclusion of the preceding paragraph suggests, we are currently living in the much ballyhooed globalized "information age" where a huge proportion of the world's information is stored and retrieved digitally in English (Graddol 1997), and where the English language functions as an international lingua franca (House 2014). We are also living in a less discussed, but equally apparent "age of proximity" where huge portions of the world's population are drawing nearer to each other, either physically through massive immigration, or virtually through digital media. Once again, English functions as the major operative language in this age of proximity. This combination of the information age and the age of proximity, with the English language acting as lingua franca, creates both positive and negative cross-cultural and cross-linguistic outcomes.

Proximity allows us to know each other better, but it can also lead to significant communication problems even among speakers whose language and culture are almost the same. As an example, I am originally from Australia. I began my TESOL career in Australia teaching at an Adult Migrant Education

Program. Often, during teaching breaks, teachers would gather in the "teacher's lounge." Perhaps after a particularly difficult class, I might complain about a student, or a lesson's content. My complaint was almost always met with commiseration, a sharing of a similar incident or concern, and then we would move on to another topic. After teaching in Australia for a number of years, I moved to Southern California for graduate school. I ended up teaching ESL part-time at an Adult Basic Education program. Teachers would also congregate during breaks. However, in this slightly different cultural event, I noticed that my complaints about a class, content, or student did not evoke commiseration, but rather helpful hints for solving the problem. My initial reaction was to feel that my well-meaning colleagues were patronizing me. It wasn't until much later that I realized that in the Australian context, my whining was interpreted as a request for commiseration whereas in the Southern Californian context, similar whining was interpreted as a plea for help. The intent of my whining was interpreted differently in different cultural contexts. As Miller (1974, p. 15) states:

> Most of our misunderstandings of other people are not due to any inability to hear them or to parse their sentences or to understand their words.... A far more important source of difficulty in communication is that we so often fail to understand a speaker's intention.

Pragmatics is the term given to the linguistics field that deals with intended meaning. Pragmatic failure occurs when interlocutors misinterpret intended meaning, as in my whining example above. In a classic article, Jenny Thomas (1983) provides a framework that helps us understand communication breakdowns, or pragmatic failure, caused by cultural differences.

> Grammatical errors may be irritating and impede communication, but at least, as a rule, they are apparent in the surface structure, so that H [hearer] is aware that an error has occurred. Once alerted to the fact that S [speaker] is not fully grammatically competent, native speakers seem to have little difficulty in making allowances for it. Pragmatic failure, on the other hand, is rarely recognized as such by non-linguists. If a non-native speaker appears to speak fluently (i.e., is grammatically competent), a native speaker is likely to attribute his/her apparent impoliteness or unfriendliness, not to any linguistic deficiency, but to boorishness or ill-will. While grammatical error may reveal a speaker to be a less than proficient language user, pragmatic failure reflects badly on him/her as a person. Misunderstandings of this nature are almost certainly at the root of unhelpful and offensive national stereotyping: "the abrasive Russian/German", "the obsequious Indian/Japanese", "the insincere American", and "the standoffish Briton".

Thomas 1983, pp. 96–97

Note that cross-cultural pragmatic failure is not seen as an "error" by both speaker/writer, or hearer/reader. Rather, the cause of the failure is attributed to a human failing or characteristic rather than a communication breakdown. With this in mind, I would now like to focus on some aspects of the English-speaking culture as well as the Korean culture. Remember, I am using Korean culture as an exemplar culture, a proxy for the cultural backgrounds of our students.

English in Culture and Culture in English

Anthropological linguists travel the world investigating exotic languages and cultures, often discovering ways that culture and language interact. Witherspoon (1980), for example, shows that, in Navajo, it is possible to say, "The man kicked the horse," but impossible to say "The horse kicked the man." Of course, theoretically "the horse kicked the man" can be said, but Navajo speakers reject the grammaticality of such a sentence. Why? Because the Navajo cultural worldview does not accept that a horse can kick a man. In that worldview, entities lower on a volition scale cannot do things to higher entities. The only way to describe such an event would be to say "The man allowed the horse to kick him." Witherspoon's article is aptly entitled "Language in Culture and Culture in Language."

If such culture and language relationships exist in Navajo, do they exist in the English language? Anna Wierzbicka is one linguist who studies the relationships between Anglo-American culture and the lexicon, grammar, and pragmatics of the English language. For example, she has shown, using a simplified semantic meta-language lexicon, that a prevailing "cultural script" of Anglo-American culture revolves around notions of personal autonomy as in, "when I do something, it is good if I do it because I want to do it, not because someone else wants me to do it" (Wierzbicka 2006, p. 52), or a related "no one can say to another person something like this about anything: I think like this about it, you have to think the same about it" (Wierzbicka 2006, p. 56). These personal autonomy cultural scripts are realized in the English language in numerous ways, including Anglo-American's use of "wh-imperatives" such as, "would you mind…?" Or "could you…?" where an imperative is disguised as a question so as to allow the person receiving the command to feel in control. This personal autonomy cultural script also suggests that any individual can make any assertion, and that the art, or rhetoric, of speaker persuasion requires the speaker to convince the hearer that what is being asserted is to be adopted by the hearer within the hearer's right of personal choice. Thus it is the speaker's/writer's responsibility to provide clear, sophisticated, and nuanced argumentation as to why a particular choice is better than another, and it is the hearer's/reader's right to accept or reject that choice. Within this cultural context, the art of argumentation becomes highly valued, especially within the educational sector.

There is, within each of us, a tendency to assume that our central cultural values, such as the personal autonomy script explicated above, are universally shared across all humanity. But, as the following discussion involving Korean culture and language will reveal, this assumption is inaccurate.

Korean in Culture and Culture in Korean

One prevailing cultural script of Korean culture involves showing considerable deference to those holding superior status in terms of sociopolitical power and/ or age. Not surprisingly, this cultural value is reflected in the lexicon, morphology, and syntax of the Korean language. For example, Yoon (2004) examines the elaborate honorific system of the language, a system that is so pervasive that no Korean language speaker can avoid thinking about age-related and positional status when functioning in Korean. Once again, using a simplified semantic meta-language, this cultural value is expressed as:

> When I want to say something to someone, it is good to think like this: there are many words. Some words can say something like this: "this person is someone above me." Some other words don't say something like this. Because of this, sometimes I have to say things with some words and not with other words. If I don't say things with these words, someone can feel bad. It is very bad if this someone feels bad because of me. Because of this, I have to know these words. It is good if I say these words when I have to say them. If I don't say these words when I have to say them, people will think bad things about me.
>
> *Yoon 2004, pp. 204–205*

Goddard and Wierzbicka (2007) provide the following related Korean cultural script that invites comparing with the Anglo-American cultural scripts mentioned above:

> When I am with some people, I have to think like this: "This person is not someone like me. This person is someone above me. Because I am with this person now I cannot do some things, I cannot say some things. I cannot say some words. If this person says to me: "I want you to do something", I can't say to them: "I don't want to do it." If this person wants me to do something, it will be good if I do it. It will be very bad if this person feels something bad because of me."

Culture in Writing

Obviously, there are major differences between the prevailing personal autonomy cultural scripts of the Anglo-American world and the hierarchically sensitive cultural scripts of Korean culture and language. Are these differences realized in the preferences each culture displays for writing extended discourse? Consider the three writing samples below. The writer in each is attempting to persuade the reader toward a course of action, or to adopt an opinion.

Text 1 is an exemplar text designed to set a standard for persuasive writing for the Irish-based Professional Development Service for Teachers.

> **Text 1: Adopting a Pet from the Pound (www.pdst.ie/node/588)**
> Owning a pet from the pound or Animal Rescue League has many advantages. First of all, a child feels good about rescuing an abandoned or abused animal and giving it a whole new life. Besides, if the animals from the pound aren't adopted right away, they might be put to sleep. Having a pet also means lots of responsibilities. A child has to feed, clean up after, brush, and exercise the pet.
>
> Another great advantage of having a pet from the pound is the price of these cute and cuddly animals. Pets from the pound cost only a few dollars while pets at a fancy pet store can cost hundreds of dollars.
>
> Once you adopt a pet from the Animal Rescue League, it will quickly become a part of your family. If you are thinking of adopting a pet, you might consider choosing a dog or a cat. Dogs and cats can bring lots of happy times to a family, and they can be excellent companions for a person who lives alone or someone who has lost a loved one. Dogs are also a wonderful source of protection. Cats are funny, and they may help to calm people down when they are sad or mad.
>
> Please consider adopting an animal. If you remember all of the advantages of adopting a pet from the pound, you might find the bird, mouse, hamster, dog, or cat of your choice.

Note how the text opens with the key assertion central to the persuasive rhetorical objective. There is no hesitation, no deference to potential readers who may be older, or have higher social status. The author is confident of her assertion. She is basically saying, "this is what I believe, and this is why you should agree with me." At the end of the first sentence, she projects what is to follow by using the phrase "many advantages." As readers, we know that we will now be provided with an elaboration of these advantages. Sure enough, these advantages follow. The text concludes with a summation and an invitation to acquiesce to the argument provided by the persuader. Throughout the text, the writer takes responsibility to make meaning clear within a "tell us what you are going to say, say it, tell us what you said" paradigm. I am confident that almost all native English speakers would have no problems following the "logic" of the text.

Now consider Text 2. This is a text taken from my 1987 article (Eggington 1987) mentioned at the beginning of this chapter. It is the English translation of a letter to the editor written by a Korean university professor submitted to a leading Korean newspaper that is published in both Korean and English. Try to locate the key assertion, and then build the logic of the text around that assertion.

> The Ministry of Home Affairs is planning to lengthen the period of training for public officials from 3 days to 6 days per year in order to solidify the spirituality of the public officials. The training is to be conducted at the Spiritual Cultural Institute which is rendered in English as the Institute for Korean Studies.
>
> A new meaning of "national" is attached to the word "spiritual." Perhaps this comes from the term, "Spiritual Culture."
>
> A member of the Korean Alphabet Society complained that the architectural design of the Institute for Korean Studies represents a Buddhist Temple and thus is not Korean. This is not so because Buddhism, though imported from India, is a Korean religion. Likewise Christianity is a Korean religion.
>
> Any attempt to label what is national and what is foreign fails.
>
> Perhaps too much emphasis on nationalism may do more harm than good.
>
> Instead of inspiring nationalism we should be appealing to universal reason and proper moral conduct. The civil spirit must take precedent over the national spirit.
>
> I am reminded of this when, changing trains at the subway, I witness the rush to occupy seats on route to the sports center where the Olympic Games are to be held. How do we enhance the nation's prestige through a sports event? As a teacher, I am partly responsible for this situation.
>
> Once you catch a taxi you have to listen to the loud radio controlled by the driver.
>
> Dear administrators, please do not talk about spiritual things unless you are interested in implementing concrete ethical conduct.

Rather than opening with the key assertion as in Text 1, the thesis statement is located toward the middle of the text, as in, "Instead of inspiring nationalism we should be appealing to universal reason and proper moral conduct. The civil spirit must take precedent over the national spirit." With the assertion identified, we can now map the following rhetorical moves: the text opens with an oblique reference to an unknown thesis statement. An additional oblique reference to the unknown thesis statement is provided. This is followed by the thesis statement which is then followed by a series of observations that support the nature of the problem that leads to the thesis statement. The text finishes with a pleading that connects the mid-text thesis statement to the end of the text. A more detailed analysis of the rhetorical structure is available in Eggington (1987).

Text 3 is taken from the September 26, 2014 edition of *The Chosun Ilbo*, one of Korea's major newspapers, published in both Korean and English.

English–Language Education Is a Rudderless Ship http://english. chosun.com/site/data/html_dir/2014/09/26/2014092601888.html

By Ahn Seok-bae from the Chosun Ilbo*'s News Desk*

Most people in northern Europe speak English fluently. According to the English Proficiency Index compiled by Education First, a global education business, Sweden ranks No. 1, followed by Norway and the Netherlands. Some 89 percent of Swedes speak fluent English, and no one in the country gets nervous when approached by a foreigner in a supermarket or in the street.

What is their secret? The education system has a lot to do with it. In Sweden, English teaching starts in elementary school, focusing on conversation, and many subjects are taught in English through all grade levels. For instance, some classes such as chemistry in high school are taught in both English and Swedish. Education authorities do not meddle in that.

Outside school, language learning takes place on TV. Swedish TV does not dub foreign-language programs but provides subtitles instead, so children get exposed to English at an early age.

But in Korea, where English-language education accounts for a huge proportion of the vast sums parents and the government spend, most people are still seized by panic when a foreigner approaches them in the street. Korea ranked a poor 24th out of 60 nations on the EPI last year.

Education First says that despite "enormous private investments," Korea has seen "minimal" effects, while the proficiency of Koreans has "declined overall."

This may be due to several reasons, but flip-flopping educational policies of successive administrations may have a lot to do with it.

In 2008, the government was all for "practical" English and announced plans to hire more native speakers in schools to teach conversation. The traditional focus on grammar shifted to more emphasis on listening and speaking. But the changes were short-lived. The number of foreigners teaching in Korean schools in fact declined, despite an investment of W39 billion (US\$1 = W1,044) in a practical approach that is about to become extinct.

This year, the goal is suddenly to make the English portion of the university entrance exams easier, in order to reduce the competition that causes parents to spend astronomical sums on crammers. The ones who end up losing due to these short-sighted policies are the future leaders of Korea.

I invite readers to locate Text 3's thesis statement, and then map the rhetorical functions of the surrounding texts. I have been reading Korean texts for many years and can follow the logic with ease. However, I suspect most Anglo-American readers will struggle.

From my perspective, both Texts 2 and 3 are pragmatic reflections of the underlying Korean cultural scripts presented above. Korean writers must be highly sensitive to the status of their readers. There are things they can say and not say, but above all, they should not offend. Consequently, a direct assertion following the Text 1 model could easily be seen as breaking a range of sociocultural norms. It is much safer and far more acceptable to "beat the bushes" as a Korean linguistics professor recently told me. The main ideas of a text are hiding somewhere in the bushes. Writers beat the bushes and readers must do likewise in order to derive meaning from the text within myriad pragmatic rhetorical moves. In that sense, Korean rhetoric follows Japanese rhetorical patterns with respect to reader versus writer responsibility (Hinds 1987). In this paradigm, different cultures place the responsibility for making meaning clear on different shoulders. Anglo-American writers in most prose genres accept responsibility for delivering a clear text. In English, however, the responsibility is placed upon the reader in verbal art genres such as poetics. In Japanese, Hinds claims, readers bear the burden of ascertaining meaning even in academic prose. Such an orientation seems evident in Texts 2 and 3.

Implications and Applications

Texts 2 and 3 are manifestations of deep cultural Korean scripts that posit the writer of any text within a relational context. Writers must consider the relationship they have with their audience in terms of sociocultural status and age. As such, being assertive is counterproductive. It is far more acceptable to be indirect, to place responsibility for ascertaining meaning on the reader, and to use reading-between-the-lines pragmatic intent as a major tool in achieving rhetorical objectives. Anglo-Americans approach Texts 2 and 3 with a set of pragmatic expectations concerning what the text will deliver. We want a clear thesis statement at the beginning, as seen in Text 1. We want the writer's intent to be "telegraphed" and delivered in ways that match our rhetorical expectations—which we subsequently label, somewhat ethnocentrically, as linear and direct discourse. When we are mystified by the supposedly random structure of a text written by someone operating outside of our cultural expectations, we can easily ascribe the cause of this miscommunication to writer deficits. Rather, I believe many underlying miscommunications associated with intercultural rhetoric are actually examples of cross-cultural pragmatic failure.

As stated a number of times, I have been using Korean rhetorical strategies as a proxy for a range of languages-other-than-English preferred rhetorical structures. Many of these non-English rhetorical patterns are built upon cultural scripts that are realized in writing through pragmatic intent. Naturally, many ESL students hold to these same cultural scripts using pragmatic strategies even when they write in English. Therein lies a problem. You may recall that one result of cross-cultural pragmatic failure is a tendency to ascribe the cause to be more personal than linguistic. A student is simply a poor writer, rather than an individual making the best choices available to her. Consequently, the first step in dealing with texts where "everything is right, but it's still wrong" is to assume that the cause is a misalignment of reader/writer expectations, often, not always resting on cross-cultural foundations. ESL writing instructors would be wise to delve into the preferred cultural and rhetorical preferences of their students, and to teach their students to be ethnographers of their own and Anglo-American writing strategies, just as teachers should attempt to be ethnographers of the writing strategies of their students. There is no magic bullet to overcoming writing problems caused by intercultural rhetorical pragmatic failure. But, as in all cross-cultural communication, understanding the cause of differences is a good beginning.

Summary

- English plays a key role in fostering positive global communication in the combined information age and age of proximity.
- Significant communication problems are caused by cross-cultural pragmatic failure which often goes unrecognized.
- Culture is in language and language is in culture.
- We can understand how language functions particularly at the pragmatic level by understanding underlying cultural scripts.
- Cultural scripts influence the ways rhetoric is developed. Korean preferred rhetorical strategies reflect deep cultural values.
- Often, being unable to follow the rhetorical strategies of a text can be ascribed to cross-cultural pragmatic failure.
- Bringing cultural values to the surface is one way to help students become ethnographers of written communication.

Discussion Questions

1. What rhetorical strategies are evident in a language other than English that you are familiar with?
2. Can these rhetorical strategies be ascribed to cultural values?
3. There is some evidence that English is the new Latin in that its preferred rhetorical strategies are influencing other languages. How would one go about measuring such a phenomenon?

Further Reading

Connor, U. (1996). *Contrastive rhetoric: Cross-cultural aspects of second-language writing.* Cambridge: Cambridge University Press.

Connor, U. (2002). New directions in contrastive rhetoric. *TESOL Quarterly, 36,* 493–510.

Eggington, W. (1987). Written academic discourse in Korean: Implications for effective communication. In U. Connor & R. B. Kaplan (Eds.), *Writing across languages: Analysis of L2 text.* Reading, MA: Addison-Wesley.

Goddard, C., & Wierzbicka, A. (2007). Semantic primes and cultural scripts in language learning and intercultural communication. In F. Sharifian & G. Palmer (Eds.), *Applied cultural linguistics: Implications for second language learning and intercultural communication.* Amsterdam: John Benjamins.

House, J. (2014) English as a global lingua franca: A threat to multilingual communication and translation? *Language Teaching, 47*(3), 363–376.

References

Connor, U. (2002). New directions in contrastive rhetoric. *TESOL Quarterly, 36,* 493–510.

Eggington, W. (1987). Written academic discourse in Korean: Implications for effective communication. In U. Connor and R. B. Kaplan (Eds.), *Writing across languages: Analysis of L2 text.* Reading, MA: Addison-Wesley.

Goddard, C., & Wierzbicka, A. (2007). Semantic primes and cultural scripts in language learning and intercultural communication. In F. Sharifian & G. Palmer (Eds.), *Applied cultural linguistics: Implications for second language learning and intercultural communication.* Amsterdam: John Benjamins.

Graddol, D. (1997). *The future of English.* London: The British Council.

Hinds, J. (1987). Reader versus writer responsibility: A new typology. In U. Connor & R. B. Kaplan (Eds.), *Writing across languages: Analysis of L2 text.* Reading, MA: Addison-Wesley.

House, J. (2014) English as a global lingua franca: A threat to multilingual communication and translation? *Language Teaching, 47*(3), 363–376.

Kaplan, R. (1966). Cultural thought patterns in intercultural education. *Language Learning, 16*(1), 1–20.

Miller, G. A. (1974). Psychology, language and levels of communication. In A. Silverstein (Ed.), *Human communication.* New York, NY: John Wiley.

Thomas, J. (1983). Cross-cultural pragmatic failure. *Applied Linguistics, 4*(2), 91–112.

Wierzbicka, A. (2006) *English: Meaning and culture.* Oxford: Oxford University Press.

Witherspoon, G. (1980). Language in culture and culture in language. *International Journal of American Linguistics, 46*(1), 1–13.

Yoon, K. J. (2004). Korean social models and the use of honorifics. *Intercultural Pragmatics, 1–2,* 189–210.

14
USING TECHNOLOGY TO TEACH ESL READERS AND WRITERS

Greg Kessler

Vignette

Language learners and teachers today are faced with a wealth of interesting, engaging, and meaningful opportunities to interact with text through the acts of reading and writing. In particular, the English language content on the internet has dramatically increased in both quantity and quality in recent years, providing a wealth of resources for both teachers and learners. Similarly, the increasing and ubiquitous use of technology for social communication has created new reading and writing contexts, tasks, and activities. Many of these new developments are seen as providing compelling and engaging reasons for learners and teachers to participate. Some research has suggested that social networking has contributed to improvements in students' reading and writing, partly due to an overall increase in the time students devote to these activities (Purcell, Buchanan, & Friedrich, 2013). At the same time, higher education institutions have invested significantly in technology to expand student access through technology enhancements, including expanded wireless networks. Students and faculty also have ubiquitous access to an increasing array of resources off campus as well. These developments have much to offer English for academic purposes (EAP) instruction; however, there are a number of potential challenges associated with internet-based reading and writing practices.

Introduction and Overview of the Challenges

Teaching second language reading and writing skills for academic purposes is challenging. Fortunately, there are numerous tools that can be used to support and promote these skills. It is not always obvious which of these may be most beneficial or appropriate for any particular teaching context. It is also not obvious how pedagogy may be best adjusted to these tools and practices.

Further, the nature of how we interact with digital text is changing, and the forms of literacy that are expected within academic contexts are becoming more diverse. These changes are in alignment with other digital shifts in our communication landscape. Consequently, teaching reading and writing skills requires teachers to develop skills associated with digital tools as well as a critical perspective on their use. In particular, social media and other collaborative technologies offer opportunities for students to interact with text in compelling ways that are already familiar to them. By mimicking social networking activities in language learning, we are able to better engage students. Such authentic practices are beginning to emerge in academic and professional contexts, which further supports the incorporation of technology in EAP settings.

Emerging Writing and Reading Contexts

The way we communicate through reading and writing has changed dramatically in recent years. Crystal (2001, 2008) describes a merging of written and spoken discourse, promoted by a variety of computer-mediated communication (CMC), that he refers to as "netspeak" (Crystal, 2001, p. 17). He suggests this may be the seed of a preferred means of communication in the future. While netspeak may not demonstrate the characteristics traditionally associated with academic writing, such CMC practices can benefit language learners in numerous ways, particularly due to the collaborative and constructive manner in which netspeak is created. This collaborative construction creates a compelling sense of participation and has many obvious correlations to the language classroom. Further, some have argued that the act of writing for a public audience can increase motivation and, therefore, the quantity and quality of writing (Bloch, 2007). There has also been a shift from text-centric discourse practices to more multimodal discourse practices throughout academia. In many cases, students are expected to do much more small-group work in academic contexts that span the language skills. Increasingly, writing is becoming less of a solitary practice and more of a shared activity (Kessler, 2009; Storch, 2013) across a spectrum of genres, topics, and purposes (Kessler, 2013). These new practices present new reading and writing contexts and opportunities, as well as expectations. For example, students may need to read one another's notes, summarize group discussions in writing, or prepare debriefings as a group.

This changing academic landscape is also noticeable in the increased reliance upon technology-based tools across academic contexts. There are numerous tools available to specifically support reading and writing. Many general-purpose technologies have become so ubiquitous in our daily lives that they are likely to find their way into academic practice. Many CMC and other social media tools have become so common that it is important for language teachers to be able to identify ways to incorporate them into teaching and learning practices. Further, we can also adapt many aspects of the compelling social tasks associated with these tools for a variety of instructional reading and writing purposes. Some significant and common activities that have emerged recently include referencing and contributing to shared knowledge bases (such as Wikipedia), navigating interconnected (or mashed-up) data sets to identify relationships between seemingly disparate information, and decoding multimodal sources that overlap text with varied visual interpretation. Such tasks promote complex understanding and critical thinking skills as well as participation and collaboration in ways that allow everyone to contribute.

Academic Expectations

It is likely that international students in academic programs will be required to communicate through a variety of CMC tools and contexts. It is becoming not only more common for students to be working on extensive group projects as part of their academic programs, but also more common for these projects to be accommodated through the use of web-based collaborative technologies such as wikis, Google Docs, Office 365, or other similar environments. In recent years there has been an increase in collaborative writing in second language learning contexts. This is a direct reflection of an increase in these CMC practices throughout academia, as well as in the professional contexts for which many EAP programs are preparing students. Many researchers have observed collaborative writing activities and found that students are likely to use the tools within these environments not only to write their papers, but also to plan their papers, share drafts and peer feedback, and offer other forms of intervention (Elola & Oskoz, 2010; Kessler, 2009; Kessler & Bikowski, 2010). Students are also likely to write differently when working individually or collaboratively (Oskoz & Elola, 2011).

Each of these contexts has its own unique set of functions, but, in general, they tend to support forms of both synchronous and asynchronous communication. Synchronous CMC (SCMC) includes communication that takes place at the same time, such as text messaging, microblogging (e.g., Twitter), and video-conferencing (e.g., Skype). Asynchronous CMC (ACMC) typically involves a greater period of time between turns and reflects practices associated with e-mail and discussion forums. ACMC and SCMC have both been researched extensively in second language and foreign language writing contexts, and they have been found to benefit language learning in different ways. SCMC requires participants to respond quickly in a manner that often resembles face-to-face spoken communication, while ACMC provides participants with time to reflect before responding, perhaps contributing to more thoughtful and in-depth engagement (Sotillo, 2000). This suggests that ACMC might be more closely aligned with established practices of providing feedback about global issues such as organization, audience, purpose, and cohesion, but that SCMC might be better aligned with addressing local issues such as word choice, grammar, and other sentence-level issues. There have been suggestions that a new form of CMC referred to as simultaneous CMC is emerging in conjunction with new tools that allow multiple authors to write simultaneously without waiting for others to finish their turns (Kessler, Bikowski, & Boggs, 2012).

New Forms of Literacy and Communication

We are witnessing not only a dramatic change in the availability of potential reading and writing contexts, but also a dramatic change in the types of writing we do within these spaces. For example, in many cases, writing is becoming more social. Composition textbooks have long presented three purposes that an author may assume: to inform, to persuade, and to entertain. I have written recently about an additional purpose that we are now witnessing: to participate (Kessler, 2013). In the traditional writing constructs, there was a clear distinction between writers and readers. Writers held a position of authority or power in this relationship. In many contemporary social contexts, this authority has become more fluid, promoting the participation of many individuals in a variety of ways. In many cases, this happens in ways that have been identified as synchronous or asynchronous. This participation can also occur simultaneously. The immediacy of feedback that is generated in these social writing and reading contexts can compel many students to participate.

Today, we also write to share and participate. Social media's participatory culture relies upon these kinds of contributions because it is co-constructed by its members. To some extent, it is this interdependence among participants that creates engagement. In order for their students to attain this kind of engagement, teachers can mimic these practices in reading and writing instruction. Reading and writing practices can take place in the social media contexts that are already familiar and accessible, or they can be created in the contexts that resemble these popular sites. These practices can also be conducted in technology-free classrooms while still retaining the engaging nature of the experience. Activities such as digital storytelling, fan fiction, or game dialogue construction can all involve or simply be inspired by technology at some stage in the process.

Overall Challenges

While it is exciting to witness the abundance and variety of tools and contexts available today for supporting reading and writing, it is also likely to be overwhelming, even for those who are most technically savvy. Others who are not intrinsically motivated to seek out new potential technologies, and align them with instructional reading and writing activities and goals, and evaluate their effectiveness are likely to benefit from guidance.

As social communication tools have increased in popularity, concern has also increased about the influence that these tools will have upon our more formal reading and writing practices. While these tools present enhancements for the experience of reading and writing, they also present many potential distractions. For example, students may easily be tempted to check e-mail or update social media statuses while engaging in an online reading task that includes hyperlinks to external information. Once this happens, it is difficult to regain a student's attention. Consequently, many teachers may simply choose not to use technology-based tools in their teaching, but with appropriate planning and thoughtful implementation, teachers can overcome these, and many other, challenges. There are, of course, other numerous challenges facing the integration of technology into EAP instruction.

Plagiarism

Recently, there has been a marked increase in attention to issues of academic dishonesty, including plagiarism. The abundance of online text has caused concern among many about the potential for plagiarism. Of course, these large, searchable collections of text can also be used to identify and prevent plagiarism. Concerns around plagiarism have become so commonplace today that we often read about them in the news, particularly when they involve politicians or academic administrators. In academic English contexts, plagiarism has been addressed extensively. It has also become a much more complicated issue than casual observers might realize. Further, nearly everything about plagiarism today is related to the use of technology. With the combination of the internet and word processing being such ubiquitous presences in academic writing, the ability to borrow, copy, or steal text has become quite simple. For some, this introduced a temptation to cheat, while, for others, this simply made it easy to appear as a cheater for making simple mistakes.

The difference between what is actually plagiarism and what is not may not always be obvious. This distinction is particularly challenging in preparing students who are nonnative speakers (NNSs) for academic programs. There are not only linguistic misunderstandings, but also conflicting cultural assumptions regarding the use of others' words. Issues of plagiarism have reached proportions where students are afraid of accidentally plagiarizing, and as a consequence, they may develop new forms of writing anxiety (Yamada, 2003). In fact, students may be so affected by the fear of accidentally plagiarizing that they may write in extremely careful and predictable ways (Yamada, 2003). Bikowski (2012) illustrates ways that technology tools can be used to help students develop skills to recognize and avoid plagiarism. These include tools such as plagiarism detectors, search engines, and online thesauri that are also useful for instructors.

Challenges in Reading Electronic Texts

There has been a lot of recent scholarly and public debate about the changing nature of reading in online and electronic formats. Coiro (2003) recognizes that electronic texts present us with benefits as well as challenges. Some have suggested that reading electronically threatens the very nature of our intellectual abilities and leaves us unable to think deeply about topics (Carr, 2010), while others have focused upon the benefits that electronic texts provide us with (Crystal, 2001; 2008). The introduction of hypertext presented us with opportunities to experience texts in a nonlinear manner with links to additional material such as media, dictionaries, collocations, and audio narration (Chun, 2006). Since the emergence of internet-based reading, there has been an ongoing discussion about the influence that these practices will have on higher education. Carr (2010) argues that reading text on electronic screens is an inferior experience when compared with reading text in printed books. He has gone so far as to state that the internet is making us stupid. There is certainly not a consensus around this perspective, however. For instance, Cobb (2007) suggests that the digital delivery of reading materials allows teachers the opportunity to adjust vocabulary to best meet students' abilities and, thus, increase their reading retention. Others have recognized the benefits of tagging vocabulary with glosses and hyperlinked metadata (Chun, 2006), as well as enhancing contextualization in vocabulary and reading activities through corpora (Huang & Liou, 2007). Chun (2006) suggests that the great wealth of text-based resources on the internet results in a body of reading material that can be organized by various topics, language levels, or any number of other criteria. Gathering and organizing texts in such a manner can help a language program, or even a single teacher, expand the reading resources in meaningful ways. Of course, lengthier or more complicated texts can also be broken down into accessible chunks and delivered to students when they are prepared for each piece. We can also manipulate the speed of such text delivery when it is beneficial, providing students at different levels with an individualized experience.

Recently, we have seen a rise in the use of mobile devices, or e-readers, throughout society. McFall (2014) suggests that good readers tend to be active readers and argues that e-books allow for more active reading. The emergence of mobile devices is also introducing significant challenges to reading. Electronic reading devices have been credited with introducing a new age of reading. These devices provide portability as well as numerous enhancements for our personalized libraries. Depending on the device they use, readers have the abilities to capture notes both in written and oral formats and interact with the text through hyperlinked dictionaries, media, and other illustrative material such as embedded videos and animations. They can also take quizzes based on what they have read. Perhaps most interestingly, readers using these devices can engage with other such readers during the act of reading, making reading more social and less solitary. In academic contexts, some have recognized that e-textbooks may provide students with a substantial cost saving (Baek & Monaghan, 2013). We can find little other research thus far in the area of reading on mobile devices, but we can anticipate many future developments in the area of reading, particularly through mobile devices and other touch-screen devices.

Challenges of Simulations and Games

The introduction of simulation and gaming concepts in education has become very popular in recent years. However, it is likely that most teachers are not prepared to implement such practices. The use of simulated environments offers EAP instructors opportunities to engage students in contextualized reading and writing activities that can help increase students' motivation. There have been a handful of interesting and innovative reading and writing projects built around gaming practices. Some of these appear to be great successes, while others fail miserably. The utilization of games is most effective when focused upon creating an engaging, compelling, and authentic experience. We can definitely anticipate the introduction of many game-influenced activities in EAP instructional contexts. Some have found that games benefit learning through embedded vocabulary practice, largely due to the rich contextual experience (Bing, 2013). Activities relying upon these rich, shared experiences, Kuhn (2013) notes, can provide students with a meaningful foundation upon which instructors can construct innovative and compelling learning experiences. These early investigations into gaming in EAP contexts are very promising, but it is important to note that while experienced game players can benefit, novice game players may struggle. Clearly, teachers who become familiar with the potential of simulations and games in EAP contexts will benefit.

Challenges of Increasing Fluidity of Skills

We must, of course, always take all skills into account when teaching EAP. We know that reading and writing are informed and supported by listening and speaking, and vice versa. We also know that receptive skills inform productive abilities. With some recent technological offerings, it may sometimes be difficult to distinguish between these traditional skills. It is not uncommon today for many individuals to rely on speech-to-text programs to record dictation or automate technological functions. Similarly, we have had audio-recorded versions of books available for many years. While it may seem obvious that the necessary reading skills associated with identifying characters, lexical items, and syntactic structures are absent when listening to a narrated book, it may not seem as obvious that such skills are absent when using speech-to-text tools.

As an author, I have relied upon these tools to gather my thoughts, frame up book chapters and articles, and even extrapolate on thoughts when typing is not convenient (e.g., while driving) or even possible (e.g., while having a broken wrist). Through this personal experience, I have come to greatly appreciate what these tools have to offer. However, as with all potential tools, there are a number of caveats that one should consider. Approaching the use of speech-to-text tools with a solid understanding of the conventions of academic writing, including brainstorming, process writing, and revision strategies, may contribute to successful use. With the advancements that are being made today in this area, it is quite likely that we will soon be seeing many more student writers using these tools, at least for preliminary drafts. In fact, the use of these tools may be extremely beneficial for students with particular learning preferences. They would, of course, be critically important for those with fewer options due to physical challenges or other challenges. Keeping an open mind about the use of these tools and similar tools that will emerge in the future is likely to be helpful for writing teachers. Of course, we can anticipate similar developments in the use of text-to-speech tools that are beginning to have some similar influences on transforming reading experience into listening practice.

Challenges of Incorporating Automated Tools

There are many recent developments in automated technology that are directly targeted at the teaching of reading and writing. These include tools that can perform an automated analysis of various aspects of writing as well as those that can allow an automated adjustment in regard to the delivery of reading materials. Automated writing evaluation (AWE) has received a good deal of attention recently (Cotos, 2012). Ware and Warschauer (2006) have found that AWE tools, at the time, promoted formulaic writing. Yet there have been some positive developments recently. Ware (2011) has found that AWE tools can reliably evaluate student writing within specific genre and contextual limitations. In the near future, we are likely to see these tools become much more effective and popular. There is much excitement about the potential for these tools in some academic circles.

However, all developments in this area are not necessarily perceived positively within academia. When EdX received significant publicity for their automated composition tool, which was initially designed to align with their massive open online courses (MOOCs), they also received a dramatic backlash from academia. Some were not only concerned that this tool would promote uninteresting formulaic writing, but also that it would be used to automate the writing that students needed to do. Essentially, this would be using an AWE tool to reverse-engineer compositions. These are valid concerns. But as with all these technological developments, we need to identify ways to inform ourselves about the potential for these tools so that we can choose which ones we will use and which we will avoid in a given situation.

By being informed about the potential of these tools, we can acknowledge the potential benefits that automated evaluation can offer instructors while also being fully aware of the threats that they may pose. Perhaps some preliminary or fundamental aspects of writing could be addressed through automated means in order to allow instructors to attend to more personal or otherwise meaningful activities. Of course, integrating such tools into one's teaching repertoire requires a functional understanding of the tools that are available in addition to the means by which they can be integrated into curricular goals and practices. As Warschauer and Grimes (2008) conclude, "Automated assessment will neither destroy nor rescue writing instruction" (p. 34). Instructors should explore and understand developments in the area of AWE in order to make informed decisions.

Implications and Applications

There is much that teachers of all language skills can learn from previous investigations into computer-assisted language learning (CALL) practice. This is particularly true in the area of reading and writing due to the significant focus on text-based materials and instruction over the past few decades. The field of CALL is far too complex and diverse to summarize within this chapter, but some salient points of focus are included here. Among the many benefits that have been recognized related to the use of technology in language teaching are the increased motivation and opportunities for out-of-class practice (Ayres, 2002). Lai and Gu (2011) recognize that there are many benefits presented through the extended use of out-of-class practice that technology can accommodate, including increased authenticity and self-regulation. Similarly, many have recognized that technology integration in language learning can help to promote student autonomy (Kessler, 2009; Reinders & Hubbard, 2013). The characteristics associated with one's autonomy as a learner include the ability to take control over one's own learning. These are the very skills that EAP instruction should be targeting. However, it is important to develop a critical awareness of our technology use and integration in the classroom. Whenever new technology tools or practices are considered, it is critical that the strengths and limitations are recognized within the concept of the proposed pedagogical goals. It is also important that we are aware of the areas that have been recognized as benefiting from technology integration. As Jamieson, Chapelle, and Preiss (2013) suggest, technology use in second language classrooms needs to accommodate language learning potential, learner fit, meaning focus, authenticity, impact, and practicality. This is not easily accomplished and is likely to present a complex and challenging task. Therefore, it is imperative that EAP reading and writing teachers develop a sophisticated awareness of the potential for digital tools.

Developing Critical Awareness

While it is important that teachers are aware of the changing landscape around reading and writing teaching and practices, it is also important that students are engaged in discussions about these topics. After all, the purpose and context of students' writing may often be directly influenced by this discussion-based knowledge. Engaging students in meaningful dialogue about these changes may reveal beneficial insights into the role that reading and writing practices play in these students' lives. This knowledge can help instructors to identify potential practices and topics that students will find compelling. This meta-cognitive type of dialogue can also be focused to help students understand important concepts such as audience, purpose, and tone.

Avoiding the Temptation of Shiny Things

Often, instructors who are inclined to incorporate technology in their instruction are fascinated with the newest gadgets. In some high-technology contexts, this approach may work for instructors and students alike, but it may likely be plagued with a number of challenges. One challenge we face as new technologies are introduced is the rate at which we can expect teachers and students to adapt and adopt. In spite of the many benefits of electronic texts, Evans and Po (2007) find that students still feel that they are better able to engage with paper texts. Of course, this is a snapshot in time. It is likely that similar future studies will reveal different findings as we become more comfortable with these emerging technologies. Consequently, it is important that we approach emerging technologies prudently. It is important that we not only be selective about our use, but also be selective about the number of different technologies that we use in any one class so that we do not overwhelm or confuse students. There is perhaps nothing worse in the field of CALL than a teacher who bombards students with every new gizmo and gadget that he or she comes across. Some have observed that students who are not as digitally literate may feel marginalized when they are presented with an overabundance of technology (Kajee & Balfour, 2011). Similarly, it is important to focus our technological intervention on the ways in which technology has proven to be effective.

Perhaps the most important thing we can do to prepare teachers to effectively use technology in their instructional contexts is to train them to think critically about what the use of any tool is and how it aligns with their pedagogical goals. This is much more complicated and demanding than simply learning how to use a specific piece of software. By aligning practices with specific teaching objectives, we can maintain appropriate, authentic, and innovative experiences. One way to work toward this goal is to involve students in the process of task and activity design as well as instructional material design. When designing digital materials, teachers can benefit from gathering student feedback throughout the process (Kessler & Plakans, 2001). Of course, there are other numerous ways to promote students' active involvement. This can be partially addressed by striving for authenticity in classroom experiences. Creating authentic experiences relies upon the authenticity of the tasks, audience, and materials (Egbert & Hanson-Smith, 1999). Another aspect of authenticity can be captured through creating collaborative experiences. These are the kinds of academic experiences in which students are increasingly participating, both during their academic studies and their professional work.

Summary

As the reader can see, the landscape of reading and writing instruction and practice through the use of technological tools is quite complicated. While there are many potential benefits for both teachers and students, there are also a number of challenges and concerns that we need to keep in mind when working with these tools and in these contexts. These technological innovations, along with an increasing awareness of how we can best meet the needs of both teachers and students, require that we rethink practices associated with the teaching of both reading and writing. Future innovations are likely to further complicate the decisions about these practices. We need to be critically aware of the circumstances that comprise our specific learning contexts so that we can do the following:

- Make informed decisions about the integration of technological innovations in ways that align well with our pedagogical goals. This also requires making pedagogical decisions that align with particular technology practices.
- Reflect upon our instructional practices related to reading and writing and anticipate the potential of emerging technological tools. This reflection may benefit from thinking beyond the confines of traditional academic reading and writing practices.
- Adjust our pedagogy and/or technology use when it is feasible and appropriate. Remember that too much change too quickly can be as detrimental as too little.
- Anticipate that future developments will continue to require our attention and reflection. While this chapter presents a number of recent innovations that can impact the teaching and practices of reading and writing, this landscape is constantly changing. New tools emerge daily. Some may have significant potential, while others may not. It is important to establish and maintain a current awareness of these tools in relation to our own teaching contexts.

Discussion Questions

1. Identify a new writing or reading context and describe how it might be used for a specific language learning activity among a specific group of learners.
2. How can we incorporate collaborative writing activities into the language classroom?
3. How might we anticipate reading and writing activities to change in the future?
4. How do you think technology has influenced your own writing habits? How might it have influenced the writing habits of your students?

Further Reading

Bloch, J. (2007). *Technologies in the second language composition classroom*. Ann Arbor, MI: University of Michigan Press.

CALICO Journal. Retrieved February 10, 2015, from http://http://journals.sfu.ca/CALICO/index.php/calico.

Chapelle, C., & Jamieson, J. (2008). *Tips for teaching with CALL: Practical approaches to computer-assisted language learning*. White Plains, NY: Pearson Education.

Computer Assisted Language Learning. Retrieved February 10, 2015, from www.tandfon-line.com/loi/ncal20#.U8cbqKiVt5E.

Healey, D., Hanson-Smith, E., Hubbard, P., Ioannou-Georgiou, S., Kessler, G., & Ware, P. (2011). *TESOL technology standards: Description, implementation, integration*. Alexandria, VA: Teaching English to Speakers of Other Languages.

Huang, Hung-Tzu, & Liou, Hsien-Chin (2007). 'Vocabulary learning in an automated graded reading program'. *Language Learning & Technology, 11*(3), 64–82.

Hubbard, P., & Levy, M. (2006). *Teacher education in CALL*. Philadelphia, PA: John Benjamins.

Kessler, G. (2013). Teaching ESL/EFL in a world of social media, mash-ups and hyper-collaboration. *TESOL Journal, 4*(4), 615–632.

Kessler, G., Elola, I., & Oskoz, A. (2012). *Technology across writing contexts and tasks*. San Marcos, TX: Computer Assisted Language Instruction Consortium.

Language Learning & Technology. Retrieved February 10, 2015, from http://llt.msu.edu.

TESOL Computer Assisted Language Learning Interest Section (CAL-IS). Retrieved February 10, 2015, from http://call-is.org.

References

Ayres, R. (2002). Learner attitudes towards the use of CALL. *Computer Assisted Language Learning, 15*(3), 241–249. doi:10.1076/call.15.3.241.8189.

Baek, E., & Monaghan, J. (2013). Journey to textbook affordability: An investigation of students' use of eTextbooks at multiple campuses. *International Review of Research in Open & Distance Learning, 14*(3), 1–26.

Bikowski, D. (2012). Exploring non-native English speaking students' use of technology to improve their paraphrasing skills and avoid plagiarism. In G. Kessler, A. Oskoz, & I. Elola (Eds.), *Technology across writing contexts and tasks*. CALICO Monograph.

Bing, J. P. K. (2013). Enhancing narrative writing skills through action-adventure video games. *Journal of Education and Practice, 4*(15), 36–42.

Bloch, J. (2007). *Technologies in the second language composition classroom.* Ann Arbor, MI: University of Michigan Press.

Carr, N. (2010). *The shallows: What the Internet is doing to our brains.* New York, NY: W.W. Norton & Company.

Chun, D. M. (2006). CALL technologies for L2 reading. In L. Ducate & N. Arnold (Eds.), *Calling on CALL: From theory and research to new directions in foreign language teaching* (pp. 69–98). San Marcos, TX: Computer Assisted Language Instruction Consortium.

Cobb, T. (2007). Computing the vocabulary demands of L2 reading. *Language Learning and Technology, 11*, 38–63.

Coiro, J. (2003). Reading comprehension on the Internet: Expanding our understanding of reading comprehension to encompass new literacies. *Reading Teacher, 56*, 458–464.

Cotos, E. (2012). Towards effective integration and positive impact of automated writing evaluation in L2 writing. In G. Kessler, A. Oskoz, & I. Elola (Eds.), *Technology across writing contexts and tasks* (Vol. 10, pp. 81–112). San Marcos, TX: CALICO.

Crystal, D. (2001). *Language and the Internet.* Cambridge: Cambridge University Press.

Crystal, D. (2008). *Txtng: The gr8 db8.* New York, NY: Oxford University Press.

Egbert, J., & Hanson-Smith, E. (Eds.). (1999). *CALL environments: Research, practice, and critical issues.* Alexandria, VA: Teaching English to Speakers of Other Languages.

Elola, I., & Oskoz, A. (2010). Collaborative writing: Fostering foreign language and writing conventions development. *Language Learning & Technology, 14*(3), 51–71.

Evans, E., & Po, J. (2007). A break in the transaction: Examining students' responses to digital texts. *Computers and Composition, 24*(1), 56–73.

Huang, Hung-Tzu, & Liou, Hsien-Chin (2007). 'Vocabulary learning in an automated graded reading program'. *Language Learning & Technology, 11*(3), 64–82.

Jamieson, J., Chapelle, C., & Preiss, S. (2013). CALL evaluation by developers, a teacher, and students. *CALICO Journal, 23*(1), 93–138. doi:10.11139/cj.23.1.93-138.

Kajee, L., & Balfour, R. (2011). Students' access to digital literacy at a South African university: Privilege and marginalization. *Southern African Linguistics and Applied Language Studies, 29*(2), 187–196. doi:10.2989/16073614.2011.633365.

Kessler, G. (2009). Student-initiated attention to form in autonomous wiki-based collaborative writing. *Language Learning & Technology, 13*(1), 79–95.

Kessler, G. (2013). Collaborative language learning in co-constructed participatory culture. *CALICO Journal, 30*(3), 307–322.

Kessler, G., & Bikowski, D. (2010). Developing collaborative autonomous language learning abilities in computer mediated language learning: Attention to meaning among students in wiki space. *Computer Assisted Language Learning, 23*, 41–58.

Kessler, G., Bikowski, D., & Boggs, J. (2012). Collaborative writing among second language learners in academic web-based projects. *Language Learning & Technology, 16*(1), 91–109.

Kessler, G., & Plakans, L. (2001). Incorporating ESOL learners' feedback and usability testing in instructor-developed CALL materials. *TESOL Journal, 10*(1), 15–20.

Kuhn, J. (2013). *Building schema: A constructivist classroom via Minecraft.* Hawai'i: CALICO, University of Hawai'i.

Lai, C., & Gu, M. (2011). Self-regulated out-of-class language learning with technology. *Computer Assisted Language Learning, 24*(4), 317–335. doi:10.1080/09588221.2011.568 417.

McFall, R. (2014). Electronic textbooks that transform how textbooks are used. *Electronic Library, 23*(1), 72–81. doi:10.1108/02640470510582754.

Oskoz, A., & Elola, I. (2011). Meeting at the wiki: The new arena for collaborative writing in foreign language courses. In M. Lee & C. McLaughlin (Eds.), *Web 2.0-based e-learning: Applying social informatics for tertiary teaching* (pp. 209–227). Hershey, PA: IGI Global.

Purcell, K., Buchanan, J., & Friedrich, L. (2013). *The impact of digital tools on student writing and how writing is taught in schools [Internet & American Lift Project]*. Washington, DC: PewResearch Center. Retrieved February 10, 2015, from www.pewinternet.org/files/old-media/Files/Reports/2013/PIP_NWP%20Writing%20and%20Tech.pdf.

Reinders, H., & Hubbard, P. (2013). CALL and learner autonomy: affordances and constraints. In M. Thomas, H. Reinders, & M. Warschauer (Eds.), *Contemporary computer assisted language learning*. London: Continuum Books.

Sotillo, S. (2000). Discourse functions and syntactic complexity in synchronous and asynchronous communication. *Language Learning & Technology, 4*(1), 82–119.

Storch, N. (2013). *Collaborative writing in L2 classrooms*. Bristol: Multilingual Matters.

Ware, P. (2011). Computer-generated feedback on student writing. *TESOL Quarterly, 45*(4), 769–775.

Ware, P., & Warschauer, M. (2006). Electronic feedback and second language writing. In K. Hyland & F. Hyland (Eds.), *Feedback and second language writing* (pp. 105–122). Cambridge: Cambridge University Press.

Warschauer, M., & Grimes, D. (2008). Automated essay scoring in the classroom. *Pedagogies, 3*, 22–36.

Yamada, K. (2003). What prevents ESL/EFL writers from avoiding plagiarism? Analyses of 10 North-American college websites. *System, 31*(2), 247–258.

15

INTEGRATED READING AND WRITING ASSESSMENT

History, Processes, and Challenges

Mark Wolfersberger and Christine Coombe

Vignette

The following scenario is fictional, but it represents a situation that is quite prevalent. An international student—we will call her Mariko—comes to the United States to study English with the goal of attending a U.S. university. She enrolls in an intensive English program at the university she is interested in attending, and spends nine months building her academic English skills. Nine months later, she passes the program's final exams in reading and writing and obtains an admissible score on the institutional TOEFL. Her university application requires several writing samples in which she outlines her reasons for wanting to attend that particular university, as well as her future life plans. She has fulfilled all of the necessary requirements and appears to have the requisite literacy skills for success. She is admitted to the university.

Mariko attends her first classes with confidence. Her prior experiences and test scores over the past nine months have demonstrated that she is capable, and she has just passed the university's English placement exam that is given to all new international students. However, once her instructors begin assigning writing, Mariko struggles. She has difficulty pulling information from course texts and using it in her writing as the various assignments require. She has difficulty understanding the various ways to organize text, and each instructor seems to want something different. She finds herself spending hours working on her writing. Frustration is setting in. "What happened?" Mariko wonders. "My performance on all the required admissions tests indicated that I could do this." An assessment specialist might wonder, "What exactly were the tests that Mariko took measuring? And, do those tests measure skills that are at the core of successful academic performance?" Let's find out.

Introduction

Recently, there has been a lot of attention focused on integrated reading–writing assessment, particularly in the domain of English for academic purposes (EAP). Although integrated assessment has been around for a long time, the changing landscape of higher education, with increasing numbers of international students, has revitalized integrated assessment as a focus of second language research agendas.

This chapter first provides some background information on the history of integrated assessment, the cognitive resources upon which reading and writing draw, and assessment methods for measuring reading and writing skills that provide a foundation for understanding integrated assessment. The subsequent section examines a core assessment issue that has recently emerged in the testing literature: the construct of integrated assessment.

Background

History of Integrated Assessment: Role of the TOEFL

In the early 1960s, language acquisition was viewed as a process of acquiring discrete skills such as grammar, vocabulary, listening, speaking, reading, and writing (Lado, 1961), and in 1964, the Educational Testing Service (ETS) launched the first version of the Test of English as a Foreign Language (TOEFL). This first version responded to the view that the basis of language skill was found in its several components (i.e., reading, writing, listening, speaking), and that language skill was somewhat divisible and compartmentalized. This perspective on language was consistent with the discrete-item, multiple-choice testing practices of the time (Enright, 2011). Even though skill integration was recognized by researchers at this early stage in the history of second language acquisition (Carroll, 1961), the testing technology of the time did not allow for large-scale testing of speaking and writing. Thus, the first version of the TOEFL did not include a writing component, partly due to the complexity of administering and scoring a large-scale writing exam. The ETS partially justified its decision to not directly test writing by arguing that the structure and written expression section of the test, which essentially measured grammatical knowledge, correlated well with writing skills (Pike, 1976). Thus, according to the ETS's argument, the grammar score obtained from discrete-item testing provided to test users, such as university admissions officers and graduate programs, some indication of a student's writing ability.

At the time, the TOEFL was quite innovative and fulfilled U.S. universities' need for information on the academic English proficiency of new international students (Davies, 2008). There was a growing influx of overseas students, and university admissions officers were looking for tools to measure applicants'

English proficiency. However, washback was a concern with the TOEFL (Alderson & Hamp-Lyons, 1996). With no TOEFL writing component, teachers were less likely to include actual writing tasks in classes that trained potential international students, and the assumed consequence was that students would lack writing skills due to less experience with writing. Another concern was directed at the correlation between performance on the test's grammar section and actual writing ability. University faculty expressed reservations about a relationship between the ability to recognize correct English usage, as measured in the grammar section, and the ability to produce academic writing, particularly at the graduate level (Angelis, 1982).

In response to these concerns, the ETS commissioned researchers to study academic writing in order to identify the types of writing tasks required of university students (*Test of Written English Guide*, 2004). The resulting research revealed that academic faculty have widely differing opinions on which writing tasks are crucial to academic success (Bridgeman & Carlson, 1984). For example, summary writing and lab reports are common in engineering and the sciences, while longer research papers are typical in psychology and MBA programs. Nevertheless, the ETS used the results of this survey to develop the writing tasks assessed in the Test of Written English (TWE).

The TWE is a direct assessment of writing that was added as an optional component to the TOEFL in 1986. Test-takers are assigned a single prompt that asks them to either take a position and argue for it, or express their opinion and support it. Reading source texts to obtain information is not part of the test. Rather, writers rely on their own background knowledge as the sole source of their essay content.

The addition of the TWE resolved some critics' concerns regarding the indirect assessment of writing. Research that compared TWE with TOEFL scores showed that while the TWE was consistent with the TOEFL in identifying more and less English-proficient test-takers, the TWE also measured a different ability than the TOEFL (Carlson, Bridgeman, Camp, & Waanders, 1985). This finding supported the argument that indirect measures of writing may correlate well with writing ability but do not measure a complete construct of writing. It also furthered the argument that writing itself was separate and distinct from other language skills.

While some concerns were resolved, others remained. One such concern was with the construct of academic writing used in TWE:

> The topics and tasks are designed to give examinees the opportunity to develop and organize ideas and to express those ideas in lexically and syntactically appropriate English. Because TWE aims to measure composition skills rather than reading comprehension skills, topics are brief, simply worded, and not based on reading passages.
>
> Test of Written English Guide, *2004, p. 6*

To some, this definition of academic writing seemed narrow. It did not measure students' ability to write in different academic genres or write for different audiences and purposes. It assumed that academic writing is simply the creation of argumentative prose. TWE scoring also seemed to be problematic because the writing score was coupled with the grammar score. This suggested that linguistic accuracy was more important than other aspects of writing such as organization and topic development (Weigle, 2002).

Another concern with the TWE was authenticity. Authenticity is the extent to which a test task resembles a real-world task (Birjandi & Ahmadi, 2013). As applied to the TWE, the extent to which the TWE is authentic is the degree to which the writing tasks resemble writing tasks given in authentic academic environments. It was well known, even through early studies on writing in academic settings, that students used source texts (both written and spoken) to write rather than relying solely on background knowledge (Spack, 1984). Thus, the authenticity of the TWE was limited by the lack of reading texts to use as a source of information on the given topic.

In responding again to the concerns of test stakeholders, the ETS made a major change to the TOEFL test design and in 2005 launched the internet-based TOEFL, or iBT. The writing portion of iBT requires test-takers to incorporate information from both a lecture and a reading text into their response to a writing prompt. Before the change, ETS had again commissioned researchers to evaluate potential changes in test design. Researchers compared the written responses of two task types: (1) independent tasks, which did not require the use of source texts, and (2) integrated tasks, which required writers to either read a text or listen to a lecture and respond. They found that both the listen–write and read–write conditions resulted in discourse that was significantly different from the writing-only condition in lexical and syntactic complexity, rhetoric, and pragmatics (Cumming et al., 2005).

The history of TOEFL development shows a marked shift in the academic writing construct. Early test design suggested that writing was closely related to grammar competence and that one's writing ability could be inferred from scores on grammar tests. The next stage showed that writing was a language skill that was independent from but related to other language skills. The third stage is characterized by a shift toward test authenticity. Academic reading and listening are used to build content knowledge that is then used as the basis for a written response to the writing prompt.

One positive result of the shift in the writing construct in the TOEFL has been a renewed interest in reading–writing relationships. Researchers have begun to ask questions to clarify the construct being measured through integrated reading–writing assessments. They have explored questions such as whether reading for a comprehension test is the same type of reading that students use to read source texts while responding to a writing prompt. The next section provides some background on reading and writing processes that underpins the answers to these questions.

Reading Processes versus Writing Processes

Reading and writing have a large overlap in the cognitive resources they draw upon. This seems natural since both deal with printed language. While it is true that this commonality causes them to draw upon many of the same cognitive resources, the ways in which they access these resources are different. At one time, reading was referred to as a receptive skill and writing a productive skill. Although this analogy is outdated and oversimplifies the complex processes involved in each skill, it demonstrates that we recognize, on the surface, that reading and writing are fundamentally different.

There are a large number of cognitive processes that must run concurrently when one reads. The processes that constitute reading can be divided into lower-level processes and higher-level processes (Grabe, 2009). Within the domain of lower level processes, the most important process is word recognition (Perfetti, 2007), and this skill is subdivided into orthographic, phonological, semantic, syntactic, and morphological processing, as well as lexical access and automaticity. Higher-order processes are more complex and include the ability to build a model of the text in which subsequent propositions are connected to previous propositions (Pressley, 2006), the ability to guide text interpretation through the use of background knowledge and contextual clues (Singer & Leon, 2007), and the ability to direct attentional processes such as strategy use and goal setting.

Writing shares some common processes with reading. For example, like reading, writing requires writers to process orthography, phonology, morphology, syntactic structure, and vocabulary (Grabe & Kaplan, 1996). It requires writers to recognize semantic relationships across propositions in order to organize a text; to apply sociolinguistic contextual knowledge, including audience and writing purpose; and to orchestrate strategy use. From this perspective, there seems to be a large overlap in the cognitive processes used for reading and writing; however, there are differences.

One of the principle differences between reading and writing is "the greater need for automaticity of subprocesses in reading and the greater need for deliberate awareness in writing" (Grabe, 2001, p. 20). For example, while knowledge of text organization is a cognitive resource common to both skills, composing text requires writers to create a new organization that matches the parameters of each writing task, while readers apply background knowledge to interpret an existing text organization (Flower, 1990). Another example is lexical access. Writing requires lexical retrieval rather than meaning recognition, whereas reading requires rapid lexical recognition to maintain the speed of cognitive processing required to build comprehension. Writing does not have the same speed of processing constraints that reading has. In fact, second language writers often use their first language to overcome problems with lexical retrieval in order to keep their writing process moving forward (Jones & Tetroe, 1987).

The differences between reading and writing are further demonstrated in how each skill is typically assessed. When assessing reading, standardized assessments typically attempt to measure components of the reading ability such as fluency and reading speed, automaticity and rapid word recognition, main-idea comprehension, recall of details, inferences, and knowledge of vocabulary and grammar (Grabe, 2009). These skills are assessed through formats such as multiple-choice questions, true/false, self-assessment questionnaires, matching, and cloze. The shift from indirect to direct measures of writing has widened the gap between the types of measures used to assess reading and writing. Writing assessment also attempts to measure components of the writing ability such as fluency, grammatical knowledge, creating textual coherence, control of tone and style, and awareness of audience and purpose (Weigle, 2002). However, these skills are measured through tasks that are very different from the types of tasks used to measure reading. Writing assessment tasks usually vary in terms of subject matter, genre, rhetorical task (e.g., narration, description, argument), level of formality, length requirement, and time allowed.

Assessment Issues

In order to better support ESL university students, we must understand the assessments they are taking so we can make better inferences about their language abilities and needs. Support begins with diagnosis and understanding, and assessment is a major tool used to obtain a diagnosis and develop understanding of needs. The following section helps us better understand these assessments by focusing specifically on the construct of reading–writing integrated assessment.

Defining the Construct

The construct is the language ability that an assessment is attempting to measure. In language testing, this ability is not directly observable, but is employed by the test-taker during a test performance (Fulcher, 2010). Thus, the outcome of an assessment should indicate the extent to which the test-taker possesses the language skills that comprise the construct of the test. When developing a test, defining the construct is important so that the test design elicits the precise language skills that are to be measured. Furthermore, defining the construct is important so that test score users know exactly which language abilities a test measures in order to accurately interpret test results (Bachman & Palmer, 1996).

In academic contexts, one impetus behind the return to reading–writing integrated assessment has been the recognition that academic writing does not occur independent of reading and listening skills. Research on writing tasks in academic contexts has shown that academic writing typically requires students to read texts (Carson, 2001), and this research has led to questions about the similarities and differences between the types of writing skills elicited by independent writing tasks, which require students to draw solely on background knowledge, and integrated writing tasks, which require students to utilize information obtained through reading and listening.

When examining holistic scores across independent and integrated writing assessments, the results are mixed, with some research finding that examinees receive similar scores (Brown, Hilgers, & Marsella, 1991) while other research found that scores were different (Esmaeili, 2002). These mixed results have led to more detailed investigations. Cumming et al. (2005) found that the products from integrated tasks contained a wider variety of lexis as well as longer words and clauses. One point of similarity was grammatical accuracy, which remained constant across task types. Moving beyond the product itself, Plakans (2008) investigated the composing processes used by examinees across both task types and found that examinees used less initial planning but more online planning for integrated tasks. During the writing-only task, examinees spent more time with initial planning in order to generate content and plan organization before composing. In contrast, while engaged in the integrated task, examinees spent little time with initial planning and frequently moved back and forth between reading source texts and composing, which allowed the source text to drive the content generation and organization.

In order to understand the reading skills used during integrated assessment, researchers have examined the reading processes involved when writing from sources. Researchers have determined that the reading processes used during a reading-to-write assessment are different from the reading processes measured in assessments of general reading comprehension. Specifically, two of these processes are mining and writerly reading (Hirvela, 2004). Mining is the process of drawing from a text information that accomplishes a specific goal, and writerly reading is reading a text as an example for the purpose of improving one's own writing. Higher-scoring writers on integrated assessments tend to employ mining and goal-setting, while weaker readers appear to focus more on word-level reading rather than on mining and writerly reading, leading to lower overall scores on integrated assessments (Plakans, 2009b).

Researchers have explored the degree to which the integrated writing construct varies across differing reading-to-write tasks, such as summary, response essay, and synthesis writing. During summary writing, writers read the source text in order to select important information and typically reproduce within the summary the organization and language features of the original text (Durst, 1987). Response essays require writers to evaluate information presented in one or more source texts and compose a response that defends a position. Response writing requires more mental operations than summary writing, including more planning and critical thinking. Scores across these two writing tasks show little correlation, suggesting that these two tasks elicit different aspects of the reading-to-write ability (Asencion Delaney, 2008). Synthesis writing involves differing mental operations from summary and response essay writing. Synthesis writing requires writers to engage in organizing a structure for their composition, selecting pertinent information from source texts, and connecting that information together in a cohesive manner that addresses the writing task (Spivey, 1990). In addition, there is evidence that L2 proficiency is a mitigating factor on L2 writing performance for synthesis writing. Writers who have lower L2 proficiency and are engaged in synthesis writing seem to struggle at the word level when reading source texts, which inhibits comprehension, and when composing text, which reduces linguistic transformations of the source texts (Plakans, 2009a).

Based on the research assembled thus far, experts have defined integrated writing tasks as having three characteristics: (1) a significant amount of language provided in source texts (e.g., not graphs or charts), (2) a requirement to incorporate information from source materials in the written response, and (3) the obligation to transform the language found in source texts (Knoch & Sitajalabhorn, 2013). Thus, an integrated assessment prompts lead writers to the source texts and provide a framework for culling information from them. However, not all writers interpret the differences between integrated and independent tasks in the same way. Some writers see a big overlap in the requirements of the tasks, while others who have more experience with academic writing find the integrated task more complex (Plakans, 2010). While this leads to differences in how writers approach integrated assessment tasks, there is as yet no research to determine whether these variations lead to differences in assessment results.

Probably the most obvious and controversial difference between writing-only and reading-to-write assessments is the effect of using a source text during an integrated writing task. The presence of a source text can lead to varying amounts of direct copying, and opponents of integrated assessment argue that direct copying can have a negative impact on the reliability and validity of test results. Research has provided some insight on this issue. Direct copying seems to be related to two factors: the writing task type and the examinee's general English proficiency level. Summary writing tasks seem to elicit less direct copying from lower proficiency writers (Asencion Delaney, 2008). It is speculated that, for summary tasks, lower proficiency examinees do not understand enough of the source text to know what to include in the summary, and thus, do less direct copying. Mid-proficiency examinees seem to do the most copying because they understand more of the source text but lack the language skills to adequately paraphrase like high proficiency writers do (Cumming, et al., 2005). Composing a response essay in which writers refer to information in the source texts in order to support a position seems to have a different effect on direct copying. Asencion Delaney (2008) found that response essays lead to more copying from lower-level writers when compared to summary writing. This result contrasts with Weigle and Parker (2012), who found no difference in the amount or type of textual borrowing across L2 proficiency levels while writing response essays. However, they did find that lower proficiency writers used longer quotations than higher proficiency writers did.

Another issue with direct copying is the potential effect it has on test scores. Direct copying is considered a test-wiseness strategy—a trick used to arrive at a correct answer rather than employing the cognitive operation elicited by the test. If test scores cannot differentiate between writers who copy and those who employ genuine discourse synthesis operations as defined by the test construct, integrated assessments are of little use. While research on this topic is still limited, it does offer some tentative results. One study of the integrated iBT writing portion found that test-takers who used more direct copying received lower scores than did those who actively interacted with the texts and used a discourse synthesis process (Yang & Plakans, 2012). Another study using iBT data found that lower-scoring writers relied heavily on the reading text and copied words and phrases from it, while higher scoring writers were able to select important ideas equally between the listening and reading texts and incorporate that information into a written response (Plakans & Gebril, 2013). A third study approached the issue from the perspective of test raters to see how they responded to direct copying when making rating decisions. The raters focused on citation mechanics and locating information and word strings within the source text across all scored samples. Additionally, for high-scoring samples, raters attended to the quality of the source use, which seemed to be the characteristic that differentiated high- and low-rated samples (Gebril & Plakans, 2014). These studies suggest that, while direct copying exists in integrated assessments, test-takers who use this strategy do not score well. It should be noted, however, that within each of these studies, there was a close alignment between the integrated writing construct, the writing task that was carefully designed to elicit the integrated writing construct, the scoring rubrics used to evaluate the assessment, and raters who were well trained in evaluating integrated assessment products. Integrated assessments that fall short in any one of these areas may not be able to reliably differentiate between test-takers who employ the integrated writing construct during the test and those who use direct copying to subvert that process.

Conclusion

In summary, the construct underlying integrated assessment tasks describes the expected behaviors of test-takers. Five behaviors form the basis of this construct: (1) writers mine source texts for information; (2) writers summarize from a single text or synthesize across multiple texts; (3) writers transform the language of source texts; (4) writers create an organizational structure that is often different from the source texts; and (5) writers connect their own ideas with those found in the source texts and create cohesion between those ideas within their composition (Knoch & Sitajalabhorn, 2013). Given the heavy emphasis on reading and source text use, this construct definition clearly delineates integrated reading–writing assessment from independent writing assessment, and it provides a strong impression that integrated assessment elicits different reading processes from more traditional forms of reading comprehension assessment.

Let us return to Mariko's story. Some details were intentionally left out because they are not details that test-takers and some test score users ever consider. These details are that the program-level final exams were independent reading and writing measures, and the likely washback effect was that the program's instructors also taught these skills independently with only minimal crossover between skills. The institutional TOEFL only measures reading and does not include a writing sample. The writing samples Mariko submitted as part of her application to the university drew upon her background knowledge and were independent of any reading or use of source texts. And the university's English placement exam recently adopted an integrated assessment task, but the scoring rubrics were not revised from the previously used assessment, which was an independent writing task. This diverted the attention of the test raters from the construct of integrated assessment, causing them to score the test as if it were an independent writing assessment. When taken together as a whole test package that attempts to give evidence regarding Mariko's ability to perform at the university, these tests are problematic because there is no evidence of Mariko's ability to compose text from sources, and composing from sources is the primary form of writing within academic writing tasks.

This chapter reviewed research that indicates that students use different reading and writing processes when engaged in a reading–writing integrated task than when they use reading and writing independently. In order to be ethical users of language test scores, it is important that we understand the differences between these assessments so that we can make sound inferences and informed decisions that impact the lives of the test-takers.

Summary

- The TOEFL, the most influential EAP test in North America, did not begin with integrated reading–writing assessment because it paralleled historical trends in discrete-item testing. Integrated assessment was precluded by limitations in test administration and test scoring technology. Today, those barriers have been overcome, and the TOEFL iBT contains integrated assessment tasks.
- Although reading and writing seem to draw upon a common core of cognitive resources, the ways in which they utilize these resources is different. As such, reading and writing assessment take different approaches to skill measurement. Integrated assessment attempts to navigate the relatively murky space between the two.

- The construct of reading–writing integrated assessment is different from the construct of writing-only assessment. Integrated assessment requires test-takers to employ a synthesis writing process in which writers return to the source texts to generate an organizational framework for the writing, select relevant information to include, and create cohesion within the composition.
- While direct copying is a concern with integrated assessment, the research thus far indicates that well-designed tests are able to differentiate between test-takers who use direct copying and those who are able to transform the language of the source texts.

Discussion Questions

1. Are you aware of any situations similar to Mariko's? What happened in the situation(s) you know about? Speculate on what role assessment could have played in making either more or less accurate inferences about a student's academic writing abilities in each situation.
2. Standardized assessments such as the TOEFL and IELTS maintain a powerful influence on the way teachers teach and students study academic English. How have these tests influenced the study or teaching of English that you have experienced or observed? Is this influence positive or negative?
3. How would you respond to someone who argued that reading and writing were separate and distinct language skills and that integrated assessment only makes it more difficult to accurately measure those skills?
4. What rationale would you give to a local program that is planning to include an integrated assessment as part of their larger assessment package?
5. University admissions officers are a prominent group of standardized English test score users, and they must make inferences from test scores regarding students' ability to function academically. What inferences do you think can be made from integrated assessments? What advice would you give to a university admissions officer regarding the use of scores from integrated assessments?

Further Reading

Cumming, A. (2013). Assessing integrated writing tasks for academic purposes: Promises and perils. *Language Assessment Quarterly, 10*, 1–8.

Grabe, W. (2003). Reading and writing relations: Second language perspectives on research and practice. In B. Kroll (Ed.), *Exploring the dynamics of second language writing* (pp. 242–262). Cambridge: Cambridge University Press.

References

Alderson, J. C., & Hamp-Lyons, L. (1996). TOEFL preparation courses: A study of washback. *Language Testing, 13*(3), 280–297.

Angelis, P. J. (1982). Academic needs and priorities for testing. *American Language Journal, 1*, 41–56.

Asencion Delaney, Y. (2008). Investigating the reading-to-write construct. *Journal of English for Academic Purposes, 7*, 140–150.

Bachman, L. F., & Palmer, A. S. (1996). *Language testing in practice: Designing and developing useful language tests.* Oxford: Oxford University Press.

Birjandi, P., & Ahmadi, H. (2013). Authenticity in second language assessment: A social-constructivist perspective. *Advances in Asian Social Science, 4*(3), 899–903.

Bridgeman, B., & Carlson, S. B. (1984). Survey of academic writing tasks. *Written Communication, 1*(2), 247–280.

Brown, J. D., Hilgers, T., & Marsella, J. (1991). Essay prompts and topics: Minimizing the effect of mean differences. *Written Communication, 8*, 533–556.

Carlson, S. B., Bridgeman, B., Camp, R., & Waanders, J. (1985) *Relationship of admission test scores to writing performance of native and nonnative speakers of English.* Princeton, NJ: Educational Testing Service.

Carroll, J. B. (1961). Fundamental considerations in testing for English proficiency of foreign students. In *Testing the English proficiency of foreign students* (pp. 31–40). Washington, DC: Center for Applied Linguistics.

Carson, J. (2001). A task analysis of reading and writing in academic contexts. In D. Belcher & A. Hirvela (Eds.), *Linking literacies: Perspectives on L2 reading–writing connections* (pp. 48–83). Ann Arbor, MI: University of Michigan Press.

Cumming, A., Kantor, R., Baba, K., Erdosy, U., Eouanzoui, K., & James, M. (2005). Differences in written discourse in independent and integrated prototype tasks for next generation TOEFL. *Assessing Writing, 10*, 5–43.

Davies, A. (2008) *Assessing academic English: Testing English proficiency 1950–1989: The IELTS solution.* Cambridge: Cambridge University Press.

Durst, R. (1987). Cognitive and linguistic demands of analytic writing. *Research in the Teaching of English, 21*, 347–376.

Enright, M. (2011) *TOEFL program history.* Princeton, NJ: Educational Testing Service.

Esmaeili, H. (2002). Integrated reading and writing tasks and ESL students' reading and writing performance in an English language test. *Canadian Modern Language Review, 58*(4), 599–622.

Flower, L. (1990). The role of task representation in reading-to-write. In L. Flower, V. Stein, J. Ackerman, M. J. Kantz, K. McCormick, & W. Peck (Eds.), *Reading to write: Exploring a cognitive and social process* (pp. 35–75). New York, NY: Oxford University Press.

Fulcher, G. (2010). *Practical language testing.* London: Hodder Education.

Gebril, A., & Plakans, L. (2014). Assembling validity evidence for assessing academic writing: Rater reactions to integrated tasks. *Assessing Writing, 21*, 56–73.

Grabe, W. (2001). Reading–writing relations: Theoretical perspectives and instructional practices. In D. Belcher & A. Hirvela (Eds.), *Linking literacies: Perspectives on L2 reading–writing connections* (pp. 15–47). Ann Arbor, MI: University of Michigan Press.

Grabe, W. (2009). *Reading in a second language: Moving from theory to practice.* New York, NY: Cambridge University Press.

Grabe, W., & Kaplan, R. (1996). *Theory and practice of writing*. New York, NY: Longman.

Hirvela, A. (2004). *Connecting reading and writing in second language writing instruction*. Ann Arbor, MI: University of Michigan Press.

Jones, S., & Tetroe, J. (1987). Composing in a second language. In A. Matsuhashi (Ed.), *Writing in real time* (pp. 34–63). Norwood, NJ: Ablex.

Knoch, U., & Sitajalabhorn, W. (2013). A closer look at integrated writing tasks: Towards a more focused definition for assessment purposes. *Assessing Writing, 18*, 300–308.

Lado, R. (1961). *Language testing*. New York, NY: McGraw-Hill.

Perfetti, C. (2007). Reading ability: Lexical quality to comprehension. *Scientific Studies of Reading, 11*, 357–383.

Pike, L. (1976) *An evaluation of alternate item formats for testing English as a foreign language*. Princeton, NJ: Educational Testing Service.

Plakans, L. (2008). Comparing composing processes in writing-only and reading-to-write test tasks. *Assessing Writing, 31*, 111–129.

Plakans, L. (2009a). Discourse synthesis in integrated second language writing assessment. *Language Testing, 26*(4), 561–587.

Plakans, L. (2009b). The role of reading strategies in integrated L2 writing tasks. *Journal of English for Academic Purposes, 8*, 252–266.

Plakans, L. (2010). Independent vs. integrated writing tasks: A comparison of task representation. *TESOL Quarterly, 44*(1), 185–194.

Plakans, L., & Gebril, A. (2013). Using multiple texts in an integrated writing assessment: Source text use as predictor of score. *Journal of Second Language Writing, 22*, 217–230.

Pressley, M. (2006). *Reading instruction that works* (3rd ed.). New York, NY: Guilford Press.

Singer, M., & Leon, J. (2007). Psychological studies of higher language processes: Behavioral and empirical approaches. In F. Schmalhofer & C. Perfetti (Eds.), *Higher level language processes in the brain* (pp. 9–25). Mahwah, NJ: Erlbaum.

Spack, R. (1984). Invention strategies and the ESL college composition student. *TESOL Quarterly, 18*(4), 649–670.

Spivey, N. N. (1990). Transforming texts: Constructive processes in reading and writing. *Written Communication, 7*, 256–287.

Test of Written English Guide (2004). Princeton, NJ: Educational Testing Service.

Weigle, S. C. (2002). *Assessing writing*. New York, NY: Cambridge University Press.

Weigle, S. C., & Parker, K. (2012). Source text borrowing in an integrated reading/writing assessment. *Journal of Second Language Writing, 21*, 118–133.

Yang, H.-C., & Plakans, L. (2012). Second language writers' strategy use and performance on an integrated reading–listening–writing task. *TESOL Quarterly, 46*(1), 80–103.

CONTRIBUTORS

Neil J Anderson is a Professor in the Department of English Language Teaching and Learning at Brigham Young University—Hawaii. His research interests include second language reading, language learner strategies, learner self-assessment, motivation in language teaching and learning, and ELT leadership development.

Maureen Snow Andrade is Associate Vice President of Academic Programs at Utah Valley University. She is a former ESL program director, department chair, and journal editor. Her academic background focuses on TESOL and the study of higher education. Her professional interests include student access and success in global higher education contexts.

Christine Coombe is a Faculty Member at Dubai Men's College in the United Arab Emirates. She is Past President of the TESOL International Association (2011–2012). Her research interests include language assessment, leadership, research, task-based teaching and learning, and teacher effectiveness.

Nicholas David received his MA in TESOL from Brigham Young University and is an ESL instructor at Divine Word College in Epworth, Iowa. He has served on the executive board of MIDTESOL, and his professional interests include ESL writing center research, ESL teaching history, and language policy.

Mark Davies is a Professor in the Department of Linguistics and English Language at Brigham Young University in Provo, Utah. He is the creator of several large corpora and corpus-based tools that are available from corpus.byu.edu, which are used by hundreds of thousands of teachers, learners, and researchers each month.

William G. Eggington is Ludwig-Weber-Siebach Humanities Professor, Department of Linguistics and English Language at Brigham Young University and, during 2013–2014, a visiting scholar at Kyung Hee University, Global Campus, South Korea. His research interests include language planning and policy, intercultural rhetoric, and forensic linguistics.

Fatima Esseili is an Assistant Professor in the Department of English at the University of Dayton. She teaches graduate and undergraduate courses in applied linguistics and composition. Her research interests include second language writing, ELT, world Englishes, and language policy.

Norman W. Evans is a Faculty Member in the Linguistics and English Language Department at Brigham Young University, where he is Coordinator of the TESOL MA program and the English Language Center. His research focuses on writing in a second language, language teaching methods, and curriculum development.

Dana Ferris is Professor of Writing at the University of California, Davis, where she directs the second language writing program and teaches undergraduate writing classes, graduate pedagogy courses, and doctoral seminars on second language writing and response to student writing. She is the author or co-author of eight books and numerous chapters and journal articles. Her most recent books include *Teaching L2 Composition* (with John Hedgcock, 2014, Routledge) and *Language Power* (2014, Bedford St. Martin's). She is also Editor-in-Chief of the new *Journal of Response to Writing*.

Dee Gardner is Associate Professor of Applied Linguistics and TESOL in the Department of Linguistics and English Language at Brigham Young University—Provo. His research and teaching interests include first and second language vocabulary, academic literacy, applied corpus linguistics, and lexical semantics.

William Grabe is Regents' Professor of Applied Linguistics and Vice President for Research at Northern Arizona University. He has published on topics in reading, writing, literacy, written discourse analysis, and content based L2 instruction. He has lectured and given teaching training workshops in over 30 countries around the world.

K. James Hartshorn has been involved in second language education in the United States and Asia for three decades. James currently serves as Associate Coordinator of Brigham Young University's English Language Center, where his professional interests include teacher development and second language acquisition with an emphasis on second language writing.

Xiangying Jiang is Associate Professor of TESOL in the Department of World Languages, Literatures and Linguistics at West Virginia University. Her research focuses on second language reading development, including comprehension strategies, discourse structure, oral reading fluency, vocabulary, and the influence of first language on second language literacy development.

Greg Kessler is Director of the Language Resource Center in the College of Arts & Sciences and Associate Professor of Computer Assisted Language Learning (CALL) in the Department of Linguistics at Ohio University. His research addresses the convergence of language, digital environments, language learning, language teacher preparation, and innovative pedagogy.

Elena Lawrick is a Faculty Member in the Communications, Art, and Humanities Division at Reading Area Community College. Elena directs the ESL Program and the Learning Center for Multilingual Students. Her research focuses on writing in a second language, innovative approaches in TESL, curriculum development, program administration, and world Englishes.

Lucie Moussu is Associate Professor in Writing Studies at the University of Alberta and Director of the Centre for Writers. Originally from Switzerland, she got her PhD at Purdue University and also worked at Ryerson University, in Toronto. Her research interests include nonnative English-speaking ESL teachers and second language writing.

Marin S. Robinson is Professor of Chemistry and Biochemistry at Northern Arizona University. She teaches organic chemistry and scientific writing and conducts research in atmospheric chemistry.

Tony Silva directs the ESL Writing Program in the Department of English at Purdue University, where he teaches graduate courses for PhD, MA, and Certificate students and writing support courses for graduate and undergraduate international students. He has also directed the Graduate Program in Second Language Studies/ESL.

Fredricka L. Stoller is Professor of English at Northern Arizona University, where she teaches in the MA TESL and PhD in Applied Linguistics programs. Her professional interests are in second language reading, disciplinary writing, project-based learning, and EAP curricula.

Mark Wolfersberger is an Associate Professor in the Department of English Language Teaching and Learning at Brigham Young University—Hawaii. He enjoys teaching second language writers as well as researching issues associated with writing in academic contexts.

INDEX

Page numbers in *italics* denote tables, those in **bold** denote figures.

Academic Word List (AWL) 153
accuracy *see* language accuracy
action research 134–5
affective variables 11, 51
anxiety 160; physical environment 119; testing environment 159; writing 155, 213
assessment, integrated: construct, the 228–32; direct copying 231, 233; history 224–7; reading-to-write versus writing-only 229–30, 233; reading-writing 224, 232; *see also* TOEFL (Test of English as a Foreign Language)
assessment plan 26, **26**
Asynchronous CMC (ACMC) *see* computer-mediated communication (CMC)
at-risk factors 9–10
attainment gap 19
Australia, English language proficiency in 22–3, 37–8
authenticity 219; definition 226; in games 215; in reading 166; in social networking activities 210; in technology 217–18; in vocabulary development 152–4
automated writing evaluation (AWE) 216–17
autonomy 156, 201–2, 217

basic interpersonal communication skills (BICS) 7

behavior of language 43–4
behavior toward language 11, 43–4, 114–15, 117–18
British English 81, 190–1
British National Corpus (BNC) 181, 189, 195

cognitive academic language proficiency (CALP) 7
collaboration: through computer-mediated communication 210–11; interdisciplinary 175–6; of students 157, 211; of teachers and advisors 11; of teachers and researchers 142; of teachers and students 86, 89; of TESOL professionals 28–9; in Writing Centers 50
Collaborative Strategic Reading (CSR) 140
communicative competence 10
component-skills approach 132
computer-assisted language learning (CALL) 217–18; *see also* technology
computer-mediated communication (CMC) 210–12
Concept-Oriented Reading Instruction (CORI) 140
conferencing, teacher–student 86–9, 91
content-based instruction 28, 105, 143
Corpus of Contemporary American English (COCA) 181, 194–5; chain of

Corpus of Contemporary American English (COCA) *continued* meaning 185; compare collocates 182–3; compare collocates and synonyms 183–4; compare synonyms 184; dialectal differences 189–90; genre 186–9; morphological properties 190; phraseological properties 190–1; *see also* WordAndPhrase
Corpus of Historical American English (COHA) 181, 195
corpus research 40, 181–2; *see also* Corpus of Contemporary American English (COCA)
culture 6–7, 117; influence on behavior and performance 114–15, 126; in English 201–2; expectations 206; in Korean 202; pragmatic failure 200–1, 206–7; in writing 202–6; *see also* scripts, cultural

dictionary entries 183, 188, 191, 195
discipline-specific genres 6, 30, 103, 105, 167; *see also* English for specific purposes (ESP)
discourse communities 5, 40, 166
discourse structure awareness 136, 138–9
dynamic written corrective feedback (DWCF) 156

Educational Testing Service (ETS) 224
embedded instruction 11, 125
English for academic purposes (EAP) 148, 165; assessment in 224; reading skills 133; research on 165–6; technology *see* technology; *see also* reading, academic; writing, academic
English Composition Profile 71
English proficiency scores 4–5, 22–3, 29
English as a second language (ESL) learners 3, 40–1; background 51, 84, 115; challenges 114–15, 165; class placement 84–6; cultural differences 114, 198–9, 213; effect of education practices on *87*, 87–8; feedback *89*, 156–7; previous study of English *83*, 83–4; research on 80–1; as *tabula rasa* 82; *see also* nonnative English language speakers (NNES); Purdue University
English for specific purposes (ESP) 165; challenges for instructors 175–6; research in 165–6; support for students 166; *see also* read–analyze and write instructional approach

entity theory *see* self-theories
environment: learning 83, 86, 117, 131; physical and social 9, 46, 119, *121*, 124; testing 159

face-to-face learning 86, 88
feedback: from alumni 31; bias for the best 158; as error treatment 156; guidelines for 156–7, 159, 160; oral versus written 88–9; for researchers 135, 142; in social writing and reading 211–12; from students 218–19; in Writing Centers 50–1, 59
first-year writing course 154, 165; at Purdue University 69, 71, 74, 82; research on 81; and self-regulated learning (SRL) 125; typical U.S. courses 83, 87; and writing skills 6
fluency: academic language 8; assessment of 228; multilingual writers 159–60; in reading 133, 136–8, 151; in writing 154–5

Generation 1, 5; students 5, 10, 52, 81
globalization 81
grammar: component of writing 166, *169*, 173, *175*; exercises 157; and extensive reading 150; and self-regulation 123; student perception of tutoring needs 57, 90; and Synchronous CMC 211; and writing ability 224–6; Writing Center tutoring 50, 52, 59
group work 11, 87, 115, 210

higher education: academic language of 96; admissions and language testing 5, 20, 22–3, 29; benefits of 3; change in 116–17; completion goals 19; corpora, uses of 181–2; enrollment rates 20, 23, 96, 114, 148; ESL students **76**, 114–15; graduation rates **9**, 19; internationalization of 81; language planning 40–1; language support 9–10, 20–1, 23, 75; NNES students 8, 19, 32; practices and challenges **24**; self-regulated learning (SRL) 120 (*see also* self-regulated learning [SRL])
higher-level processes 138, 227
higher-order concerns (HOCs) 50, 52, 90
Highlighter 153
holistic approach 11, 113, 120

idioms 182–3, 188–9, **189**

incremental theory *see* self-theories
institutional framework for English language development **27**; foundational steps **25–6**, 23–7; implementation strategies 29–32; influencing concepts 27–9
integrated instruction 28, 72, 152
International English Language Testing System (IELTS) 37–8, 51, 84, 92n2
International English Programs (IEPs) 96, 105–7
international students: assumptions about 4–6, 82; in Australia 22–3; challenges 114–15; enrollment rates 20, 23, 76, 96, 114; and ESL courses 4, 70–2, 85; literature on 6; at Purdue University *see* Purdue University; testing of 224–5; *see also* nonnative English language speakers (NNES)

Korean culture 36, 198–9, 202–6

language accuracy 51, 122, 155–6, 160
language acquisition, linguistic theory of 7–8, 25, 38
Language Planning 39–41; *see also* language-in-education plan, example of
language support 49, 180–1; deficiency of 20–1; ESL courses 85–6; fluency 154–5; institution-wide approach for 10–11; at Purdue University *see* Purdue University; read–analyze and write approach 166; in reading and writing 209–10; resources for 30; self-regulated learning (SRL) 117 (*see also* self-regulated learning [SRL]); in vocabulary development 153–4; Writing Center/Lab 90, *58*
language-in-education plan, example of 41–5
language-use profile 43–4
Learner Corpora 181
lexical signaling 138–9
lingua franca 199
longitudinal experimental instructional studies 133–4
low-code/high-code usage 40–1; *see also* reading, academic
lower-level processes 227
lower-order concerns (LOCs) 90–1
Lumia Foundation for Education 19

metacognition 158; awareness 106, 140, 157; processes for comprehension 106; and self-regulation 117; strategies 160

metalanguage 158
methods of learning 9, 118, *121*, 123
morphological adjustments 41, 190
motivation 43, 51; definition 117–18; and entity theory 122; ESL writing course, registering for 85; and language proficiency 6; and reading 103, 137, 140; role of 106; and self-theories 8; and self-regulated learning (SRL) 9, **120**, *121*, 122–3; and technology 215, 217; and vocabulary 138; and writing 210
multilingual students 148; challenges in literacy 148–9; vocabulary 152; writing 154–5, 159; *see also* international students
multimodal discourse practices 210–11

native speakers (NSs) 41, 51, 54–7
netspeak *see* computer-mediated communication (CMC)
nonnative English language speakers (NNES) 4, 19; assumptions about needs and abilities 4–6, 13; institution-wide approach for 10; linguistic and cultural issues 6–7; support for 10–11, 20–1, 23; testing of 20, 22; tracking of 19, 21–2, 23, 31–2; writing skills of 6; *see also* English as a second language (ESL) learners; multilingual students

Organisation for Economic Co-operation and Development, the (OECD) 96

peer reviews: forms for 177n3; self-editing strategies 157; in the Sequenced Writing Project 86–7; student perceptions of *87*, 87; for writing tasks 86, 174, 211
performance: culture 115; evaluation of 120, 122; orientation on grades 8, 115 (*see also* self-theories: entity theory); SRL, dimension of 9, 118–19, *121*, 124
pilot instructional research 134
plagiarism 60, 149, 213
pragmatic failure 200–1, 206–7
Purdue University: administration 68; challenges 73–6; courses 70–3, 82–3; enrollment **73–4**; ESL Writing Program of 65, 77, 89–90; first-year composition 82–3; history 65–8; instructors 69; Office of Writing Review (OWR) 67; Online Writing Lab (OWL) 73; students 69–70; Writing Lab 90

quasiexperimental instructional studies *see* longitudinal experimental instructional studies

read–analyze and write instructional approach 166–7, **167**, 176; essential elements of writing 168–73, *169*, *175*, 177n2; scaffolding 156, 167–8; writing 174
reading: electronic texts 214–15; extensive 151; intensive 150–3; L2 research on 149; new contexts and forms of 210–12; processes 227; response writing 229–30; technology for teaching 214–17
reading, academic 97; amount 98–100, *99*, **99–101**, 107; challenges *103*, 103–4, 107; expectations *101*, 101–2, 107; preparation for success in 105–6; research findings 130–1
reading comprehension 122, 136; discourse knowledge 138–9; fluency 136–7; reading-to-write tasks 229; recognition vocabulary 137–8, 149, 152–3; research on 131 (*see also* research–instruction cycle); strategic reading 140–1 (*see also* strategic reading)
reading–writing relations 166, 226–8
registers 40–1, 189
research–instruction cycle 131, **132**, 141–2; assessment 135; challenges 136–7; feasibility research 134; implementation of findings 134–5; recommendations for research 135–6; theory development 131–2; theory verification 133
roles, teacher and student 24, 89, 97, 115–17

scripts, cultural 201–7
second language (L2): learners 96, 159; reading 130, 132; reading expectations 102; research on 80–1; *see also* English as a second language (ESL) learners
self-editing 50, 154, 156–7
self-regulated learning (SRL) **120**, 217; categories of 117–18, 120; culture, effect of 115; definition 8, 11, 113, 117, 126; dimensions of 9, 118–20, *121*; implementation of 125–6; learners 117; learning strategies 119–20, *121*; student reactions to 122–5
self-theories 8, 12; entity theory 8, 11, 120, 122; incremental theory 8, 120, 122

Sequenced Writing Project 86
Sheltered Instruction Observation Protocol (SIOP) 11, 45
sociolinguistic surveys 43
Standard American English 81–2
strategic reading: definition 140; strategies *141*; success in academic reading 105–6; teaching 141
strategies 9, 119; change, facilitating 116; digital/multimodal 157; feedback 160; framework for English development, instituting 29; metacognitive- and metalinguistic-awareness 160; reading *141*, 151–2, 106; rhetorical analysis 157; self-editing 156; self-regulated learning (SRL) 118–20, *121*; for students 11, 118; for teachers 30; test-taking 231; training 157–8; vocabulary learning 152–3
Synchronous CMC (SCMC) *see* computer-mediated communication (CMC)

tabula rasa 82
technology 11, 180–1; audio books 215; automated writing evaluation (AWE) 216–17; challenges 212–13; corpora 181 (*see also* Corpus of Contemporary American English [COCA]); e-instruction 30, 86, 88; electronic/digital text 100, 153, 214–15; selective adoption of 218; simulations and games 215; social media 210, 212; speech-to-text programs 215–6; and testing 224, 232
testing, high-stakes 156, 159; *see also* TOEFL (Test of English as a Foreign Language)
text-centric discourse practices 210
thesaurus: entries 183–4, 195; errors 154
time management 9, 114, 118, *121*, 123
TOEFL (Test of English as a Foreign Language) 51, 92n2, 165; history 224–7; iBT 226, 231; indicator of 5, 232; Test of Written English (TWE) 225; scores, use of 65, 71; *see also* assessment, integrated
Tom Cobb's Compleat Lexical Tutor 193
Transactional Strategies Instruction (TSI) 140

United States, education ranking of 18–19

vocabulary: academic 6, 180; awareness and strategies *121*, 152–3; books on

teaching 149; building recognition 137–8; corpus-based resources 181 (*see also* Corpus of Contemporary American Usage [COCA]); development framework 138; in electronic text 214; embedded practice 215; productive 153–4; and reading challenges *103*, 104; and reading comprehension 132, 136, 152; recognition 132–3, 136, 138, 149; in simulations and games 215; and text analyzers 153
Vocabulary Profiler 153

washback 232, 225
WordAndPhrase 181, 191–4, **192–4**; *see also* Corpus of Contemporary American English (COCA)
writing: anxiety 213; challenges 148–9, 153–4; changes in 212–3; culture in 202–3, 206; ESL background in 51–2, 81–2; essay writing 86–7, 89; independent tasks 229; integrated tasks 229–30; new contexts and forms of 210–12; processes 227; at Purdue University 70–2; summary writing 229–30; synthesis writing 230; technology for teaching 215–17; tutoring 50, 57–8
writing, academic 97, 210; audience and purpose 169–70; books on 149; competence 149; content 173; corpora, use of 183, 186–7, 194; fluency 154–5; grammar and mechanics 173; organization 171; skills, improvement of 6; writing conventions 172
Writing Across the Curriculum 41, 165
Writing Centers/Labs (WC or WL) 46, 49; content versus correctness 50, 55, 57, 59, 90; and native speakers (NS) 52–4, 56–7; pedagogy 50, 59; at Purdue University 73; student perceptions of 56–7, 90; student requests 90–1; tutor perceptions of 52–5, **53–4**, *54*; websites of 57–8, *58*